The
SOURCE

The
SOURCE

Creation—Eternal Design or Infinite Accident?

John Clayton
Nils Jansma

HOWARD
PUBLISHING CO.

Our purpose at Howard Publishing is to:

- *Increase faith* in the hearts of growing Christians
- *Inspire holiness* in the lives of believers
- *Instill hope* in the hearts of struggling people everywhere

Because He's coming again!

The Source © 2001 by John Clayton
All rights reserved. Printed in the United States of America

Published by Howard Publishing Co., Inc.
3117 North 7th Street, West Monroe, Louisiana 71291-2227

02 03 04 05 06 07 08 09 10   10 9 8 7 6 5 4 3 2

Edited by S. L. Jansma
Interior design by Stephanie Denney

Library of Congress Cataloging-in-Publication Data
Clayton, John, 1938–
    The source : creation—eternal design or infinite accident? / John Clayton.
        p. cm.
    Includes bibliographical references and index.
    ISBN 1-58229-193-4 (pbk.)
        1. God—Proof, Teleological. 2. Bible and science. 3. Creation. I. Title.

    BT103 .C39 2001
    231.7'652—dc21   00-054090

Scripture quotations not otherwise marked are from the Holy Bible, New International Version © 1973, 1978, 1984 by International Bible Society. Used by permission of Zondervan Bible Publishers. Other Scripture quotations are from the Holy Bible, Authorized King James Version (KJV), © 1961 by the National Printing Co.; and the New American Standard Bible (NAS), © 1995 by The Lockman Foundation.

Contents

Illustrations

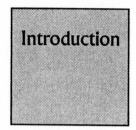

THE NEED
FOR ANSWERS

"What intelligent person could possibly believe in an old man floating around up in the sky, blasting things into existence here on earth?" That was just one question I remember my mother asking me when I was a child.

My parents, Elizabeth and Stafford Clayton, were marvelous people. There was no divorce, no unfaithfulness, and no neglect in my family. As we did things together, my mother and father would ask me questions like the one above because both of them rejected the existence of a personal God, and they raised me to do the same.

From the beginning, I believed there was no God because of my parents' teaching. As I matured and observed the hypocritical lifestyle of many so-called Christians, I became more convinced than ever that only superstitious, ignorant, or self-serving people professed a belief in God. In retrospect, those who said they believed in God and the Bible and then lived a life in total defiance of or indifference to what God

1

teaches did more to uphold the cause of atheism than the atheists themselves. Conversely, I knew that my life was consistent with what I believed, and what I believed was reasonable, logical, and certainly defendable.

THE JOURNEY

When I entered Indiana University as a physical science major, I had the privilege of having two distinguished, respected men of science teach me astronomy and biology. On one occasion, I asked my astronomy professor which theory he believed was most convincing about the generation of matter from nothing. He told me this was a question for the philosopher or the theologian; it was not a question that a scientist should try to answer.

On another occasion, I asked my biology professor a similar question. "How did the structure or the generation of DNA occur?" To my surprise, I received a similar response: "That doesn't fall within the realm of science." From this point on, I began to realize that science also had its limitations. In fact, for questions about the natural causes of matter and life, science had no answers at all.

The next series of events in my life led me closer to the outcome that the famous British scientist, Lord Kelvin, predicted. He said, "If you think strongly enough, you will be forced by science to believe in God" (Cothran 1958, 37).

About this time, I met a committed Christian, whose claims about God and the Bible added additional incentives for me to question my belief system. I subsequently left no stone unturned, so to speak, in my six-year journey from atheism to Christianity. During this time, I devoted myself to studying science, the Bible, and the sacred writings of all the major religions. While a sophomore in college, I read the Bible through from cover to cover four times for the explicit purpose of finding scientific contradictions in it. I found none.

As I read, I also began to realize that most of the things I had been told about God and about religion were not taught in the Bible. For example, the Bible did not say that God was an old man floating around in the sky blasting things into existence. The Bible said, "God is spirit," (John 4:24) and God is not made of flesh and blood (1 Corinthians 15:50).

Today I believe very profoundly in the God of the Bible. Nevertheless, I still believe my position is consistent, logical, and defendable in every way. That is why I have spent the last thirty years in a ministry designed to educate Christians about atheism and science. I also offer a challenge to atheists to investigate and see how a study of science can actually lead to belief in God.

A DIFFERENT PERSPECTIVE

Nils Jansma, geotechnical engineer and geologist, joined me in the process of writing this book. In addition to his scientific specialties, his childhood and young adult experiences bring an entirely different perspective to the subject. Growing up in a family who professed belief in God for many generations, he found it hard to understand why anyone wouldn't believe in God as creator. Yet his college years brought intellectual challenges, and in his search for truth he eventually ended up at one of my lectures. He asked numerous questions from the audience, and over the next years, our paths crossed several times. In the process of writing this book, his research and attention to detail have proved invaluable.

THE DILEMMA

Our combined perspectives have equipped us to understand the dilemma facing both Christians and non-Christians today.

Due to the incredible advances in technology over the past thirty years, some scientific discoveries have proved to be a mixed blessing for Christians. On the one hand, for certain Christians, these discoveries have called into question their interpretation of the first chapter of Genesis, causing them to view science as an enemy to their faith. On the other hand, for another group of Christians, these discoveries have provided such overwhelming evidence for the existence of a creator that they ask, "How could anyone *not* believe in God?" Yet at the same time, atheists who see this same information react with a knowing smile and say, "There is no God."

THE APPROACH

With three such differing views toward science and the existence of God, we need to find an approach to the subject that excludes as much emotion as possible and includes as much solid evidence as we have from the scientific world today.

In view of our training in the sciences, we believe the problem of God's existence can be approached in the same way a research scientist might approach an attempt to discover a new particle in the nucleus of an atom. When studying atoms, we are dealing with something we cannot see or manipulate by conventional means. Yet by looking for measurable properties of subatomic particles, we can find convincing evidence that they do exist. If we can prove the existence of the neutrino, which we accept in nuclear science in a more-or-less absolute way, then we can also prove the existence of God using similar techniques and logic.

The Christian can be assured that good science is not an enemy to faith in God; in fact, God invites us to learn about him through his creation. The Bible says in Romans 1:20, "For since the creation of the world God's invisible qualities—his eternal power and divine nature—have been clearly seen, being understood from what has been made."

In this book, we are confident the evidence will show that the believer's intellectual position is more rational and better supported scientifically than that of the atheist. When the same methods and procedures used in science and technology are applied intelligently to the question of God's existence, only one conclusion can be reached—that God is real and that he is the God of the Bible.

Where, then, do we begin? A good place would be at the beginning—or was there a beginning to the universe?

Chapter

1

THE COSMOS AND
THE CREATION

Those who like to indulge in philosophical debate might wish to contest the idea that any kind of existence is real. I have had skeptics ask me, "How do you know you exist?" This question reminds me of the story I heard about a father who called his son to ask how his college classes were going.

"Pretty well," said the son, "except philosophy."

"What's the problem there?" asked the father.

The son responded, "Well, every time the professor tries to call roll, we get into a debate about whether we really exist!"

We are assuming that most people reading this material believe that they exist. We do not wish to quibble in our discussion about "absolute proof." With that as a starting assumption, all of us have a very limited choice about the origin of our existence. Either the matter from which the universe and we are made had a beginning or it did not have a beginning. There is no other reasonable choice possible.

COSMOLOGICAL FACTS

Any discussion about the origin of matter involves the very stuff of which the universe is made. As a result, we first need to review some basic cosmological facts before we can appreciate the arguments for whether or not matter had a beginning.

The following facts can be found in any basic astronomy book.

- The size of our galaxy and the tremendous size of the cosmos in general is essential to the survival of all we see. Without great distances between them, the stars, galaxies, planets, and the vast galactic clouds of matter that are all around us in space would be drawn together by gravitational attraction. Ultimately all matter would be reduced to one enormous blob of virtually infinite density. So we need lots of space.

© Anglo-Australian Observatory

Figure 1.1: A Spiral Galaxy Similar to the Milky Way, from the Top, Showing Our Solar System's Approximate Location

© IAC/RGO/Malin

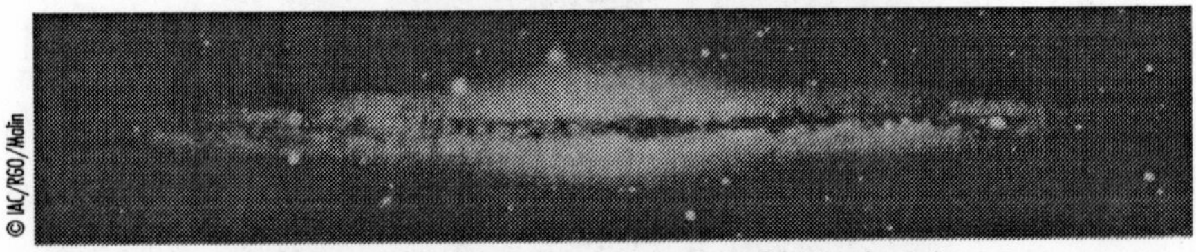

Figure 1.2: A Spiral Galaxy Similar to the Milky Way, from the Side, Showing Our Solar System's Approximate Location

- The earth is part of a rotating system of planets that orbit a star we call the sun. The sun is but one of an estimated 100 billion stars all revolving in a spiral-shaped disk we refer to as the Milky Way galaxy. (See figures 1.1 and 1.2.)

  The Xs in figures 1.1 and 1.2 show the approximate location of our solar system with its sun and all nine planets rotating around it. To get an idea of how big this system is, you could take the smallest pin you can find and poke a hole in the center of the X in figure 1.1. However, the tiny hole would be many times larger than *our entire solar system*. This experiment helps us to get a feel for the relative size of our earth when compared to our galaxy.

- Because the distances in space are so vast, scientists use a unit called the light-year to measure them. A light-year is the distance that light travels in one year. For example, our galaxy shown in figures 1.1 and 1.2 is approximately 100 thousand light-years in diameter. If we were to convert this number into miles, we would find that our galaxy is 588,000,000,000,000,000 miles across. (See the shaded box

Calculating the Diameter of Our Galaxy

Multiply the speed of light in a vacuum (186,317.6 miles per second) by the number of seconds in an hour (3600) to get the speed in miles per hour.

Then multiply your answer by the number of hours in a day (23 hours, 56 minutes, 47 seconds).

When you get that worked out, multiply again by the number of days in a year (roughly 365.25) and you will have the distance that light travels in one year.

This number is approximately 5,880,000,000,000 miles, and it must be multiplied again by 100,000 (the diameter of the Milky Way) to get the diameter of our galaxy.

Thus we determine that the diameter of the galaxy is something on the order of 588,000,000,000,000,000 miles.

titled "Calculating the Diameter of Our Galaxy" to learn how that number is figured.)

- Even this unfathomable number is microscopic when compared to the dimensions of the universe. If you were to take a very powerful telescope and look out into the constellation Hercules, you would see hundreds of hazy splotches of light.

  In 1997, the Hubble telescope looked into a region of space that was thought to be completely empty. Astronomers were astounded to see more splotches of light similar to the Hercules cluster. Each of those splotches of light is believed to be a galaxy up to 100,000 light-years in diameter and composed of 100 billion stars. We now know that there are millions of galaxies like these scattered across the seemingly endless space of the universe.

- Not surprisingly, our small segment of space contains two cloudlike galaxies called the large and small Magellanic Clouds, which are our closest neighbors. Another nearby galaxy, known as Andromeda, is about 2.2 million light-years from earth. It is very interesting to us because it is almost a twin to our own Milky Way galaxy except that it has a diameter twice as large ("Andromeda" 1998).

The following comparison will illustrate the magnitude of 2.2 million light-years. If you were to send a radio signal to a friend of yours living in Andromeda and your friend were to send you an answer the instant he received your message, you would have to wait at least 4,400,000 years for the reply. Remember that this message was sent both ways by one of the fastest transport systems we know—a radio wave that could orbit the earth over seven times in one second! It should be obvious to all that these distances are exceedingly large and that the creation of the universe represents an immeasurable effort on the part of God. In this respect, its size and grandeur serve as ever-present reminders of God's great love for his human creation (Psalms 8:3–4; 19:1; 97:6; 136:5–9).

BIBLICAL POSITION

When faced with the unfathomable vastness of space and all the apparent volume of matter in the universe, those who believe in the Bible and those who reject the notion of a creator will no doubt have very different responses. An atheist might say that the universe has existed forever and, therefore, is self-existent and does not need a creator (Humanist Manifesto I). The argument is that although matter may have been recycled again and again, the basic stuff of which we are made has existed forever.

On the other hand, the Bible clearly takes the position that we had a beginning. "In the beginning God created the heavens and the earth" (Genesis 1:1). "I am the Alpha and the Omega,...the Beginning and the End" (Revelation 22:13). Notice that the Bible also states that there will be an end. In 2 Peter 3:10–12, we read:

> But the day of the Lord will come as a thief in the night; in the which the heavens shall pass away with a great noise, and the elements shall melt with fervent heat, the earth also and the works that are therein shall be burned up. Seeing then that all these things shall be dissolved, what manner of persons ought ye to be in all holy conversation and godliness, looking for and hasting unto the coming of the day of God, wherein the heavens being on fire shall be dissolved, and the elements shall melt with fervent heat? (KJV)

The Bible portrays time as having a beginning and an end. There are even references to events before time began (1 Corinthians 2:7; Colossians 1:16–18; and John 1:1–5) and references to things that will occur after time ends (Revelation 10:6 KJV; 2 Peter 3:8–11; Hebrews 9:26–27). This idea of time having a beginning and an end is unique to the Bible. Most religious systems, along with many atheists, portray time as cyclic—repeating over and over in one way or another.

If the Bible was inspired by the Creator of the universe, then scientific discoveries should verify that matter had a beginning. What do these discoveries show?

Expanding Universe

The most incredible thing about the size of the universe discussed earlier is that it is getting larger with every passing second. If the universe is getting larger by expanding like a giant balloon, then the space between all the galaxies is also expanding. Look at figure 1.3 showing our galaxy and four others in relation to us. All of them are moving in the same general direction, but not at the same speed.

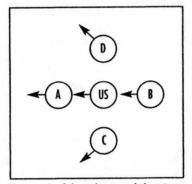

Figure 1.3: The Speeds of the Galaxies and Their Positions in Space

If we are in the center (us) and moving to the left (◄—), galaxy A is moving faster than we are, since it is in front of us and also moving to the left. It is pulling away from us because it got a bigger push at the start.

Similarly, because galaxy B is behind us, it is moving in the same direction as we are, but at a slower speed. So we are likewise pulling away from it. Galaxies C and D are likely to be moving at the same speed along with us. However, since their trajectory relative to the center of the universe is different from ours, they would also appear to be pulling away from us. It is when we analyze all these different movement rates and directions that we conclude that the universe, in general, is expanding like a giant balloon.

With this in mind, let us consider another situation. Suppose that we observed three galaxies located at positions A, B, and C as illustrated in figure 1.4. If they are positioned in such a way that they form a triangle today, then they will form a bigger triangle tomorrow and a still bigger triangle the day after tomorrow, because the universe is becoming larger with every passing second.

Conversely, if we could run time backward, then yesterday the three galaxies would have been closer together than they are today, and even closer still the day before yesterday. As we keep going backward in time, obviously we will eventually end up at a point—a beginning—at what a physicist would call a singularity.

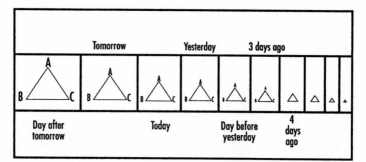

Figure 1.4: Three Galaxies over a Period of Time Showing Their Relative Positions

Big Bang

What logical interpretation can be made of this data? Even a casual look at figure 1.3 tells us that the pattern we observe is what some type of explosion would produce. That is why in 1929, the famous astronomer Edwin Hubble arrived at the same conclusion. His analysis led to the proposal of a big bang event as the origin of the cosmos. The actual term *big bang* was coined by Fred Hoyle in a 1950 BBC radio series entitled *The Nature of the Universe*. Since Hoyle believed the universe had always existed, he used the expression "big bang" to mock the theory that the universe had suddenly emerged. Ironically, the name caught on and subsequently became respectable (Barrow 1994, 34).

Today the big bang theory says that between 14 and 22 billion years ago, a singularity, suddenly and without any known explanation, became visible and produced something like a gigantic, seemingly controlled explosion. The content of this singularity, though being much smaller than a period on this page, contained the entire universe in energy form, including space itself. This pure energy rapidly expanded and was transformed, in accord with Einstein's theory, into all the galaxies, stars, and planets that we see about us.

In the 1990s, a number of supporting evidences for the big bang were discovered. The Cosmic Background Explorer project (COBE) found that temperature measurements of free space were exactly what a big bang event would produce (Dooling 1998). The distribution of galaxies and patterns of movement all agree with the big bang theory, leaving it as the best explanation we have for the distribution of the stars and galaxies we see in space.

If the big bang theory is accurate, does it support or deny God's existence as Creator? No matter how sophisticated this theory becomes, there are two fundamental questions that remain unanswered—What apparently exploded? and Where did it come from? It should be evident, then, that the big bang theory does not explain creation; it assumes creation, thereby giving support to the existence of the Creator.

Additionally, in the early 1990s, physical models of the big bang were developed that would not work until 10^{-43} seconds after it began. This is called Planck Time after the German theoretical physicist Max Karl Ernst Ludwig Planck. It marks the transition between reality and the unknown. There is currently no mathematical way to define matter before Planck Time. This has led Stephen Hawking, a world renowned theoretical physicist, to say that this period marked the beginning of both space and time. Before this instant, there is no way to explain physical relationships or to predict time-related, cause-and-effect phenomena. So if the big bang theory is correct, it proves that there was a beginning. However, as Hawking has also said, it offers no explanation for what blew up (1988, 9). It only shows that matter is not eternal.

Amount of Hydrogen

Along with the big bang, there is other evidence indicating that the universe had a beginning. One example is the energy system of the cosmos. The sun is an incredible furnace made of its own fuel. Every second that passes allows 661 million tons of the sun's hydrogen to fuse into 657 million tons of helium, as shown in figures 1.5 and 1.6 below. The remaining 4 million tons of matter are released as energy in the form of electromagnetic radiation, which includes visible light (Audouze and Israel 1988, 24). In spite of this huge release of energy, the sun is only about 50% into its relevant life cycle. We know this by comparing the sun's gravity-mass with its energy-mass conversion rate. Though the sun can still supply useful heat for another five billion years, it is most reliable during the present midlife phase, which turns out to be absolutely essential for human life to survive.

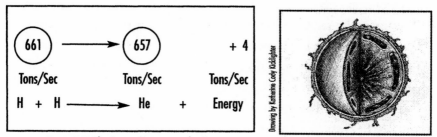

Figure 1.5: The Fusion Process on the Sun   Figure 1.6: The Sun in Cross Section

Not only is the fusion of hydrogen the process that fires the sun, but it is also the starting process that drives all known energy reactions in space. Every star in every galaxy generates its energy by this same process. We know of no other energy production of any kind that can fire stars. If every star in the sky is using hydrogen as its basic fuel and if, as a result, multibillions of tons of hydrogen are being consumed per second all over the universe, what must be true of the total hydrogen supply in the cosmos?

What would happen if we were to fill up the gas tank in our car and drive and drive without putting in more gas? Obviously, we would soon come to an unavoidable stop. Likewise, if the universe has always been, we would long since have exhausted our hydrogen supply.

Nevertheless, hydrogen is still the most abundant material in the universe. We see it everywhere we look in space. In radio astronomy, the most common frequency received is 1,420 megacycles, which corresponds to the 21 centimeter wavelength of hydrogen as determined by a spectrometer. This is an express message from outer space indicating that enormous quantities of hydrogen are still out there.

Second Law of Thermodynamics

Another proof that the creation had a beginning is the second law of thermodynamics. It states that in a closed system, things tend to move toward a condition of disorder. For example, when you buy a new car, it is supposed to be in a perfect state. There are no loose nuts or bolts, no scratches or dents, no dirt, and no wear and tear on the engine or brakes.

What is the situation ten years later? The car has slowly become a disordered wreck. It has loose nuts and bolts, scratches, dents, wear and tear, and possibly will no longer run. When this happens, we say that the car has worn out or died. This process occurs in every aspect of our lives. Our bodies become disordered with age and ultimately death results. Chemists see this happening in atoms and molecules, and physicists and engineers can measure statistically the disorder of the systems with which they work.

However, these are not valid examples of a closed system. The car we described has had energy added to it with fuel, and a mechanic may have reversed some of the disorder by tightening loose bolts. Similarly, our bodies take in food and medicine and thus are not closed either. Even the earth is not a closed system, because it receives huge amounts of energy from the sun.

What about the universe? Is it a closed system? From an atheistic viewpoint, it would have to be, because there would be no outside source of energy available to renew it. In harmony with this viewpoint, Carl Sagan said, "The cosmos is everything that was, or is, or ever will be" (1980, 257). This statement by the well-known atheist embodies a classic definition of a closed system. No organizing energy can be applied to a system that is defined as "everything that was, or is, or ever will be."

If that definition is accepted, what has to be true of the cosmos as far as the second law of thermodynamics is concerned? Clearly, since it is a closed system, it is obviously running down. As it ages, the available energy decreases and its disorder increases. This means that the cosmos must have started sometime in the past because if the cosmos had always been here, it would now be totally disordered and freezing cold. Heat death would have set in, and we would not see any of the functional energy systems that make our existence possible. Therefore, thermodynamically, the universe had to have a beginning.

ATHEISTIC POSITION
Oscillating Universe

The atheist will be quick to point out that the oscillating universe would be a way to avoid the conclusion that the cosmos had a beginning. The idea behind this theory is that the universe appears to explode with a big bang, expand, and then eventually stop due to the internal gravity of its own mass.

It then starts collapsing back upon itself, finally reaching that point where it somehow explodes again in another big bang, and the whole process begins all over again. We could write an entire book on this idea alone, but for our discussion, we will only point out some of the basic facts that make the oscillating universe impossible to believe from a scientific standpoint.

Hubble's Law

Both Hubble's Law and physical observations do not support the oscillating universe theory. Hubble's Law says the farther out in space you go, the faster things move ($V=hR$, where V is velocity, h is a constant, and R is the distance). When we see objects a great distance out in space, we find that they are moving with enormous velocities—in some cases close to the speed of light.

These galaxies are moving so rapidly that there is not enough gravitational pull to stop their motion. In fact, their velocity is many times greater than what the known mass in the universe could reasonably reverse. Additionally, as of August 1998, it has been determined by two reliable, independent sources that the rate of the galaxies is accelerating (Easterbrook 1998). This has led to the undeniable conclusion that the "universe will expand forever" ("Top Scientific Advance of Year" 1998, 1).

Missing Mass

Some might think that these conclusions could be invalidated if a huge amount of previously unknown matter could be discovered in space. All kinds of attempts have been made to locate a missing mass, from cold dark matter to neutrinos to black holes. However, if such mass were available for discovery, the galaxies would not be accelerating as they are. Therefore, the missing mass is just that—missing.

Distribution of Space

Another problem for the oscillating universe is that space is not isotropic (the same in all directions). Estimates of the mass of the universe have been based on the assumption that space is uniformly distributed with equal numbers of galaxies distributed across the cosmos.

Recent measurements have shown huge regions of space that are totally void of galaxies. This is because combinations of galaxies apparently line up to form a series of walls with empty space between them. What this means is that the total mass is even less than had been originally assumed, which is possibly one reason why the galaxies are still accelerating.

Black Holes

Even if some mechanism were found to collapse the existing universe, black holes make repeat big bangs impossible. If a huge amount of matter in space is collected in a single mass, it will have a huge gravitational force associated with it. The more mass there is, the more gravity there will be. If a mass becomes large enough, its gravitational field will exceed the strong push/pull balancing forces that hold the components of atomic nuclei in their respective positions. When this happens, all the nuclei collapse. The matter involved becomes compressed to a smaller and smaller volume, with the gravitational field continuing to become more and more intense, thus forming a black hole.

In 1998, the Hubble telescope gave us an actual photograph of a black hole in action. In a wide-field view of the merged Centaurus A galaxy, also called NGC 5128, there is evidence of galactic cannibalism. The photograph from space shows a massive black hole feeding on a smaller, adjacent galaxy. The suspected black hole is believed to contain billions of stars compacted into a volume just slightly larger than our solar system ("Hubble Provides Views of Black Hole" 1998). Black holes are no longer just theoretical. The Hubble telescope has shown them to be real objects.

A star the size of our sun could be reduced to the size of a thumbtack by such a process. If that happened, the space around the mass could be warped or bent by the huge gravity field, so that even light itself could not escape from the object. The boundary around the black hole is a theoretical surface called an "event horizon." With light unable to cross the event horizon, the object would be a black hole in space from which *nothing could escape*. By definition, we cannot get a big bang from a black hole, which is what would have to happen in an oscillating universe.

Declining Energy

Even if a black hole could explode again, an oscillating universe would still run down due to an eventual loss of energy. Each time the universe exploded, collapsed, and exploded again, it would emit some of its energy in the form of radiation that would be forever lost. As a result, the total energy of each big bang cycle would decrease until there would be no usable energy left.

In an attempt to explain this problem away, many imaginative ideas have been proposed about the geometry of space. However, declining energy remains an apparently insurmountable barrier to the oscillating universe theory. It is inescapable that the second law of thermodynamics will eventually result in the heat death of any closed-system process that repeats itself over and over. Thus we can conclude that the universe, as we know it, is not an oscillating system. It will continue to expand indefinitely.

Certainly the discoveries of the future will improve our understanding of the details involved in these processes, but the fact that the universe will never collapse upon itself remains a solid proof that we had a beginning. With that in mind, we can use the following chart as a guide in answering the next series of questions.

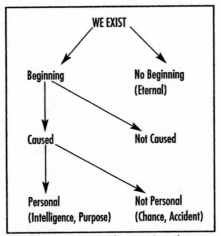

Figure 1.7: The Logic Flow of a Cosmological Argument

If the universe had a beginning, and we have every reason to believe it did according to the evidence, was that beginning caused or not caused? If it were caused, was the cause personal or nonpersonal? If it were a personal cause, we would expect certain attributes to be present in the creation, such as intelligence, purpose, design, and planning. If it were a nonpersonal cause, then none of these attributes would be found. Instead, the creation would be totally a product of chance, with no apparent purpose or intelligent reasoning behind it. So the next question to answer is, Do we have evidence supporting a design or a non-design hypothesis? That is the subject of our next chapter.

THE DESIGN OF PLANET EARTH

If we conclude that the universe had a beginning, we must then ask whether that beginning was caused or not caused. The Bible's position that the cosmos was created by God clearly recognizes that there was a cause and identifies what that cause was. (See figure 1.7.)

This assertion contrasts sharply with those who would maintain that, out of an absolute void (no force, mass, or energy) and by an unknown principle of science, matter just popped into existence. Which of these explanations sounds the most plausible? First, we should ask if it is even possible for matter to come from nothing. The answer is no, not if we are going to be able to rely on the universal laws governing matter. This fact is critical to the question at hand, because from an atheistic point of view, these are the only laws there are.

Of these laws, certain ones are recognized as being the foundations of all scientific disciplines. The law of conservation of matter/energy, for example, is the foundation of chemistry. If matter can spontaneously pop into existence out of nothing, then the foundation of chemistry is compromised and no longer reliable.

The law of conservation of angular momentum is the foundation of most of the physical sciences, particularly atomic physics. If matter can naturally come into existence out of nothing, endowed with the property of angular momentum, then all of physics is likewise uncertain and therefore unreliable.

Electronics is based upon the law of conservation of electrical charge. If matter possessing charges can mysteriously come into existence out of nothing, then all of electronics would be equally mysterious. There are many other conservation laws. In all cases, to accept the idea that matter was not caused means to deny that we can consistently rely on any scientific observation. Such a conclusion is not worthy of serious consideration if we are to think pragmatically and base our conclusions on available evidence.

Therefore, we can rationally conclude that the creation had a beginning and that the beginning was caused. So the final question remains, Was that cause personal or was it nonpersonal? If it were a personal cause, we would expect attributes like the Bible describes to be present in the creation—intelligence, purpose, design, and planning. If it were a nonpersonal cause, none of these attributes would be seen. The creation would be completely the product of chance, with no purpose or intelligence or reasoning behind it. It would be as Julian Huxley has written:

> We are as much a product of blind forces as is the falling of a stone to earth or the ebb and flow of the tides. We have just happened, and man was made flesh by a long series of singularly beneficial accidents. (Smith 1976)

Whenever we use phrases like "just happened" or "a series of accidents" as Mr. Huxley did, we are speaking about the odds of something happening by chance alone. Since the probability of such events taking place by chance can be measured or predicted mathematically, we can test the reliability of these assertions.

CONDITIONS NECESSARY FOR A LIFE-SUPPORTING PLANET

Let us examine, then, a few of the variables necessary for producing a life-supporting planet and then calculate the mathematical probabilities of such a functional planet developing by chance alone from the big bang. First we will calculate the probability for each variable individually. At the end of our discussion, we will calculate the odds for all of the variables occurring simultaneously.

Normally, the calculations for probability would be based on many, many factors with regard to the entire universe. However, these calculations result in extremely large numbers that are not necessary to make the point. To keep the following probabilities smaller and simpler, we will use only a few familiar examples that are based on conservative, common-sense values.

The Right Kind of Galaxy

In a discussion about life in space, we need to realize that not all galaxies are the same. Figure 2.1 shows four different kinds of galaxies.

Our galaxy, the Milky Way, is a type b spiral galaxy. That means our galaxy looks like a pinwheel of medium tightness in the winding of its arms. Interestingly, spiral galaxies are relatively rare in space.

Some eighty out of every one hundred galaxies are classified as elliptical galaxies. Unlike spiral galaxies, elliptical galaxies are made up of older stars and contain very little dust and only limited amounts of other solid materials. There is nothing in an elliptical galaxy from which to produce a planet, let alone to make life to put on that planet.

Similar problems exist for the other types of galaxies listed, as well as some we have not listed. Seyfert galaxies, for example, explode every so often, shattering everything in and around them. There is good evidence available showing that well under 1 percent of all galaxies in space have the conditions necessary to sustain life. If we accept a figure of 1 percent, that means that the odds of having the big bang produce the right kind of galaxy by chance alone are 1 in 100.

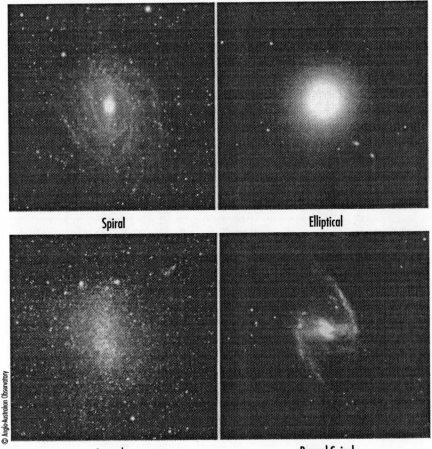

Spiral

Elliptical

Irregular

Barred Spiral

© Anglo-Australian Observatory

Figure 2.1: Four Types of Galaxies

The Right Position in the Galaxy

Figure 2.2 demonstrates that the position of our earth in the galaxy is essential to our survival. The sketch is a side view of our galaxy as seen from a great distance in space. The X marks the position of our solar system within the Milky Way galaxy. Throughout most of our galaxy, the gravitational and magnetic forces are so intense that a solar system like ours could not remain intact.

Only in two doughnut-shaped areas located outside the central bulge of the galaxy could a solar system like ours safely exist. In figure 2.2, these "doughnuts" are shaded in to emphasize their approximate location. Taking the calculated volume of our galaxy and dividing it by the volume of the shaded areas gives a value of approximately 150. (See appendix 1.) Therefore, the odds of having a solar system located in one of those doughnuts are 1 in 150.

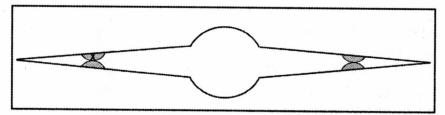

Figure 2.2: The Milky Way Galaxy, from the Side, Showing Our Solar System's Location

The Right Kind of Star

Another factor we must include in our calculations relates to the kind of star needed to serve as the sun of our solar system. Of the 100 billion stars in any given galaxy, only a very small percent would be identical or nearly identical to our sun with the proper size, radiation, and temperature needed to support the kinds of systems found on the earth. For instance, the Hubble telescope revealed in 1996 that 70% of all stars are red dwarfs, 10% are white dwarfs, and 15% are K dwarfs. That means that 95% of all stars are too small and cold to support a functional solar system.

Someone might respond that this should not be a factor because a planet could simply be closer to a colder star. However, there is a limit to how close a star can be to a planet without its gravitational force destroying the planet. This limit is called Roche's Limit. It is the closest distance in which a planet can be situated from its parent star (sun) and not be torn apart by tidal bulges developed within its crustal skin.

Dwarf stars would require a planet to be too close to survive, because the planet would have to be inside Roche's Limit to be warm enough to support life as we know it. With the elimination of all 95% of the suspected dwarf stars from our calculation, we are left with about 5 billion (5% of 100 billion) stars in our galaxy that may include a sun like ours.

A significant number of these remaining stars would also include binary or trinary stars, blue stars, and red giants like Betelgeuse in the Orion constellation. Binary or trinary groups are multiple stars orbiting one another. They, too, would destroy any planetary satellite like our earth. Because blue stars emit too much destructive heat and radiation and red giants are much too large, they would not qualify as eligible substitutes for our sun either.

The star we need would have to be just hot enough to allow for a suitable planet to orbit outside Roche's Limit and yet be at a distance that would sustain life-supporting temperatures. Therefore, if we generously assume that 100 million of the remaining 5 billion stars were possible replacements for our sun, we would have a galactic probability ratio of 1 to 1,000.

The Right Distance from the Sun

Studies of Venus have shown that our distance from the sun is critical to the existence of life. Venus is a near twin to the earth in many ways, but its closeness to the sun and its slow, backward rotation rate have left the planet with a dense cloud cover made out of sulfuric acid, causing ground temperatures to rise up to 900°F.

Earth's distance from the sun also becomes crucial when we consider how important water is for sustaining life. For water to exist in a liquid state, a very specific temperature range must be maintained. The freezing point of water is 32°F (0°C) and its boiling point is 212°F (100°C). This requires that our distance to the sun has to be a distance that will keep the average ground temperature well above 32° at night and significantly below 212° during the day.

If we were any closer to the sun than we are, all of our water would be in the vapor state. If we were any farther away from the sun than we are, our water would exist only as solid ice. Since there are ten planets in our solar system (counting the asteroid belt as a planet), only one of these ten is at the right distance for water to continuously exist as a liquid. Based upon this, we could conservatively say that the odds of having a planet the right distance from the sun are 1 in 10.

The Right Planetary Tilt

Another essential design feature is the tilt or inclination of the earth's axis. This tilt, along with the distribution of landmasses and the chemical properties of water, is also critical to maintaining a reliable range of temperatures on the earth's surface.

In figure 2.3, we see a sketch of the shape of the earth's orbit around the sun. Our summer in the Northern Hemisphere occurs when the earth is at point A. Notice that we are farther from the sun at this time.

At point B, we see the situation is quite different during summer in the Southern Hemisphere. The earth is closer to the sun than it was at point A. It would seem, then, that there would be a great deal more heat accumulated in the Southern Hemisphere during its summer than there would be in the Northern Hemisphere. This is, in fact, what would happen if there were not two significant design features incorporated within the earth's physical makeup to prevent it—the distribution of landmasses and the heat retention properties of land and water.

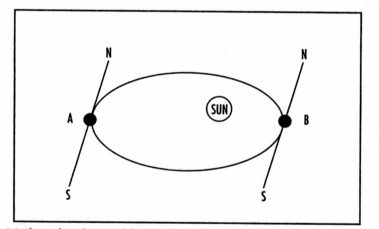

Figure 2.3: The Earth's Orbit around the Sun with the Northern Hemisphere Tilted toward the Sun in A and the Southern Hemisphere Tilted toward the Sun in B (Exaggerated Scale)

The Right Land-and-Water Distribution

A casual look at any world map shows that most of the landmass of planet earth is in the Northern Hemisphere. This naturally leaves most of the Southern Hemisphere covered by water. Water has a large heat capacity, whereas land does not. This means that water both absorbs and releases a lot of heat slowly. Landmasses, on the other hand, do just the opposite.

Therefore, when the Southern Hemisphere is close to the sun, most of the sun's intense heat is dissipated when it reflects off the water. Some of the heat that the water does absorb is circulated to the colder Northern Hemisphere by ocean currents. If water were not concentrated in the Southern Hemisphere, this heat dissipation and transfer system would not work.

These two properties, working in conjunction with the earth's tilted axis, help to moderate global temperatures. The northern landmass area absorbs maximum solar energy when the earth is farthest from the sun, while the southern waters both store and reflect heat when the earth is closest.

It is because of earth's tilt and the complementary heat retaining properties of land and water that we experience the four seasons and other climatic variations essential to life. Since these combined features are unique to planet earth, the odds of them occurring in our solar system are again 1 in 10.

More Right Conditions for the Earth

Mars has demonstrated for us what a thin atmosphere does to help shape a planet's surface. Neil Cummins of the astronomy department at the University of Maine has shown that, without a large solitary moon, a planet cannot maintain the tilt of its axis critical to the mixing of atmospheric gases—another factor that has apparently rendered Mars inhospitable for life. Our studies of the atmospheres of other planets have proven how carefully designed our earth is, with some twenty-six different atmospheric layers, each serving a separate function essential to preserving life.

In addition, charged particles raining down from space, from the sun, and from other stars are repelled by the earth's magnetic field. This may be our most important shielding device next to the atmosphere itself. Again, using our solar system as a basis, the odds of these three features happening by chance are 1 in 10, respectively.

We have also discovered that our supermassive planets of Jupiter, Saturn, Uranus, and Neptune passively serve a vital purpose as they use their huge gravitational fields to draw invading comets away from possible collisions with earth. We conservatively give this a probability factor of 1 in 40.

Finally, no life-bearing planet or system could exist anywhere near a black hole. As we have already discussed in chapter 1, because of a black hole's tremendous gravitational field, not even light can escape from it. Our only evidence of its existence is that we see matter being swallowed up by it. If a black hole came near a star like our sun, it would instantly destroy both the sun and our earth, along with all the other planets in our solar system. We estimate that the odds of a planet not being near a black hole are less than 1 in 250.

Thus far, we have discussed only a few of the necessary conditions needed for our planet to support life. While there are many, many more we could mention, the ones we have considered are sufficient to prove our point. Figure 2.4 summarizes eleven of the more obvious essential characteristics, along with the odds of their occurring by chance alone.

PROBABILITIES FOR CHANCE PRODUCING A LIFE-SUPPORTING PLANET

At this point, someone might say, "These odds are all well within the realm of possibility, so you are proving very little by listing them." This is certainly true. All of these events could possibly have happened individually. In the case of a life-supporting planet, however, they all must be happening at the same time and place, which changes things considerably.

How to Figure Probabilities

In order to appreciate how small the probabilities become when so many events must take place simultaneously, we need to review a few basic rules of probability. If I have a deck of cards that is thoroughly shuffled, and I ask you to draw the ace of spades blindly from the deck, what are the probabilities of your doing so? One out of fifty-two (1/52).

Now suppose I ask you to draw the ace of spades twice in a row, shuffling the deck each time.

In other words, you draw the ace, I shuffle it back into the deck, and you draw it again—twice in a row. What are the odds now? The answer is 1/52 x 1/52 or 1/2,704. When two things have to occur in a row or simultaneously, you multiply the individual probabilities together. The odds of drawing the same ace four times in a row would be 1/52 x 1/52 x 1/52 x 1/52, which equals 1/7,311,616.

```
Being in the right kind of galaxy. . . . . . . . . . . 1 in 100
Being in the right place in the galaxy . . . . . . . 1 in 150
Having the right kind of star. . . . . . . . . . . . . . 1 in 1,000
Being the right distance from the star . . . . . . . 1 in 10
Having the proper planetary mass . . . . . . . . . 1 in 10
Having the proper planetary spin . . . . . . . . . . 1 in 10
Having the proper planetary tilt . . . . . . . . . . . 1 in 10
Having comet-sweeping planets . . . . . . . . . . . 1 in 40
Not being near a black hole . . . . . . . . . . . . . . 1 in 250
Having a large solitary moon . . . . . . . . . . . . . 1 in 10
Possessing a magnetic field capable
    of shielding . . . . . . . . . . . . . . . . . . . . . . . 1 in 10

Total Odds. . . . . . . . . . . 1 in 150,000,000,000,000,000
```

Figure 2.4: Estimated Odds of Selected Variables Vital to an Earth-like Planet Occurring by Chance

Let us consider the short list of probabilities for each variable in figure 2.4. We can now use it to calculate the odds of having all of the beneficial features occurring together to produce a life-supporting planet. Like the cards, all these conditions have to be satisfied simultaneously or in a row, so to speak. We have to multiply all the odds or probabilities together as we did with the cards. Even with these very conservative figures, the probabilities would be 1 in 150 thousand million million (1.5×10^{17}).

This figure includes only conditions necessary to support life on the earth. It does not include all the other precise chemical balances needed in the composition of the atom and the elements making up matter. And it does not include the factors needed for life itself, as demonstrated in its complex chemical codes for DNA and RNA.

Odds for Betting a Life

However, with just this small sample of eleven necessary characteristics we have used here, we find the odds for a chance occurrence are far greater than anything we humans would care to bet our lives on. For example, parachute clubs have often stated that the odds of surviving a fall without a parachute from 10,000 feet are one in ten million.

If I offered you a billion dollars (tax free) to jump out of an airplane at 10,000 feet without a parachute, with the proviso that you had to live to collect it, would you accept the offer? Not if you were in your right mind, I'm sure. Obviously, the odds of survival are much too small for any rational person to accept. Yet the odds of there being an "accidental" planet hospitable for life using only the few parameters we have considered are *15 billion* times less likely than surviving a free-fall from an airplane.

With odds like these, you have to wonder why anyone would choose chance over design. It seems that the evidence clearly testifies to the intervention of a personal, intelligent planner and designer, whom the Bible calls the God of heaven and earth. In the chapters to follow, we will consider even more conditions necessary for life. When all of these essentials are analyzed, the odds in favor of the existence of God become so great that they far exceed not only the total number of possible stars, but even all the atoms that make up the cosmos.

Chapter

3

DESIGN IN THE CHEMISTRY OF MATTER

Before one of the billions of galaxies in the expanding universe could provide the perfect location for our planet earth to support life, matter had to come into existence. By "matter" we mean atoms and molecules, the forces binding them together, and the laws governing their interactions. A brief examination of what scientists believe took place regarding the creation of matter within the first few seconds and then minutes of the big bang will add even more convincing proof of intelligent design inherent in creation.

THE FOUR FUNDAMENTAL FORCES

All matter in our universe is composed of atoms. Each atom contains a certain number of neutrons, protons, and electrons, which are themselves made of even smaller units. For the sake of simplicity, however, we will ignore these smaller units and just focus on the three classic components: the neutron, proton, and electron.

Everything that happens in the universe and in our world is based upon the interaction of atoms combining with other atoms to form molecules. The forces that bind together particles within the atom, that control all the possible combinations of atoms, and that determine their rates of decay are known as the four fundamental forces of physics.

These forces can be expressed mathematically in the basic equations of physics. There are a number of physical constants that show up in these equations which must be *very* precise for matter to exist in a way that can sustain life. This precision becomes obvious with a closer examination of the four forces.

The Strong Force

The strong force does not reach far—only the distance across a single atom—but it serves as the glue of the universe. It is the force that holds the protons and neutrons together in the nucleus of the atom.

The precise strength of this force is crucial for the existence of life. If it were any weaker, atoms would not form at all. If it were stronger, all matter could conceivably clump together into one giant nucleus.

The Weak Force

The weak force works interactively with the strong force and has to do with radioactive decay of elements. It is 100,000 times weaker than the strong force and works over very short distances. This confines its action to individual subatomic particles. Nevertheless, the delicate disturbances it makes cause a neutron to transmute into a proton, which results in the production of elements like nitrogen, oxygen, and carbon, all of which are vital for life.

The Electromagnetic Force

Each of the building blocks of the atom has a different electrical charge. The proton has a positive charge, the electron has a negative charge, and the neutron is neutral. Both electricity and magnetism demonstrate that like charges repel and opposite charges attract.

It is the electromagnetic force that keeps the negatively charged electrons orbiting the positively charged nucleus of the atom. If this electromagnetic force were any weaker, electrons would fly off into space and the atom would not exist. If it were any stronger, electrons would be bound so tightly to the nucleus they could not be shared with other atoms. As a result, no molecules would be able to form.

Not only are the strong force and the electromagnetic force precisely balanced individually, they have also been beautifully designed to work together as a team within the atom. The strong force on its own should draw multiple protons in the nucleus together into one lump. What keeps them distinct?

Since like charges repel and all protons are positively charged, the electromagnetic repulsion force keeps the protons separated from each other. The atom, all molecules, and life itself hang in this perfect balance of forces. (See appendix 2.) (Note: In the late '60s and early '70s, the electromagnetic and weak forces were *mathematically* merged into the single "electroweak force.")

Gravity

While everything in the universe—absolutely everything—is subject to the force of gravity, it is more relevant in this discussion to describe the effect of gravity on large objects, such as stars and planets in space. With this in mind, we could say that gravity is to the universe as the strong force is to the atom. Gravity is the glue that holds galaxies together.

The strength of the force of gravity depends upon the separation distance and the respective mass of objects (how many protons and neutrons they contain). The greater the mass, the more gravity it produces. That is why the sun, which is very massive, exerts such a strong attraction on the earth, as well as all the other planets revolving around it. (See appendix 2.)

We have said that the strong force in the atom is balanced by electromagnetism, which keeps the protons from clumping together. In the universe, however, the balancing factor preventing gravity from attracting all matter into one gigantic clump is the relative expanding motion caused by the big bang.

If the initial acceleration from the big bang had been any less, the force of gravity would have consolidated everything before any discrete galaxies could have formed. Conversely, if the explosive force of the big bang had been even slightly greater, the gravitational force would not have been strong enough to pull atoms together. As it is, the delicate balance between gravity and the expansive motion is perfect—just right for matter and, finally, for galaxies to form.

THE BIG BANG TIME LINE

Before the big bang event, scientists theorize that all the matter of the universe was compressed into an infinitesimally small point called a singularity. Immediately after the start of its explosive expansion, it is believed that all four of the fundamental forces were united in a single force referred to as the Unified Force. There were no atoms or particles, only energy that was *very, very* hot (10^{29} K [On the Kelvin (K) temperature scale, 0 K marks absolute zero, 273 K marks the freezing point of water, and 373 K marks the boiling point of water in metric degrees.]).

Figure 3.1 illustrates the order and approximate time periods in which the cataclysmic events took place.

Notice the period representing the *first second* after the big bang. Within that first second, through a highly complex process involving many transitional events, the Unified Force split into the four fundamental forces we discussed, and the *exact number* of discrete electrons, protons, and neutrons formed. In this arrangement, protons and electrons form first, with neutrons to follow. Neutrons are nothing more than a proton and an electron compressed together.

Scientists who study quantum mechanics presently believe that the basic properties necessary to unite these fundamental forces need at least seven other dimensions in order to produce matter as we know it. The necessity for these other dimensions has important implications for the existence and domain of God, as we will discuss in chapter 5. (See appendix 3 for additional information.)

Three minutes after the big bang, the universe had cooled enough for protons and neutrons to unite and form nuclei. By 300,000 years, the universal temperature had cooled to 3,000 K, allowing the first simple atoms like hydrogen and helium to form. Since then, for the past 10 to 20 billion years, the universe as we know it with stars, galaxies, and planets has been expanding into what we see today.

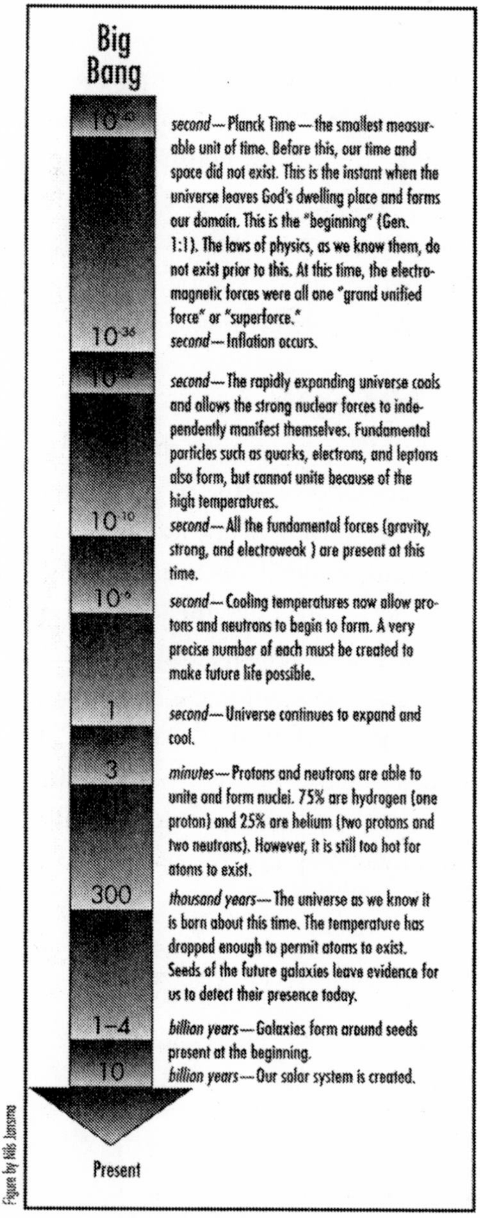

It is important to note here that some people mistakenly view this process as being godless evolution. This is certainly not the case, any more than it would be to explain the existence of the great pyramids in Egypt. Just because something takes a long time to build does not mean it was caused by evolution. There is nothing unpredictably random or unplanned about the building of either the great pyramids or the universe. The precision with which the various components of the universe are formed is truly

Big Bang

10^{-43} second — Planck Time — the smallest measurable unit of time. Before this, our time and space did not exist. This is the instant when the universe leaves God's dwelling place and forms our domain. This is the "beginning" (Gen. 1:1). The laws of physics, as we know them, do not exist prior to this. At this time, the electromagnetic forces were all one "grand unified force" or "superforce."

10^{-36} second — Inflation occurs.

10^{-35} second — The rapidly expanding universe cools and allows the strong nuclear forces to independently manifest themselves. Fundamental particles such as quarks, electrons, and leptons also form, but cannot unite because of the high temperatures.

10^{-10} second — All the fundamental forces (gravity, strong, and electroweak) are present at this time.

10^{-6} second — Cooling temperatures now allow protons and neutrons to begin to form. A very precise number of each must be created to make future life possible.

1 second — Universe continues to expand and cool.

3 minutes — Protons and neutrons are able to unite and form nuclei. 75% are hydrogen (one proton) and 25% are helium (two protons and two neutrons). However, it is still too hot for atoms to exist.

300 thousand years — The universe as we know it is born about this time. The temperature has dropped enough to permit atoms to exist. Seeds of the future galaxies leave evidence for us to detect their presence today.

1-4 billion years — Galaxies form around seeds present at the beginning.

10 billion years — Our solar system is created.

Present

Figure 3.1: Big Bang Time Line

Figure by Niels Bonsma

amazing and clearly manifests the "finger of God" in all that has been accomplished (Psalm 8:3).

This is exemplified by the extremely delicate balancing of the four fundamental forces that came into existence within the *first second* of the big bang event. After that, at least twenty-eight other equally fine-tuned characteristics had to occur regarding matter in order to produce our present universe and life itself. If we attribute the big bang to blind, unintelligent chance, how could all of the various constants (fine-tuned numerical relationships) have arrived at such precise values on the very first try? For instance, the unusual structure of the water molecule well illustrates the effect of the perfect balance between forces, along with the obvious intervention of a designer-creator, God.

THE WATER MOLECULE

At first glance, the water molecule seems to be very simple. It is made up of only two elements, hydrogen and oxygen. In one water molecule, two atoms of hydrogen share electrons with one atom of oxygen (H_2O). Often molecules share electrons equally. If this were true for water, the arrangement of the atoms would look like the illustration in figure 3.2. The oxygen would be tightly bound by hydrogen.

However, because both the oxygen and hydrogen atoms have room for an extra electron within their inner orbital shells, they bind together differently. Since oxygen has a more massive nucleus, its attraction for electrons is greater than that of hydrogen. As a result, there is an angle of 105° between the hydrogen atoms, as pictured in figure 3.3.

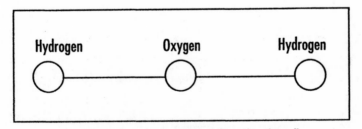

Figure 3.2: Water Molecule if Electrons Were Shared Equally

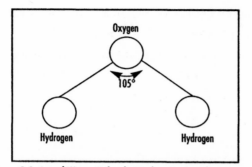

Figure 3.3: Actual Water Molecule Displays Design Characteristics

Solvency Property

One immediate result of this arrangement (called a polar arrangement) is that it allows water to dissolve things. Salt, for example, has the chemical formula Na (sodium) Cl (chloride). When salt is placed in water, the sodium is pulled toward the oxygen end of the water molecule and the chloride toward the hydrogen end, as shown in figure 3.4.

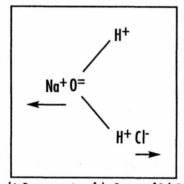

Figure 3.4: A Graphic Representation of the Process of Salt Dissolving in Water

This dissolving process causes the sodium chloride molecule to be torn apart by its attraction to both hydrogen and oxygen. If the water molecule were arranged as shown in figure 3.2, the oxygen atom would be too tightly bound to the hydrogen to attract the sodium, so the salt would not dissolve.

This solvency property of water is very important. Nutrients in the soil must be dissolved in water before they can be absorbed by plants.

The blood in our bodies is 83% water, and it carries dissolved nutrients to all parts of our bodies. A drop of rainwater falling through the air dissolves atmospheric gases, affecting the quality of our land, lakes, and rivers. In other words, all life on earth depends upon this very unusual design feature of the water molecule.

Freezing Property

As if that were not enough, the way water freezes is another manifestation of its unusual atomic arrangement. Water is one of the few materials in nature that freezes from the top down. Most liquids become more dense as they cool, and they sink in the process. Water does, too, until it reaches 40°F (4°C). At this temperature, the water molecules begin to lock on to each other, forming ice crystals.

If water were nonpolar, its rearrangement into ice might look like that shown in figure 3.5. With the polar structure water actually possesses, the distribution of frozen water molecules looks like that shown in figure 3.6.

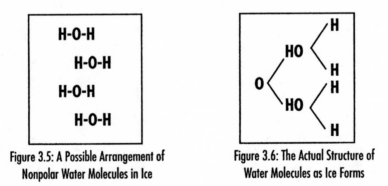

Figure 3.5: A Possible Arrangement of Nonpolar Water Molecules in Ice

Figure 3.6: The Actual Structure of Water Molecules as Ice Forms

This latter arrangement takes up more space, which means that its density is less. For this reason, ice floats and forms on the surface of the water instead of at the bottom.

The importance of water freezing from the top down may not be obvious at first glance. Think of the consequences, though, if water froze from the bottom up. First of all, it would allow year-round evaporation, since water evaporates much more rapidly than ice. The climate changes caused by the extra moisture in the air would be severe in areas near large bodies of water.

Second, and even more important, many animals living in saltwater or freshwater environments would not be able to survive. Their food supply and much of their protection from predators would be eliminated. Third, icebergs would not float. Ice would sink to the bottom where colder water temperatures would allow it to accumulate over time, upsetting currents in the sea that depend upon uninhibited convection.

This brief review should make it obvious that life on earth is dependent upon the unusual design features of the atoms in the water molecule. Rather than believing that the cosmos began by pure chance, would it not be more reasonable to recognize that the powerful hand of an engineering God carefully crafted every design feature? If this is evident in the formation of the universe, it is even more evident in the creation of life, as we shall see in the next chapter.

Chapter

4

DESIGN AS
EVIDENCED IN LIFE

A simple examination of the material making up the universe shows intelligent design in the perfect balance found to exist among all the natural forces. In like manner, the complexities inherent in life on this earth testify to the powerful, personal hand of an engineering God who has mathematically expressed his design features in every exquisite detail.

DESIGN WITHIN THE CELL
Definition of Life

In order to appreciate the design in life, we first need to define exactly what we mean when we say "life." Do we mean an organism that can move, eat, breathe, reproduce, and respond to external stimuli? The problem with that definition is that some living bacteria do not breathe and some nonliving molecules reproduce. To resolve the problem, we will define life as consisting of three essential components. 1) A living organism must be enclosed by a membrane or skin that separates it from its environment. 2) The organism must contain information molecules, such as DNA (deoxyribonucleic acid) and RNA (ribonucleic acid). 3) The organism must possess the chemical tools with which it can replicate itself on the cellular level.

This definition shows that life is irreducibly complex. If any one of the three components is missing, life does not exist. So if it can be proven that even one of the above essentials could not form by random occurrence, then life itself could not come into existence by chance. Since so much research has been done in recent years on DNA and RNA, we will focus on the second component for life listed above.

The Complexity of the Cell

Back in Darwin's time when it was believed that the cell was nothing more than a simple blob of protoplasm, it was much easier for biologists to assume that the first cells had evolved from basic chemicals rather quickly and easily. Scientists made a series of what they then considered relatively small leaps from primordial soup to simple molecules to more complex molecules to a cell membrane to a cell. From a cell, they figured that life would proliferate in earnest.

These simplistic assumptions can no longer be made. We now know that a single cell with a nucleus is the microscopic equivalent of an entire high-tech, industrialized city. It is surrounded by a wall armed with a tight security system, selectively allowing raw materials to enter and manufactured products to leave. The city contains a factory in production around the clock, tied to a trillion other similar factories by a mysterious communications network that dictates repair schedules and keeps track of all inventory.

A special library within each city is filled with detailed blueprints for every piece of machinery and maintenance equipment it uses. In living organisms, this information includes every minute characteristic of the organism, from the number of hairs on a human body to the shape, size, and function of every organ, including the unique pattern of each fingerprint.

Directions for all of this activity are encoded in DNA, the genetic material of each cell, that is wound into the shape of a double helix within the microscopically small nucleus. DNA also supplies detailed instructions on how to make and distribute all the necessary complex proteins that organisms need to use as building materials and as enzymes to carry out millions of functions that keep the host organism alive and healthy. This process is called protein synthesis, a highly sophisticated, intricately designed process that takes place trillions of times a day within the cells of a human body.

To make matters even more complicated, the "language" of DNA is expressed in chemicals that are called nucleotides, and the "language" of proteins is expressed in chemical complexes called amino acids. To manufacture proteins, a translation from one language to the other is necessary. This is where the RNA molecules come in. They translate the four nucleotides of DNA into the twenty amino acids used to build proteins. These twenty amino acids combine in unique configurations to produce thousands of proteins. (For more information, see the shaded box titled "Meters of DNA in the Human Cell.")

Stanley Miller's Experiment

With this newfound knowledge of the complexity of the cell, scientists have had a much more difficult problem in explaining how the

---

Meters of DNA in the Human Cell

A human cell contains about 2 meters of DNA. The human body is composed of approximately 10^{13} cells, and therefore contains about 2 times 10^{13} meters of DNA. Some idea of the extreme length of this DNA can be understood by comparing it with the distance from earth to the sun, which is 1.5 times 10^{11} meters. That means that the DNA in our bodies could stretch to the sun and back about 50 times.

How efficiently is this DNA packed into each cell? The 2 meters of DNA in a human cell is packed into 46 chromosomes, all in a nucleus 0.006 millimeters in diameter! (Griffiths et al. 1993, 468).

cell could possibly have come into existence by chance. In an attempt to solve this problem, they thought about how to synthesize amino acids, because amino acids are the building blocks of proteins, and proteins are essential for life.

With this goal in mind, in 1953, a graduate student at the University of Chicago named Stanley Miller simulated in the laboratory the atmospheric gases he believed had existed soon after the earth's formation three or four billion years ago. (We should note here that those assumptions he made about the composition of earth's atmosphere back in 1953 appear to be no longer valid, based on current evidence.)

To the gases contained in the apparatus shown in figure 4.1, Miller added a pool of water and an electric current to correspond to lightning, which could have acted as an energy source on the primitive earth. After boiling the water and sparking the gases for about a week, he found that the reddish water produced contained several kinds of

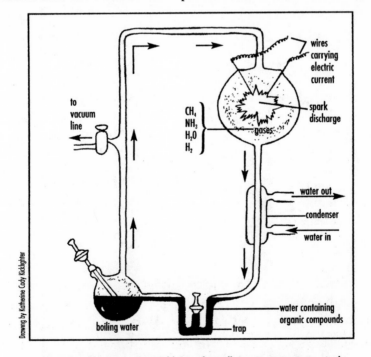

Figure 4.1: The Apparatus Used by Stanley Miller to Generate Amino Acids

amino acids. Scientists worldwide were ecstatic because it appeared that the early earth would have had the potential for producing life-supporting proteins by natural means.

Probabilities for Protein

As a result of that experiment forty years ago, we would expect that by now there would be a mountain of evidence showing the possible progression from amino acids to complex proteins, along with promising research relating to the emergence of RNA and DNA. Instead, researchers using the best equipment available to simulate conditions on the prebiotic (lifeless) earth have continually failed to naturally produce even one essential protein from random combinations of amino acids. Why?

Peter Radetsky comments on this question in *Earth* magazine.

Today his [Miller's] scenario is regarded with misgivings. One reason is that geologists now think that the primordial atmosphere consisted mainly of carbon dioxide and nitrogen, gases that are less reactive than those used in the 1953 experiment. And even if Miller's atmosphere could have existed, how do you get simple molecules such as amino acids to go through the necessary chemical changes that will convert them into more complicated compounds, or polymers, such as proteins? Miller himself throws up his hands at that part of the puzzle. "It's a problem," he sighs with exasperation. "How do you make polymers? That's not so easy." (1998, 34)

We might ask, then, based upon probabilities, how easy would it be for a protein to randomly form in nature? Biologists tell us the odds are one chance in 10^{160} (1 with 160 zeros after it). Applying chemical kinetics, this would require something like 10^{243} years for one occurrence.

Yet the fossil record appears to give evidence of *completed cells* (not merely proteins) functioning within 100 to 500 million years after the primitive earth cooled enough to allow for stable chemical reactions to take place. Some are even saying now that chemical life must have evolved, not in millions of years, but in thousands.

However, according to the laws of probability, even 500 million years is not nearly enough time for the natural development of such a complicated structure as the cell. Mathematicians generally agree that

Linear Sequence of an E. coli Protein

									10										20
Met-	Glu-	Arg-	Tyr-	Glu-	Ser-	Leu-	Phe-	Ala-	Gln-	Leu-	Lys-	Glu-	Arg-	Lys-	Glu-	Gly-	Ala-	Phe-	Val-
									30										40
Pro-	Phe-	Val-	Thr-	Leu-	Gly-	Asp-	Pro-	Gly-	Ile-	Glu-	Gln-	Ser-	Leu-	Lys-	Ile-	Ile-	Asp-	Thr-	Leu-
									50										60
Ile-	Glu-	Ala-	Gly-	Ala-	Asp-	Ala-	Leu-	Glu-	Leu-	Gly-	Ile-	Pro-	Phe-	Ser-	Asp-	Pro-	Leu-	Ala-	Asp-
									70										80
Gly-	Pro-	Thr-	Ile-	Gln-	Asn-	Ala-	Thr-	Leu-	Arg-	Ala-	Phe-	Ala-	Ala-	Gly-	Val-	Thr-	Pro-	Ala-	Gln-
									90										100
Cys-	Phe-	Glu-	Met-	Leu-	Ala-	Leu-	Ile-	Arg-	Gln-	Lys-	His-	Pro-	Thr-	Ile-	Pro-	Ile-	Gly-	Leu-	Leu-
									110										120
Met-	Tyr-	Ala-	Asn-	Leu-	Val-	Phe-	Asn-	Lys-	Gly-	Ile-	Asp-	Glu-	Phe-	Tyr-	Ala-	Gln-	Cys-	Glu-	Lys-
									130										140
Val-	Gly-	Val-	Asp-	Ser-	Val-	Leu-	Val-	Ala-	Asp-	Val-	Pro-	Val-	Gln-	Glu-	Ser-	Ala-	Pro-	Phe-	Arg-
									150										160
Gln-	Ala-	Ala-	Leu-	Arg-	His-	Asn-	Val-	Ala-	Pro-	Ile-	Phe-	Ile-	Cys-	Pro-	Pro-	Asn-	Ala-	Asp-	Asp-
									170										180
Asp-	Leu-	Leu-	Arg-	Gln-	Ile-	Ala-	Ser-	Tyr-	Gly-	Arg-	Gly-	Tyr-	Thr-	Tyr-	Leu-	Leu-	Ser-	Arg-	Ala-
									190										200
Gly-	Val-	Thr-	Gly-	Ala-	Glu-	Asn-	Arg-	Ala-	Ala-	Leu-	Pro-	Leu-	Asn-	His-	Leu-	Val-	Ala-	Lys-	Leu-
									210										220
Lys-	Glu-	Tyr-	Asn-	Ala-	Ala-	Pro-	Pro-	Leu-	Gln-	Gly-	Phe-	Gly-	Ile-	Ser-	Ala-	Pro-	Asp-	Gln-	Val-
									230										240
Lys-	Ala-	Ala-	Ile-	Asp-	Ala-	Gly-	Ala-	Ala-	Gly-	Ala-	Ile-	Ser-	Gly-	Ser-	Ala-	Ile-	Val-	Lys-	Ile-
									250										260
Ile-	Glu-	Gln-	His-	Asn-	Ile-	Glu-	Pro-	Glu-	Lys-	Met-	Leu-	Ala-	Ala-	Leu-	Lys-	Val-	Phe-	Val-	Gln-
									268										
Pro-	Met-	Lys-	Ala-	Ala-	Thr-	Arg-	Ser												

Linear sequence of one protein called the E. coli tryptophan synthetase protein. It is made up of 268 amino acids that must bond to each other in the precise order listed above. Notice how similar the arrangement is to a computer program. If such an encoded message were received from outer space, there would be no doubt about the intelligence of the sender. Yet some scientists want us to believe that the entire cell including this sophisticated message came about by random chance.

anything with a probability of less than one in 10^{50} is equivalent to total impossibility. The figure, then, of 10^{243} years puts the odds of one protein occurring by chance far beyond what any rational person could accept. And one protein is a far cry from the complexities of life.

As scientists have recognized the need to borrow more time, they have proposed theories suggesting that life arrived on earth from outer space, either on a spaceship or in cometary dust. However, as Christian de Duve commented, "Even if life came from elsewhere, we would still have to account for its first development. Thus we might as well assume that life started on earth" (1995, 1). Needless to say, with that assumption, the problem of insufficient time still looms as large as ever.

For Christians, the idea that life came to earth from outer space makes perfect sense, if by "outer space" we mean from a source beyond our universe. The Bible is silent regarding the existence of any other life in the material universe, which means at present there is no information available to us one way or the other. But the Bible is far from silent regarding the source of all life in the person of God, whose dwelling is outside the bounds of the universe he created.

One rebuttal to the arguments we have been presenting is to say that, no matter what the odds are, in an infinite universe, it will happen. Yet as enormous as the cosmos is, it is neither infinitely large nor infinitely old. Calculations show that there are not enough stars in the cosmos to allow chance to be a working factor in explaining the design we see. (See appendix 4.)

DESIGN IN NATURE

So far our discussion of design has concentrated on statistics showing that chance alone cannot adequately explain the creation as we understand it. Another approach is to review the evidence for design found in nature. While we cannot readily put numbers on such evidence, we can appeal to the common sense and fairness of the observer.

For example, watching the birth of a baby can be an awe-inspiring experience that may speak powerfully to some observers about the Creator's plan and design. The skeptic will regard this awesome event as simply an example of conformity to the laws of nature. For many of us, that explanation does not go far enough. More is needed to explain the complexity often found in the natural world. The following examples will help us see the skillful hand of a master designer manifest within and among the various species found in the world around us.

Evolution

The ability of life as a whole to adapt to a changing earth shows features that strongly suggest a designer. The built-in number of available mutation points in life's genetic coding is critical for the continued survival of the species. These mutation points are just one of the ways an animal's DNA is able to change quickly to meet new environmental demands.

Fortunately, the genetic composition of life is designed so that when climate changes, oceans advance, vegetation is modified, or predators are introduced, life can adapt and go on. This ability to change is called microevolution. Without it, life would have disappeared from the earth long ago.

A classic example of this kind of design is present in humans themselves. As far as we know, humans originated in tropical climate areas. We have every reason to believe that earth's original men and women possessed considerable amounts of an adaptive skin pigment called melanin. This genetically determined material is important to the survival of humans near the equator.

Dark pigmentation gives protection against solar radiation, ultraviolet light, skin cancer, and/or vitamin D poisoning. When the sun shines on a white person, all of the components of the sun's radiation are absorbed into the person's metabolism. In a black person, however, the sun's radiation products are absorbed into the melanin of his or her skin, thus avoiding sun poisoning.

For this reason, people living at the equator who have white skin need external protection, or they cannot survive. Black people, though, are ideally suited for that environment. Even a casual look reveals to us the "latitude effect" on skin color. With some exceptions, as one moves north from the Congo to Egypt, Palestine, Greece, Portugal, Germany and Sweden, the skin color gets lighter, the eye color bluer, and the hair color blonder. Genetic evidence has added to the view that all humans descended from one female ancestor, whom even the scientists have called "Mother Eve." If all humans share a common female ancestor and yet there are multiple races on the earth, it is obvious that all humans have microevolved and adapted to their various environments.

The point of all this, of course, is that if humans had not been created with the ability to adapt or, as many scientists would say, to evolve, they could never have left the environment of their origin. This evolutionary design feature is too wonderfully arranged to be attributed to chance and is, therefore, clear evidence of design.

Symbiosis

One area that strongly resists a totally natural explanation is the area of symbiotic relationships. A symbiotic relationship is one in which two organisms live in such a close relationship that one cannot live without the other and vice versa. Certain plants cannot live without certain insects that pollinate them or clean them or store up certain nutrients for them. At the same time, the plant provides nourishment and/or protection for the insect. Sometimes such relationships exist between two plants or two animals, like the man-of-war jellyfish and the tiny fish that live among its tentacles and yet never get stung. These types of two-way symbiotic relationships are difficult to explain by natural causes because the question automatically arises, Which came first?

If you agree that there are problems answering this question with two codependent life forms, how much more difficult do you think it would be to explain the simultaneous evolution of three? Yet this is what we find with a leaf-cutting ant species in South America whose colonies may contain up to eight million ants, a number which surprisingly represents the collective biomass of an adult cow.

These particular ants cultivate mushrooms as a farmer cultivates crops, using leaf cuttings instead of soil. The ants are not able to eat the leaves because the leaves contain a natural insecticide. Neither can the mushrooms live on the leaves because the surface of the leaves is coated with a prohibitive wax.

To make the relationship work, the ants must carefully avoid the poison as they scrape the wax off the leaves. Without the wax, the leaves are able to decay into a mulch in which the mushrooms can grow. The mushrooms, in turn, harmlessly absorb the insecticide, converting it into an edible food for the ants called gongylidia. Neither creature could live without the other. Scientists have known about the dual nature of this symbiosis for a long time.

However, recent studies have revealed another partner necessary to sustain the ant/mushroom relationship (Schultz 1999, 747–748; Currie et al. 1999, 701–704). The mushrooms have a parasite enemy that would normally destroy them, but they can be protected with an antibiotic produced by a special bacterium that, coincidentally, lives on the ants' bodies. So the bacterium depends upon the host ant's body for life. The ant depends upon the food produced by the mushrooms for life. And the mushrooms depend upon the ants' farming practices and the ants' pet bacterium for life.

This three-way relationship is irreducibly complex. If any one of the partners is missing, the entire group dies. The only way such a co-dependent society could be produced is by intelligent design. Any other attempted explanation quickly becomes a quest for the impossible dream.

Ecosystematic Design

In this day of ecological concern, nearly everyone is aware of the many delicate balances maintained in nature. Minor changes in one part of an ecological system can adversely affect the whole system. Therefore, it is very important that critical, life-supporting functions be reliable. Such reliability should be convincing evidence of design, as shown in the following examples.

Photosynthesis

Photosynthesis is the fundamental support for all life on earth. It is not only the starting point for all food chains through its amazing use of light and inorganic chemicals to generate organic food materials, but it also produces the oxygen needed for animal life to continue to exist.

Because we now understand the chemical instability of the whole photosynthetic process and its susceptibility to outside disturbances, we should be impressed with an intricacy of design that clearly could not have happened by accident. To hypothesize that by some strange series of natural processes a system such as this was created by chance is more unbelievable than expecting DNA to arise by chance in Stanley Miller's apparatus. Instead, it is far more probable that this universal supporter of all ecosystems is the product of the creator or designer of the cosmos.

Unique Animal Adaptations

Everyone is familiar with the ability of air conditioners to keep us cool on hot summer days. Air conditioners use a type of heat exchanger that allows warm air to flow through a cold radiator-like device and cool the air. Some animals are equipped with similar heat-exchanging systems that, instead of cooling them, help to conserve their body heat because they live in extremely cold environments.

For example, birds wading in cold water can lose a lot of heat through their legs. Arctic animals like seals, dolphins, and whales can lose life-supporting heat through their flippers. The tongues of gray whales also face a problem with heat loss when cold Arctic water rushes over them as the whales feed. Because there is very little insulating fat on their tongues, the potential for heat loss is critically high. How do the whales survive?

The actual heat exchangers in animals are called retia and are comprised of two layers of blood vessels (arteries and veins) that flow in opposite directions. As the cold blood leaves an exposed organ, such as the whale's flipper or tongue, it comes very close to a dense layer of blood vessels traveling in the opposite direction. This allows the warm blood leaving the animal's body and entering the flipper or tongue to transfer much of its heat to the returning cold blood.

How efficient is this heat transferring system? In regard to the whale's tongue, researchers have found that the tongue loses less heat than the rest of the whale's heavily insulated body. Without such a heat exchanger, the whale could not survive. Is this just a coincidence? Air-conditioning systems do not just happen by chance. Living heat exchangers are yet another example of intelligent design in nature (Heyning and Mead 1997, 1138–1139; see also Schmidt-Nielsen 1997).

Without a designer, it is difficult to explain how the angler fish got the wormlike appendage it suspends in front of itself to attract other fish within its "gobbling range." How did it survive before it got its built-in fishing tackle?

The same question arises about the archer fish that spits streams of water at insects, knocking them out of the trees above the water so it can catch and eat them. The amazing feature this fish possesses is its special set of bifocal eyes that allows it to see above and below the water at the same time. Without these special eyes, it could never hit its target. Which came first, the ability to spit or the ability to see in both media?

There have been evolutionary hypotheses advanced to explain some of these behaviors, but they require so many imaginary and conditional explanations that they become unbelievable. Skeptics like Richard Dawkins believe that if they can give an evolutionary chance explanation for design features such as these, no matter how imaginative or bizarre, they have destroyed the design argument (1986). However, just giving a possible explanation does not prove anything. It is only a vague faith-based conjecture or guess and not a convincing proof that evolutionary chance is the causal agent.

Instinct

Probably the most obvious examples of creative design are the instincts of animals and insects. Instinct may be defined as a behavioral characteristic inherent in a living organism that is neither learned nor accomplished by conscious thought. So ingenious and sophisticated are these instincts in animals that they clearly show they are the work of a designer. Intuitively, it should be apparent that such instincts could not have been developed by a step-by-step process based upon random chance.

For instance, marsupial mammals (animals with pouches) demonstrate a nearly miraculous instinct just by being born. Within a few weeks after conception, the fetus of a kangaroo comes into the world. Even though it is still only partially formed and well under an inch long, it crawls from the uterine environment to the belly pouch in which it will live until it is nearly an adult.

This long journey (many, many times the baby's body length) is accomplished totally without sight and without any learning or help from its mother. The only equipment the tiny creature possesses is its unusually developed, strong forelimbs and claws. During its incredible journey and while it is maturing in the pouch, its younger brothers and sisters, conceived at the same time, are put on hold in the mother's womb until the new baby either dies or leaves as an adult. At that time, one of the waiting siblings then resumes its development by making another long and arduous trip up the mother's belly.

Instinct is equally remarkable in the navigational systems of animals. Birds and turtles can travel thousands of miles in all kinds of weather and to places they have never been before. They are known to successfully return to their place of birth, even though they may have been removed from that location long before they were old enough to know where they were. How can such abilities be acquired? Not by random chance, but by built-in design features inherent in the animals.

Even more simple forms like bees and ants show truly remarkable evidence of design in their instincts. Of all the engineering shapes humans can use to build structures, there is only one recognized to be optimum in both cost and strength—the hexagon. Humans have come to this conclusion by a trial-and-error process. Various structural shapes have been subjected to stress analyses, using complex mathematical calculations, including calculus, to examine the results. The bee, how-ever, has been constructing a hexagonal structure in the most economical way from the beginning. Trial-and-error learning for the bee would have been fatal.

Instincts, then, clearly show evidence of design. They are unlearned yet precise. They are specific features arranged for a particu-lar ecosystem, and their design can be of tremendous sophistication. If we recognize these as design features, then we must concede the exis-tence of an intelligent designer, a God who is solely responsible for cre-ating all life and its remarkable complexities.

At this point, if we look back at figure 2.1, we can continue our logical argument for the existence of God. So far in our discussion, we have shown that scientific evidence supports the Bible's position that there was a beginning to the creation. If there was a beginning, then logically there had to be a cause or a causer. Through our brief exami-nation of nature, we have seen that the causer is a superior intellectual being who incorporated intelligence, reasoning, planning, design, and order into all that he created. We have not made this point by arguing religiously, but rather on the basis of scientific evidence. The next logi-cal step, then, is to explore the nature of that intelligence, which we will do in the following chapter.

THE NATURE OF GOD

If the arguments presented so far in this discussion have provided convincing evidence for the existence of a Creator, the question that naturally follows would be: If there is a God, who or what kind of being is he? Unfortunately, many people throughout history have anthropomorphized God by using features limited by our time and space environment to define and describe him.

They ask questions such as, What color of skin does God have? What sex is God? How can God hear my prayers and the prayers of a man in China at the same time? Where did God come from? Is God dead, as some have claimed? Or, as the Russian cosmonaut asked, "Why didn't I see God while I was in orbit?" Attributing these human characteristics to God has caused atheists to accuse believers of creating God in their image to fill their need for security and hope.

Not only has this misconception of God contributed to the apparent atheistic cause that abounds in the world, but it is also a major cause for religious division. Yet the Bible does not describe God in this way. Instead, it places him outside our universe in another dimension.

This description puts the Bible on the cutting edge of modern-day physics. The current, widely held theory says that for the universe to have come into existence, at least seven other dimensions must exist beyond the four dimensions of length, width, height, and time. Mathematicians have predicted these eleven spacial dimensions in order to unify the four fundamental forces in what they call the Grand Unified Theory (GUT). Since the God who created the universe must exist outside its boundaries, he would have to occupy at least a twelfth dimension. The following biblical texts clearly acknowledge this extra-dimensional characteristic of God.

From the beginning, God has been invisible (1 Timothy 1:17) and has forbidden humans to make any kind of image of him (Deuteronomy 5:8–9). No man can see him and live, we are told (Exodus 33:20). He is not made of flesh (Acts 17:22–29); he is light (Isaiah 60:19); he is love (1 John 4:8). We dwell in him (Acts 17:28), and he lives in our hearts (Romans 8:11), having unlimited time (2 Peter 3:8) to hear every prayer ascending to his throne (2 Chronicles 30:27).

wow

In harmony with our laws of science, he created matter out of pure energy (Hebrews 11:3). He is also unlike anything or anyone we humans can relate to because he is a compound being. He has revealed himself to us in three separate, coexisting persons, yet he is only one God. And perhaps most difficult for any finite person to grasp, he had no beginning and will have no end (Psalm 90:2).

This last scripture in Psalm 90:2 becomes clearer when we adjust our perspective. From the perspective of humans, the God of the Bible has always existed. If God created time and brought it into our universe from another dimension, then he existed before time. In the absence of time, a "beginning" and an "end" are superfluous.

THE ANALOGY OF FLATLAND

In order to illustrate the problems associated with visualizing another dimension beyond our three-dimensional world of length, width, and height, Edwin Abbott wrote a book titled *Flatland* in which a two-dimensional man lives on a sheet of paper that comprises his two-dimensional world. On the surface of the paper, there is only length and width. There is no such thing as thickness or height. We see the man living there as a profile only. He cannot rotate his neck in any way to see above the front surface or below the back surface of the paper.

Application to Another Dimension

Setting the Scene

One day, the man in Flatland is visited by a sphere, which has a three-dimensional shape. It crosses Flatland at right angles in the man's living room, and he is incredulous. Just as a tennis ball dipped in paint and touched to a sheet of paper would produce a dot on that paper, so, too, the movement of the sphere touching the surface of Flatland would at first only produce a dot. (See figure 5.1.)

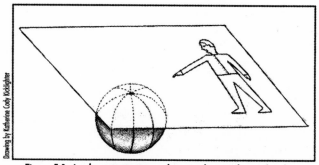

Figure 5.1: A sphere tangent to a plane produces a dot on the plane.
The man in Flatland sees only the dot.

The dot appears with no apparent cause from the man's viewpoint. A dot in Flatland is considered to be solid matter. The man himself is made up of a series of dots. That is what a line is. As far as he is concerned, matter has just appeared out of nothing, much like the concept of the singularity scientists use to explain the big bang.

From our perspective, the dot becomes a circle that keeps growing in size as the sphere passes through the plane. (See figure 5.2.) After penetrating as far as its equator, the circle then becomes progressively smaller until it turns back into a dot once again, just before it disappears.

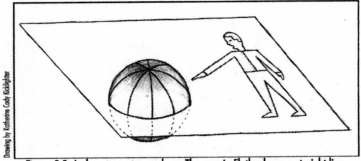

Figure 5.2: A plane truncates a sphere. The man in Flatland sees a straight line.

(See figure 5.3.) However, because our man is only a two-dimensional character, he does not actually see a circle. He only sees a dot grow into a line and then contract back into a dot again before disappearing.

Figure 5.3: As the sphere moves through the plane, the apparent line gets smaller and smaller, until the man in Flatland once again sees only a dot.

The man is terrified because he does not understand what is happening. All of the laws of science that state that matter cannot be created or destroyed have been violated. What he sees is for him a true miracle.

Speaking to the Sphere

Suppose now that the man in Flatland decides to talk to the sphere before it completes its passage through the plane. Talking to a sphere is a unique experience in itself, because its voice comes from all around the man and even from inside him as the sound waves cross his plane. After recovering from this strange encounter, the man asks, "What are you?"

The sphere says, "I'll show you. Draw a circle on your floor."

This is not easy for the man to do. His perception of a circle is a constantly curving line without corners that returns to its origin. As we have said, he cannot see all of the circle at once; he can only see the side facing him. The only way he could see a whole circle would be to get inside it. If he were to draw a circle around himself, though, he could never get out. People in Flatland can accidentally commit suicide by drawing circles around themselves from which they cannot get out. In our three-dimensional world, it would be like accidentally locking yourself in an abandoned refrigerator.

As a result, it takes the man a long time to draw the circle. The sphere is very impatient because he could have done it much faster. Finally, the circle is completed, and the sphere says, "It's about time. Now I want you to rotate the circle."

What he has in mind is for the man in Flatland to rotate the circle perpendicular to the paper, in the third dimension. But what the man in Flatland does, instead, is rotate the circumference of the circle, spinning it like a record on a record player.

"No, no! Rotate it the other way, in a third dimension perpendicular to your floor," says the sphere.

"I don't understand!" cries the man in Flatland. "There is no such thing as a 'third dimension,'" and for him this is true. There is no such thing as an up and down in a thickness direction and absolutely no way for him to comprehend what the sphere is talking about or, for that matter, even what the sphere is. The only reality he can understand is the world or dimensions in which he lives. The only way he can comprehend the sphere is in understanding the properties of the sphere as they appear in his dimension—in the paper.

Application to God

The reason Abbott wrote this story and the reason I have told it is to provide us with a foundation upon which we can build a better understanding of God. When we read, "In the beginning God created the heavens and the earth" (Genesis 1:1), we are reading a description analogous to Flatland. The concept is that God is a being who exists in a higher dimension than we do. We can only understand the properties of God as they appear in our dimension—our limited three-dimensional world.

The Person of God

God has the same kind of relationship to us as the sphere had to Flatland. He touched our little "Flatland," so to speak, and in violation of all of our laws of science, created matter out of nothing other than pure energy. Being in a higher dimension makes God so superior to us that what is natural and ordinary for him is miraculous to us. The Bible recognizes this insightful concept and uses it in every single description of God. Notice how God is described:

God is light (1 John 1:5).

God is love (1 John 4:8, 16).

God is a spirit (John 4:24).

God is not flesh and blood (Matthew 16:17).

God is not a man (Numbers 23:19).

God is the word (John 1:1).

God is unseen (1 John 4:12).

We are frequently confronted with material things we cannot detect in a direct way, yet despite this, we have learned a great deal about them. For example, we have learned much about atoms, photons, electrons, neutrinos, and other subatomic particles by indirectly discovering many of their physical properties.

Knowing an electron's charge, spin, mass, and speed (all of which can be measured indirectly), gives us a workable, though not absolute, picture of what the electron is like. By understanding such properties, we have been able to harness the power of atoms to build atomic bombs, electrons to make television sets, and photons to build lasers.

Likewise, knowing the power of God can be derived from knowing and appreciating his properties. The Bible is the only book that gives us the properties of God. Words like *love, spirit, patience, goodness,* and *justice* describe properties of God. The Bible is not vague about God, but is using accepted scientific techniques when it describes to us how he acts and when it delineates his characteristics in terms we can understand.

Metaphors for God

The descriptions of God from Genesis to Revelation are totally nonphysical and nonanthropomorphic (not like man). It is true that when we are being told how God acts, sometimes we do see anthropomorphic terms used, like "the hand of God" or "the face of God." But these terms are being used in the same way that we might speak of the "long arm of the law" or the "face of America." Biblical descriptions giving God human characteristics are only metaphors.

For instance, when the Book of Daniel (7:9, 13, 22) and the Book of Revelation represent God as being ancient, they are calling attention to his agelessness (Psalm 90:2; Revelation 4:9). When God is depicted as having white hair, it is because, in the cultural setting in which the Bible was written, age demanded respect and inspired veneration (Proverbs 20:29). None of these verses is intended to be a literal description of God. The God of the Bible is beyond physical description, and that is why he commanded his followers not to make images of him (Exodus 20:4).

THE DIMENSION OF TIME

We have the same problem as the man in Flatland when we try to comprehend such a complex being as God, especially a being who never had a beginning. In order to understand this concept a little better, we need to learn some facts about time and how it passes. Have you ever tried to define the word *time*? We have the same conceptual problem with time that we have with God. We cannot see time, smell it, taste it, feel it, or hear it.

Time is like the extra third dimension we considered in our illustration of Flatland. That is why time is said to be a "fourth" dimension because it is an additional measurement component, just like the other three dimensions. However, it does not measure size; it measures location.

In our world, it is physically impossible for two different masses to occupy the same location at the same time. They can occupy the same location at different times, but not at the same time. You and I can both sit on the same chair, but not at the same time, as most of us learned in kindergarten during a game of musical chairs.

Since we can measure our other three dimensions with a ruler and actually "see" them, time becomes very mysterious when described as a fourth dimension. But the fact that we do not perceive time directly through our senses, like seeing or hearing, does not mean that time does not exist. The atheist, like the Russian cosmonaut who refused to accept the existence of God because he could not perceive him through his senses, is not being very consistent. He certainly would not reject time on that basis even though the concept of time involves the same problem of perception.

THE VARIABILITY OF TIME

In 1905, a young patent clerk named Albert Einstein propounded a theory that not only resulted in substantially changing our concept of the physical world, but also gave us a new tool to pry into God's domain. Einstein's assertions had a profound impact on the physical sciences. One part of his work dealt with the variable nature of time and space when considered on the cosmic level.

Einstein proved that time is not fixed, but varies depending upon the speed at which an object or person is traveling. That is why someone who is sent into space at 99.9999% of the speed of light for only 50 years by his watch, could find, when he returned, that 20,000 years had passed on earth. (See appendix 5.) Time is no longer viewed as being a fixed, unchanging quantity that goes on and on forever. It is, instead, a variable that can be controlled by outside factors, such as the speed at which an object or a person is moving. This revolutionary concept is no longer considered just a theory.

Example of the Neutron

As proof, let us look at an experiment that has been done with certain subatomic particles. A single neutron, for example, under static conditions can exist for only about eighteen minutes before it disintegrates to form a proton and an electron, plus some antimatter. When accelerated in a particle accelerator to very high speeds, however, the neutron "lives" considerably longer.

Depending upon the accelerated velocity, the neutron's existence or life is prolonged in comparison with our time as predicted by Einstein's theory. This finding validates our example of a person's life being similarly extended if he or she is accelerated to near the velocity of light. Numerous other observable experiments like this one have added credence to Einstein's concept of time, supporting the novel idea that time is not fixed, but can vary or change with circumstances.

Position of God toward Time

What relevance does this scientific reality have regarding our concept of God? One of the things that confused me most about God when I was an atheist was his relationship to time as described in the Bible. We see the statement, "But, beloved, be not ignorant of this one thing, that one day is with the Lord as a thousand years, and a thousand years as one day" (2 Peter 3:8 KJV). Jude speaks of God as existing "before all time" (Jude 1:25 NAS), and Genesis 1:1 boldly says, "In the beginning God created..."

The Bible describes God as a being who relates to time the way we relate to a wall. Just as we can see the beginning of the wall, the end of the wall, and all points in between, so, too, God can see the beginning and end of time and all points or events in between (Isaiah 46:9–10). John Williams has described God as having "all of eternity in which to listen to the last split-second prayer sent up by a pilot as his plane crashes in flames" (1968, 45).

Is such a description of God reasonable? By examining time in the light of Albert Einstein's equations, we can see that it is. Humans have experimentally shown time to be manipulative, if only to a limited extent. So if humans can slow time even slightly, could not God manipulate it more fully? Since God is the creator of time, can we not expect him to know a great deal more about it than we do? Absolutely, especially since the inspired biblical description of God's relationship to time has proved to be scientifically rational.

THE PRINCIPLE OF EQUIVALENCE
In Our Dimension

A second part of Einstein's work can verify the nature of God in another way. The principle of equivalence maintains that time and space are inseparably linked. If I ask you how far it is from Chicago to Indianapolis, you might say 180 miles, or you might say three hours. You are measuring by geometric methods in one case and by relative time in the other. Both are valid.

Let me illustrate it to you another way. Suppose I could wave a magic wand and stop time, but you could continue to function in a normal way. Think of what you could do! You could get into your car and drive all the way across the country without any time passing. That would mean that you would be there and here—in both places—at the same time.

If you could stop time, there would be no limit to what you could accomplish. What is it that keeps you from doing everything you want to do? It is time, is it not? How often have you said, "If only I had time, I'd do…" Time limits how much space we can cover or, in other words, how much we can actually achieve with our lives.

In God's Dimension

If we apply this time/space framework to God, an amazing biblical concept emerges. Since God is not restricted in any way by time, then he must also be unbounded in space. Every point in space must be "here and now" for God. The Bible has consistently upheld this view. In Jeremiah 23:23–24, we read, "'Am I only a God nearby,' declares the LORD, 'and not a God far away?... Do I not fill heaven and earth?' declares the LORD."

What is Jeremiah saying in this passage? That God is here and there and everywhere—all places—at the same time. That is why we refer to God as being "omnipresent." This biblical insight, therefore, is totally consistent with the best scientific evidence we have confirming the relationship between time and space. The idea that "In him we live and move and have our being" (Acts 17:28) fits such a concept, as do all of the biblical references to the relationship of God to time and space. (See also Psalm 139.)

Understanding this aspect of God allows us to answer a myriad of questions about him. Obviously references to God's skin color, his sex, or any other physical characteristic are no longer relevant. We are not dealing with a God who has any three-dimensional human need or weakness. He has all the best characteristics of all races and sexes and is deficient in nothing.

God cannot die, because death is dependent upon time. If time does not pass for God, death is impossible. God had no beginning because *beginning* by definition implies time. Since he existed before time began, he has always been. Therefore, he can speak of events that took place before time began (1 Corinthians 2:7; Titus 1:2; Jude 1:25). This is why only God and Jesus can say, "I am the Alpha and the Omega,...the Beginning and the End" (Revelation 22:13).

We call this timeless state *eternity*. Eternity is not how long it would take an ant to move Mount Everest, grain by grain, from Los Angeles to New York and back again. Eternity is not how long a lecture or a sermon is, though sometimes it may seem that way. Eternity is that higher order or dimension where time does not exist at all!

If time does not exist, then all of the negative things that go along with time would not exist either. There would be no more death, pain, tears, or crying, because all these things are related to our time-bound, three-dimensional world. Revelation 21:1 gives precisely this description of what will happen at the end of time, calling this higher dimension or domain a "new heaven and a new earth."

The God who created both the heavens and the earth invites us to learn even more about him through studying the natural world around us.

> But ask the animals, and they will teach you, or the birds of the air, and they will tell you; or speak to the earth, and it will teach you, or let the fish of the sea inform you. Which of all these does not know that the hand of the LORD has done this? (Job 12:7–9)

If we are going to let the earth and its inhabitants tell us about the handiwork of God, we should become familiar with the "language" they speak. When we hear terms like sedimentary rock, trace fossils, and radiometric dating, we need a basic understanding of what such terms mean and how reliable the science of geology is in telling us about the history of the earth and life upon it. The next chapter will provide a brief introduction to geology and will prepare us to compare the latest findings with the Bible's account of creation.

THE LANGUAGE
OF THE EARTH

The response of humans to God's invitation in the Book of Job to "speak to the earth, and it will teach you" (Job 12:7–9) has resulted in a fascinating quest over the years. To early readers of the text, the earth taught them about the presence of God through obvious, outward manifestations of God's awe-inspiring power in the form of earthquakes, volcanic eruptions, storms, and other displays of nature's mighty forces.

RELATIVE DATING
Steno's Discovery

During the past several hundred years, however, the earth has spoken to us ever more clearly as we have gradually learned to read about its history encoded within the layers of its rocks. To begin with, in 1669, an Italian physician named Nicolaus Steno formalized a method for determining the relative ages of these layers.

Although he could not discover the absolute ages of the rocks, Steno was able to begin placing strata of rock in their proper sequence or order, from oldest to youngest, depending upon their positions relative to each other. With the exception of catastrophic events, such as earthquakes or landslides, rocks buried deepest in the earth are deposited first, followed in succession by increasingly younger layers above them, ending with the youngest on top. As time progressed, knowledge about the conditions that formed these various types of rock revealed even more about earth's history. (See appendix 6.)

Example of Limestone

For example, one type of limestone forms in warm, shallow, quiet seas when a rich mixture of dissolved calcium combines with carbon and oxygen. This precipitation of limestone is an ongoing process still seen today. Geologists experimentally calculate that it takes approximately 2,250 years for one foot of such limestone to form (Landes and Hussey 1956, 388).

Therefore, the discovery of an uninterrupted layer of this type of limestone in the earth 100 feet thick would indicate that for about 225,000 years, conditions at that location supported a warm, shallow sea. To find a layer of another type of rock above it would tell us that, later in earth's history, temperature and weather patterns changed, cre-

Rock Formation

Igneous rocks are formed naturally from magma or the hot, semiliquid rock located below the earth's crust. On land, igneous rocks can be granitelike material or they can be lava. On the seafloor, they are generally basaltic rocks.

Sedimentary rocks are formed by erosion from rocks or by material from plants and animals, chemically altered by interaction with water and pressure to become a solid mass.

Metamorphic rocks are formed by sedimentary rocks subjected to intense heat and pressure that causes them to approach their melting point.

ating a different environment. While finding such deposits provided a local window into the past, it was nearly impossible to match up or correlate these deposits with rocks of similar age in other parts of the world. Making such associations, however, would be necessary to give an overall picture of earth history.

FOSSILS
Definition

Here is where fossils become very important. Standard geology textbooks, museums, or encyclopedia tell us that a fossil is any representation of former animal or plant life, such as a bone or an imprint of a leaf or textured skin. When an animal or plant dies, it is usually consumed by other animals or it decomposes on its own. In some instances, though, it dies and is rapidly buried in a moist place. When moisture conditions are just right, all of its slowly decaying parts are replaced by new, rocklike minerals, which replicate the plant or animal in a remarkably durable and detailed way.

Sometimes the remains of the actual organism are no longer present, but only the cast or mold of its body remains. Other times, all we find are imprints of what the organism left behind, like a footprint, dung, or a nest. These items are called trace fossils. It is important to keep in mind that both fossils and trace fossils are very rare when compared to the total number of plants and animals that have ever lived.

Though fossils and trace fossils are rare, the lessons evident in the fossil record are many and varied. We see strange animals that are very different from animals living today, and we also see that the conditions under which they lived were likewise very different. When I pursued my advanced degree in earth science, I was able to experience these differences firsthand by observing much of the geology of North America.

Since then, I have been fortunate enough to travel throughout Europe and Australia as well, and have managed to collect large numbers of fossils from all kinds of living things and all sorts of geologic formations. I have seen the fossils of tropical animals in Alaska. In several places, I have seen coal deposits containing deeply embedded dinosaurs. I have seen the eggs of dinosaurs with fossilized babies still inside at various stages of embryonic development. This proves to me that dinosaurs actually lived, and their fossilized remains tell us a great deal about how they lived.

Index Fossils

In the late 1700s, a canal builder named William Smith noticed something about the fossils he observed that made him stop and take a closer look. Each layer of rock contained distinctive fossils unlike those in the strata above or below. This discovery eventually led geologists to formulate the principle known as fauna or biotic succession: Fossil organisms generally succeed one another in a definite order—from simple to complex—so that any time period can be recognized by its fossil content. The order of these fossils is so consistent on every major landmass that scientists can now divide earth history into specific eons or epochs based upon the appearance of these "index fossils," as they are called (Tarbuck and Lutgens 1993, 182–191). (See figure 6.1.)

One of the most revealing places to read a history of the earth in layers of rock is in the Grand Canyon, which is more than a mile deep. A person floating along the Colorado River can see, at river level, a distinctive rock type called schist. Schist is a metamorphic rock, meaning that it was reformed by heat and pressure in the depths of the earth more than a billion years ago. It contains no animal fossils.

As the traveler looks up, conspicuous layers of sedimentary rock are evident. In one area, there is a clear line where an ancient flood plain produced a sedimentary rock called shale. This was followed by a desert environment that formed windblown sandstone. Still later, a warm, shallow sea produced the type of limestone we have already discussed. Each layer contains unique fossils of creatures that lived in that particular environment—little marine creatures in the limestone and lizard tracks in the sandstone. These unique fossils can be used to establish the relative ages of rocks containing the same fossils that are located in other parts of the earth.

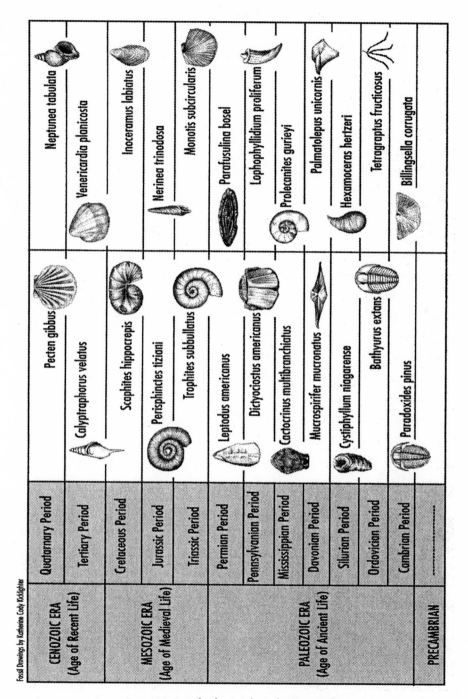

Fossil Drawings by Katherine Cooly Kicklighter

Figure 6.1: Typical Index Fossils Used as Time Markers

Microevolution

Another lesson we learn from index fossils is that there is a factual basis for one type of evolution. On a trip in the Grand Canyon several years ago, a friend of mine named Alan Doty (an Arizona resident who is an expert on the Grand Canyon) showed me numerous fossils of brachiopod remains in a rock outcrop near the top of the Canyon. A brachiopod is an ocean creature that looks a little like a clam. All of the fossils we observed that day were of the same creature. Sometime later, Dr. John McDowell (a boatman for Hatch Expeditions and a retired geology professor from Tulane University) showed me a similar rock slab of brachiopods near the bottom of the Canyon.

These two brachiopods were about the same size, but were radically different in detail and so have different names. One is called eospirifer and the other is called olenothyrus. They also have different shapes and different grooves in their shells, along with other less apparent variations. It is obvious that they are as dissimilar as a Great Dane is from a St. Bernard.

These animals are different because of microevolution. Microevolution is a design feature of the DNA molecule that, by means of the laws of heredity, allows organisms to adapt to different environments. This adaptation can be seen in everything from horses to bacteria, and we see it taking place today in cattle, dogs, and even in human racial variations. The Bible also tells us about this kind of change when it records what Jacob did with Laban's flocks in Genesis 30. While most would call this a simple breeding practice, it still fits the definition of evolutionary change.

Microevolution explains why there are so many different breeds of dogs. On the other hand, the theory of macroevolution is the same as the theory of Darwinian evolution, a distinction not made in most textbooks on the subject, including high school biology texts. So when we hear the term "fact of evolution," it is important to recognize that this refers to microevolution only. Microevolution is the fact of evolution that the Bible teaches and that can be seen in fossils or on any farm today. As we have observed in the Grand Canyon, fossils prove to us the undeniable fact that animals can adapt to their environments and change over time.

Unfortunately, evolutionary scientists have unreasonably extrapolated these minor adaptive changes into evidence that they say supports their theory. This theoretical extrapolation is the subject of intense debate among both scientists and religionists, and the favored "in" theory changes from time to time. The important point for us to remember is that living things can and do change naturally over time within specific limits.

THE GEOLOGIC COLUMN
Definition

After William Smith discovered the unique distribution of fossils in the earth, the worldwide scientific community began to add up the maximum thicknesses of all the known formations containing similar index fossils. Careful records were kept and comparisons were made. Once a maximum thickness for each particular index fossil was established, the length of time the organism had existed on earth could be estimated by multiplying the total thickness of the strata by the number of years it would take for that rock to form naturally.

At present, the accumulated sediment since abundant life appeared on earth equals a thickness of approximately 85 miles (Smith 1981, 393). This does not mean that there is one place on earth where 85 miles of sediment can be measured all in one piece, because most of the earth's surface has been eroded and recycled many times over. In other words, each successive layer of sedimentary rock for the most part is composed of eroded and/or chemically altered material from preceding sedimentary layers.

The 85 miles of observed sediment is simply the sum total of all the uneroded, unaltered, well-preserved strata containing index fossils found worldwide. Layers representing every time period have been encountered and, when pieced together, give us one continuous geologic column of history. The approximate length of time required for these 85 miles of sediment to form naturally is close to 550 million years, covering the period from the first appearance of life to the present.

Problem with Time

For the majority of people who accept the Bible as the word of God, the idea that life has been on earth for as long as 550 million years is not a problem. They believe the Bible was written to tell us that God is the one who created life, but not necessarily to tell us when he did it. They turn to modern science to supply this less important information.

A smaller, yet significant, number of Christians take issue with a figure of 550 million years because they interpret the Bible to say that the earth and life on it are young and cannot be older than 10,000 years. They base their belief in large part upon the work of Anglican Archbishop James Ussher who, in 1654, fixed the date for the earth's creation at 4,004 B.C. He figured this date by carefully counting all the relevant family generations listed in the Bible.

Although Ussher stated the limitations associated with his approach, the dates he calculated were quickly placed in the margins of the King James Version of the Bible without qualification. This led many to believe that the dates given were part of the text itself and, therefore, inspired by God. Ussher's date of 4,004 B.C. for the earth's creation would mean that, at present, the earth is only about 6,000 years old. More recently, a 10,000-year age has been proposed to allow for misunderstandings in counting the generations. (For more information on the unreliability of Ussher's calculations in using the Bible to determine the age of the earth, see chapter 11 under the heading "Biblical Chronologies.")

With such diverse ages—4.5 billion years for the age of the earth and 550 million years for the age of life compared to 10,000 years for both the earth and life—it is important for us to consider the validity of modern scientific dating methods. This is important because time is very much involved in letting the earth speak to us in the form of available evidence.

RADIOMETRIC DATING
Definition

It was not until the discovery of radioactivity around the year 1900 that a powerful new tool for dating could be added to the relative dating method begun by Steno. By measuring rates of radioactive decay, geologists were able to place numerical ages on specific rocks.

Refined over the years, this process is now known as absolute or radiometric dating. To date, there are about forty different methods available for use on rocks, ten of which are widely used. Choosing which technique to use depends largely upon the material being tested. The Potassium-Argon method is the most popular, because igneous rocks contain abundant amounts of potassium. This test is relatively easy to perform and is less expensive than alternative methods. However, because argon is a gas, it is not good for dating porous or easily weatherable rocks. Instead, the Rubidium-Strontium test is used since Strontium-87 is not a gas.

Carbon-14 Method

The Carbon-14 method is used to date organic material like rope, pottery, ashes, or bones. It has been a valid dating method since the 1960s, with considerable improvements having been made in the '70s and '80s. High precision calibration curves based on tree ring and other analyses have made possible extremely accurate Carbon-14 dates, back to 5,210 B.C. (within [+/-] 20 years in some cases). Tests run on materials beyond this date can be in error up to 20% or more.

For example, an assigned age of 30,000 years using Carbon-14 may be anywhere between 24,000 and 36,000 years old. The older the date, the greater the possible range of error. Fortunately, most people comparing geological evidence with the Bible are satisfied with narrowing a date down to the nearest one or two thousand years. Bones are only datable up to 28,000 years (Wolpoff 1999, 12), with an age of 70,000 years being the upper limit for any carbon-based material at this time.

Comparing the results of multiple tests performed by more than one laboratory on a single item can overcome problems inherent in the Carbon-14 method. If similar tests are also conducted on other specimens found in the vicinity, the accuracy of the original date can be cross-checked.

Cross-Checking Continental Deposits

The age of volcanic rocks can usually be determined because their radioactive clock is set to zero through the heating/cooling process during eruption. This characteristic of volcanic rocks is important in verifying the accuracy of modern scientific dating methods.

For example, when a volcanic eruption occurs, it often spreads a layer of lava or ash over an area being built up by sediments. After the eruption, sedimentary rocks continue to form as they did before, now burying the layer of lava. This sequence of events may continue for many thousands of years.

Today when geologists take a cross section of this undisturbed formation, they can verify their dates by using both relative and radiometric dating. First, they estimate how long one layer of sedimentary rock would take to form naturally. Then they use radiometric dating to determine the age of the layers of lava above and below the section of sedimentary rock. The difference in the ages of the lava should match the estimated formation time of the sedimentary rock in between.

Not only has this check-and-balance system proven to be reliable throughout the geologic column, several other tests have also confirmed the accuracy of the dates assigned. Top layers of lava consistently test younger than those below. Whenever there are age-datable materials within the sediments, their ages also fit in between the ages of the two confining lava layers. And finally, the radiometric age of sedimentary rocks containing index fossils must agree with the age of similarly indexed sediments, no matter where they are located in the world.

Cross-Checking Seafloor Material

The same consistent results are obtained when geologists use seafloor spreading to calculate the tectonic movement of continents and the age of the ocean floor. When continents begin to separate, as it is believed Pangea did as early as 240 million years ago (see chapter 9), an ocean floor starts to develop.

As shown in figure 6.2, new basaltic rocks are continuously being formed in the middle of the spreading centers. This new emerging rock fills the gap caused by the conveyor-like mantle rock as it transports the ocean crust toward the respective continents, where it is subducted (pulled down) under the continental boundary into the depths below. Radiometric dating bears this out, because the rocks dated nearest the spreading center are the youngest, with the oldest rocks appearing over by the continents.

According to Lamb and Sington, scientists have measured the rate of movement at the spreading center between Africa and South America and found it to be about 1.58 inches per year (1998, 55). The distance between the continents has grown to a little over 3,000 miles. When radiometric dating is applied to the coastlines, the rocks are determined to be 125 million years old.

To check the accuracy of this dating procedure, we simply multiply the separation rate of 1.58 inches by 125 million to see how far the continents should have moved apart. When we convert inches to miles, the answer is a little over 3,000 miles. This is the measured distance between Africa and South America, verifying the reliability of the radiometric dating methods used.

The ocean floor provides another way to cross-check age dating and, at the same time, substantiate prior conditions existing on earth. Geologists drill down through the ocean floor and extract uninterrupted core samples from as deep as 2,000 feet. The deep-sea ooze that forms on the ocean floor and solidifies over the years is composed of a continuous rain of material from the surface, as well as a collection of the organisms living near the ocean bottom. This solidified ooze can

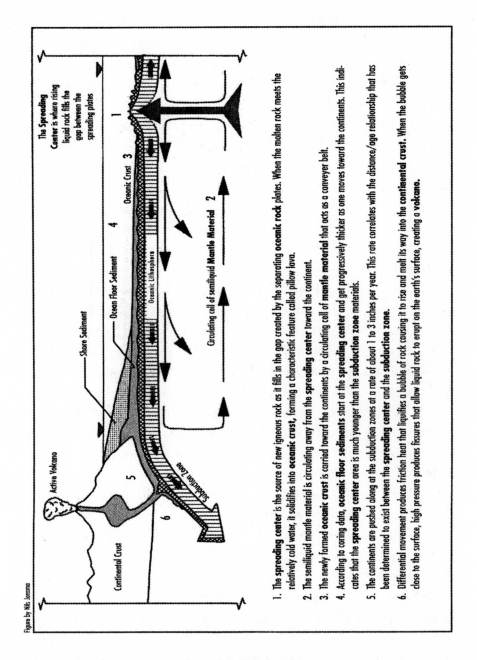

Figure by Kris Jarosma

1. The **spreading center** is the source of new igneous rock as it fills in the gap created by the separating **oceanic rock** plates. When the molten rock meets the relatively cold water, it solidifies into **oceanic crust**, forming a characteristic feature called pillow lava.

2. The semiliquid mantle material is circulating away from the **spreading center** toward the continent.

3. The newly formed **oceanic crust** is carried toward the continents by a circulating cell of **mantle material** that acts as a conveyer belt.

4. According to coring data, **oceanic floor sediments** start at the **spreading center** and get progressively thicker as one moves toward the continents. This indicates that the **spreading center** area is much younger than the **subduction zone** materials.

5. The continents are pushed along at the subduction zones at a rate of about 1 to 3 inches per year. This rate correlates with the distance/age relationship that has been determined to exist between the **spreading center** and the **subduction zone.**

6. Differential movement produces friction heat that liquifies a bubble of rock causing it to rise and melt its way into the **continental crust.** When the bubble gets close to the surface, high pressure produces fissures that allow liquid rock to erupt on the earth's surface, creating a **volcano.**

Figure 6.2: Seafloor Spreading

tell us a great deal about what was taking place on the earth and also approximately when the events occurred (Chernicoff and Venkatakrishnan 1995, 173).

Oxygen Isotope Ratios

To understand how marine fossils are used to determine water temperature, we need to know something about the oxygen atom. Oxygen is composed mainly of a light isotope weighing sixteen mass units (Oxygen-16). However, a small percentage of all oxygen weighs eighteen mass units (Oxygen-18). In water, the ratio of Oxygen-18 to Oxygen-16 (Oxygen-18/Oxygen-16) is proportional to the water's temperature. The heavier Oxygen-18 atom does not evaporate as fast as the lighter Oxygen-16 atom, so the Oxygen-18/Oxygen-16 ratio is greater in cold water than in warm.

Conveniently, because many fossils are made up of calcium carbonate, which contains oxygen atoms, we can measure the Oxygen-18/Oxygen-16 ratio in their solid body parts and determine the water temperature in which the fossil creatures lived. A similar complementary condition applies to the polar icecaps. Where the Oxygen-18/Oxygen-16 ratio is high in the ocean, it is low in the polar ice for that year. In this way, the ages of the two different types of core material can be cross-referenced.

For instance, the ocean temperature at various times in earth history is determined by analyzing the oxygen isotope ratio present in marine fossils. Ocean temperature, especially at the bottom, reveals much about weather conditions and overall air temperatures on earth and is indicative of various events, such as ice ages or warming trends. Volcanic eruptions, asteroid collisions, and similar massive catastrophes can also be recognized in ocean cores because of the deposits they scatter over the ocean's surface in the form of ash, dust, or other debris.

Some of these telltale layers can be dated radiometrically and compared to corresponding layers in continental rocks, thus cross-checking both geological events and the dates assigned to them. Based upon a combined length of more than 60 miles of core samples recovered by the research ship *Glomar Challenger* during a fifteen-year period (Chernicoff and Venkatakrishnan 1995, 337), along with numerous independent borings by private oil companies, the evidence strongly suggests that ocean-floor rocks extend in age from zero years (currently forming) back to about 200 million years for some rocks located near continental subduction zones.

Cross-Checking Polar Icecaps

The same information contained in layers of deep-sea ooze can be found to a limited extent in the polar icecaps, because each year a layer of snow is deposited at the poles that leaves us with an annual record of related events. Airborne material from volcanic eruptions and asteroid collisions settles on the polar ice, as well as on the ocean. These similar layers become correlation "markers" that can be radiometrically dated. In this way, ocean-core records can be checked against corresponding ice-core records for verification.

An analysis of the oxygen isotope ratio similar to that performed on marine fossils can be applied to the snow that became ice in the polar icecaps. The information it gives us regarding the earth's temperatures should also cross-check with corresponding temperatures and time periods found in ocean cores. When ice cores and ocean cores agree regarding time periods, cataclysmic events, and temperatures, they provide powerful proof for the validity of the dating methods currently in use (Lamb and Sington 1998, 150–154).

Cross-Checking Milankovitch Cycles

If the evidence for an ancient earth as found in the rocks, the ocean, and the polar ice could also be cross-checked by astronomical cycles, then proof for long time periods in earth history would be truly overwhelming. At present, scientists are studying the Milankovitch cycles involving the earth's orbit as a possible cause for the timing of the ice ages on earth (Lamb and Sington 1998, 159–163). Just as specific alignments of the sun and moon produce

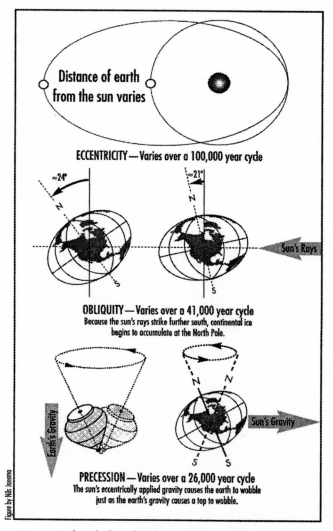

Figure 6.3: The Milankovitch Cycles in Paleoclimate (Exaggerated Scale)

extremely high or low tides on earth, so the earth's orbit and tilt in relation to the sun, when in specific alignments, can produce extreme temperatures on earth. During such cycles, the sun's effective brightness can vary up to 25% (Bowling 1987, 1). Figure 6.3 illustrates the relative position of the earth to the sun, as predicted by the Milankovitch Cycle theory.

Interestingly, the last five ice ages seem to follow a 100,000 year period, just as Serbian mathematician Milutin Milankovitch hypothesized in 1920. When his astronomical cycles are cross-checked with the oxygen isotope ratio present in ocean and ice cores, both sources support the same time periods for the onset and conclusion of the various ice ages.

This is not to say that these astronomical cycles completely explain the periodicity and scope of the ice ages (Lamb and Sington 1998, 162; Condie and Slone 1998, 423), but when it comes to finding their correlation with the physical evidence preserved within the earth's deposits, the results are surely more than coincidental. The lengths of the cycles are not imaginative conjecture. They have been computed mathematically and confirmed to be accurate by observation.

Examining Current Dating Methods

The same claim of accuracy can be made for all the dating methods described above. Some procedures, if done incorrectly or if based upon bad data, are self-checking because they simply do not give an unambiguous result. However, the vast majority of age tests conducted today agree internally, as well as with the relative dating scheme based upon Steno's laws. As stated, higher elevation rocks consistently test younger and lower layers test older. Additionally, datable deep sea and ice cores cross-check with one another and agree with corresponding radiometrically determined dates to within acceptable accuracy limits. These tests are conducted by many different laboratories throughout the world, and yet their results are consistent and repeatable.

When the above methods were first introduced, they were crude and lacked the sophistication we see today. As a result, young-earth advocates at the time quickly focused on the weaknesses of the dating techniques and thereby discredited the entire dating concept.

This position is no longer valid. Because the processes involved were based solidly upon the physical laws of science and the procedures and equipment have steadily improved, there is no longer any credible challenge to most of the tens of thousands of tests that have been made to date. Circumstances producing wrong ages are becoming well understood and compensated for whenever possible. If such refinements are not possible, then the proposed date results are generally qualified or ignored.

With this history of radiometric dating, the probability of accuracy is very high (MacRae 1998). That is why most Christians allow the earth to speak through the evidence indicating that abundant animal life, as depicted in the fossil record, began suddenly about 550 million years ago.

Those Christians who disagree and require a 10,000-year-old earth are faced with the daunting task of discrediting the dating methods and coming up with an alternative explanation for the fossil record. Such an attempted explanation called "flood geology" is discussed in appendix 7. For now, a word of warning will suffice regarding arguments presented to discredit current dating methods.

When evaluating these critical arguments, the reader should make sure that reference sources used to challenge a given testing procedure are current and not from the 1950s, when analytical equipment had vacuum tubes and computers were an expensive novelty. Much progress has been made since then. Because of this, when conflicting dating results from different decades are all thrown together and assigned equal validity, a red flag should be raised. And finally, a few exceptional examples should not be used to reach the sweeping conclusion that all radiometric dating is unreliable (Schimmrich 1998).

Since state-of-the-art technology has made it possible for the earth to speak to us in amazingly sophisticated language, how can the Bible, with its account of creation written almost four thousand years ago, have any relevance on the subject of how the earth and life on it came into existence?

In order to more fully appreciate the timeless aspect of the biblical account and how well it harmonizes with modern scientific theories, we first need to acknowledge the Bible's self-imposed limitations. A brief examination of the Book of Genesis in regard to its religious features and its original audience will help us comprehend the broad categorical harmonies between the Bible and science.

THE LANGUAGE
OF THE BIBLE

Ancient creation myths in general describe monster gods and goddesses, Frost-Giants, and feathered serpents creating the earth and humans from dismembered goddesses, trees, and tears. The Genesis account contrasts sharply with these stories, even though the Bible does not claim to be a book of science.

In 2 Timothy 3:16–17, the Bible does make the claim, "All Scripture is God-breathed and is useful for teaching, rebuking, correcting and training in righteousness, so that the man of God may be thoroughly equipped for every good work."

The Bible teaches about how God's relationship with us and how our relationship with him will motivate us to reflect his love in doing good works for others. It tells us why we are here on the earth and where we are going. That is the reason some commentators have said that the Bible tells us about the Who and Why of creation, and science supplies the What, How, and When.

The Book of Genesis is the first in a five-book section of the Bible known as the Pentateuch. The author is presumed to be Moses, who wrote and/or compiled the Genesis information around 1300–1500 B.C. in the vicinity of the land of Egypt. The introduction describes one supreme God who created the heavens and the earth without giving prominence to the gods of Egypt, particularly the sun. This was a strong theological statement against Egyptian polytheism and sun worship. God's creation framework of a seven-day week with its symbolic seventh day of rest also set the example for the sabbath law soon to be given to the nation of Israel at Mount Sinai.

An Unpolluted Creation Account

"This first chapter [of Genesis] is so ancient that it does not contain mythical or legendary matter; these elements are entirely absent. It bears the markings of having been written before myth and legend had time to grow, and not as is often stated, at a later date when it had to be stripped of the mythical and legendary elements inherent in every other account of Creation extant. This account is so original that it does not bear a trace of any system of philosophy. Yet it is so profound that it is capable of correcting philosophical systems. It is so ancient that it contains nothing that is merely nationalistic; neither Babylonian, Egyptian, nor Jewish modes of thought find a place in it, for it was written before clans, nations, or philosophies originated. Surely, we must regard it as the original, of which the other extant accounts are merely corrupted copies. Others incorporate their national philosophies in crude polytheistic and mythological form. This is pure. Genesis 1 is as primitive as the first human. It is the threshold of written history" (Wiseman 1985, 90).

ORIGINAL AUDIENCE
Scientific World-View

Recognizing this religious purpose in the Genesis account of creation makes us realize that the book should not be viewed as a scientific treatise written to challenge the technological minds of our day. It was originally penned to be understood by both shepherds and scholars whose world-view was shaped by the primitive cultures in which they lived.

Not appreciating this causes some modern critics of the Bible to complain because, in their opinion, Genesis is not nearly complicated enough to be from God. They believe it should read something like, "In the beginning God synthesized DNA in a kaolinite matrix, enzymatically catalyzed by..."

If those were the words used to reveal God's creative acts to Moses, think how difficult it would have been for Moses to understand the relevance of what God said. Such specialized language would have confused and puzzled people for ages until humans advanced enough in scientific knowledge to comprehend its significance. Fortunately, God's mission was not to confuse and misdirect Moses or any readers of the text who followed him.

As it was, no ancient reader had ever seen the earth from outer space or had leafed through a world atlas or consulted a globe. In fact, in the entire Bible, there is no original-language word for planet earth. Because of limited traveling experiences, most people's idea of the ends of the earth often consisted of what they could see from the top of the highest local hill. The heavens were equally limited by their observations, with the sun and moon appearing to be bright discs traveling across a tentlike sky.

Against this background, the first chapters of Genesis become both simple and profound. The basic message is that one supreme God created everything, including the first man and woman. They were set apart from all other living things because they were created in the very image of their maker. God omitted many of the details regarding when, where, and why he chose to create the first couple in this way. He gave what appears to be just enough information to satisfy our basic curiosity about where we came from and where we are going.

Language Differences

We also need to understand that the Bible was not written in English for an American audience. It was written in Hebrew for all audiences, and that means translation is necessary. Any time a translation is made, certain problems arise. Let me demonstrate this to you with Spanish.

I know nothing about Spanish, so when I hear, "Juan tiene frio," I have to look up what it means. When I find that the words literally mean, "John has cold," I wonder if it means that John has a cold (that he is ill) or if it means that John is cold (that he is shivering).

My wife, who took Spanish in high school, tells me that it means, "John is cold." I ask her, "How do you know that?" and she replies, "I took Spanish in school, and they explained that the culture would understand it that way."

Another example that is more complicated would be, "Juan me cae bien gordo." Literally translated, this phrase reads, "John me falls well fat." This is not a comment about my weight, it simply means, "I don't like John very much." From these examples, it should be apparent that literal translations can easily give mistaken concepts if the culture from which the translation is made is not considered.

Bara

Contextual translation such as this becomes very relevant to a literal understanding of Genesis 1. In the original Hebrew language, there are two concepts about how God brings things into existence. One way God operates is by a miraculous process that only God can do. The Hebrew word *bara* was used to indicate this process.

Bara is never used in reference to something humans can do. It is a term reserved exclusively to describe God's actions in the creation. The Jewish Publication Society says, "The Hebrew *bara* is used in the Bible exclusively of divine creativity. It signifies that the product is absolutely novel and unexampled, depends solely upon God for its coming into existence and is beyond the human capacity to reproduce" (Sarna, 1989).

The Jewish scholar Leiden says, "We have in our holy language no other term for 'the bringing forth of something from nothing' but *bara*" (1960). Appendix 8 contains the King James translation of Genesis 1 with the words in Hebrew written above the words in English. You will notice that *bara* is used in Genesis 1:1 and again in Genesis 1:21 and 1:27.

Asah and Yatsar

In addition to *bara,* there is another way God can bring things into existence. This is a process that does not always involve a miracle, but rather is a shaping or molding of something already created. The Hebrew words used to describe this process are *asah* and *yatsar.* These words are not used just in reference to accomplishments that only God can do; they are also used in reference to things that humans can do.

We see examples of *asah* in phrases like "make me laugh," "make a feast," and "make war." These are generally not miracles, but ordinary actions that humans can take by personal choice. In the biblical record, God also *asahs* much of what is described in Genesis 1:2–19.

Yatsar is used in Genesis 2:7, 8, and 19 and means to mold or squeeze into shape as a potter would work with clay. Many people have not taken the Bible literally in regard to the meaning of these three Hebrew words as they are used in the creation account. Rather, the assertion is made that *bara* and *asah* both mean to create miraculously in a way that only God can do.

One of the texts often used to argue against a literal interpretation is the scripture that discusses the formation of man. In Genesis 1:27, we are told that God created (*bara*) man in his own image; and yet in Genesis 2:7, the Bible says God formed (*yatsar*) man from the dust of the ground. Are these two verses referring to the same thing?

The answer is emphatically *no!* Genesis 1:27 is describing that which is in God's image—the spiritual makeup of humans. Genesis 2:7 is referring to man's body—that which is made of the dust of the earth and will eventually return to the dust. The two words are relating to completely different subjects.

A further challenge might come from Genesis 1:26 where God says, "Let us make (*asah*) man in our image..." In this context, the statement is made within the Godhead, not in the physical world. The *us* in the passage is the Father, Son, and Holy Spirit and is spoken from their point of view. The process is not miraculous to them because it is something they ordinarily do in their heavenly realm.

In other words, it is said that God created the universe out of nothing. However, we now know that matter and energy are equivalent. Therefore, God did not create out of nothing. From his perspective, he "made" *(asah)* the human spirit out of himself, so to speak, since he is the source of all energy (Isaiah 40:26; Hebrews 12:9). From our perspective, though, God literally created *(bara)* the human spirit because it was not formed from anything material, but came directly from his dimension or dwelling place, which is outside our tangible universe (John 14:2).

How Much Energy Exists in Our Universe?

The amount of energy in our universe is incalculable, since the amount of pure energy used in the creation of only one gram of matter (1/450th of a pound) is equal to 2.5 times the amount of energy generated by Niagara Falls in one day. This would be 10 million kilowatts of energy (Willmington).

To be sure that we do not misunderstand this vital point regarding the two aspects of creation, the Bible ends the creation story by saying that God "rested from all his work which God created *[bara]* and made *[asah]*" (Genesis 2:3). According to God, both processes were used. First, everything was created somewhere within the big bang event, and then, over time, the material universe was formed or made out of that which was originally created.

HISTORICAL NARRATIVE STYLE

Before we begin to consider the creation account in greater detail, we need to clearly understand Genesis 1:1–2. Some have interpreted these verses to imply that "In the beginning God created the heavens and the earth" (and the following verses will tell you how he did it). Of course, we should recognize that the latter words have been added.

What do the scriptures actually say? Genesis 1:1–2 begin a historical narrative written in historical style. Notice the wording:

When? "In the beginning"

What happened? "God created the heavens and the earth."

What happened next? "The earth was (or became, as some versions say) without form and void; and darkness was upon the face of the deep."

What happened next? "And the Spirit of God moved upon the face of the waters."

These are historical events written in a historical sequence. They are not summary verses of what is to follow. Something is happening in each of the statements that are made in verses 1 and 2, and the things that are happening are undated and untimed.

Genesis 1:1 Includes the Sequence of Genesis 1:3–31

So as we consider the following material, we must realize that the heavens and the earth have already been formed and planet earth has been completely prepared for humans in the first two verses of Genesis. This means that Genesis 1:3–31 applies mainly to the world of humans and the animals with which they are familiar. This is shown by the list in appendix 8 entitled "Words and Definitions," which enumerates the literal meanings of the words used in the Genesis account. As you look down the list, you will notice that all of the animals described would be familiar to the writer and to Adam and Eve. For example, the word *behemah* always refers to an ungulate (hoofed animal) and is rendered *cattle* in most translations. We will discuss this matter in more detail in chapter 11, titled "Let Humans Speak."

Though the verses of Genesis 1:3–31 directly and literally apply to the creative week in which God miraculously created the Garden of Eden and man and woman in it, the order of the events listed in those verses also applies in general to God's overall preparation of the earth for humans during the long period of activity included within Genesis 1:1. That is to say, God used the same order or sequence of events when he first prepared the entire earth for humans that he did when he prepared a particular area of the earth (the Garden of Eden) for the first man and woman. We make this distinction because the language used in Hebrew when referring to the creation of the plants and animals specifically applies to the "world" of Adam and Eve.

In order to follow our discussion of Genesis 1, it may be helpful to use the biblical text with the Hebrew words listed in appendix 8. The first sentence is a creation (*bara*) verse, not a making (*asah*) verse. The things created, according to verse 1, are the heavens (*shamayim*) and the earth. From an observer's point of view, this means that everything above and everything below was brought into existence by a miraculous act of God. It is interesting that the Hebrew word *shamayim*, according to *Young's Analytical Concordance*, has a root that means "heaved up things." Whatever the understanding of the ancients might have been, today it is remarkable that this description so clearly fits the big bang expansion.

If the *shamayim* takes in everything in the sky, this naturally includes the sun, moon, and the stars. Someone might argue that these objects are not described until verses 14 through 19, but notice that the specific word used in these particular verses is making (*asah*), not creating (*bara*). The objects were created in verse 1, the light reached the earth from these objects in verse 3, but apparently not clearly enough to establish "signs, seasons, days, and years" until verses 14 through 19.

Those who argue that *bara* and *asah* mean the same thing have to invent a light source for verse 3 because they claim the sun and moon did not come into existence until verses 14 through 19. Conversely, if we take the account literally and do not compromise the original use of these words, we do not have to invent a light for verse 3. Scientific theories based upon evidence from historical geology support the literal interpretation of this text.

Division of Waters Vertically

The universe started with a big bang event that induced the expansion we see taking place today. The development of our solar system seems to have occurred sequentially as the Bible describes it, with the heavens being created before the earth.

Research has clearly established that the earth was very hot when it first formed. The water that emerged from within its interior helped cool it down by an evaporation process, during which the earth would have been enshrouded with clouds serving to obscure the sun, moon, and stars (Job 26:7–9; 38:4–9). Historically, the evidence shows that atmospheric moisture reached its peak shortly after the earth was formed.

The Bible follows this identical sequence when it describes the creation of the heavens and the earth (including the sun, moon, and stars) and then says that God separated the waters from the waters (Genesis 1:6–7), producing two zones—waters above and below the heavens (what we might think of as the sky region below the clouds). These waters above the heavens would have obscured the sun, moon, and stars until atmospheric conditions much later in earth's history changed to make these heavenly bodies clearly visible (Genesis 1:14–19). Thus we see that there is absolute agreement between the Bible and science when we examine the facts. This is also true regarding the sequence used later to describe how life was created.

Division of Waters Horizontally

After the formation and subsequent cooling of the earth, we are told that the planet was modified (Genesis 1:6–10). There is no indication of any new creation here—only modification of existing material to produce a life-supporting environment.

We have already made reference to the division of the waters vertically when God used the evaporation process to "divide the waters from the waters." Next in sequence, verses 9 and 10 describe the division of waters horizontally with the separation of land and water. The water is said to be "gathered together" in one place, and dry land appears in another.

All the geological evidence we have indicates that this actually happened. The present arrangement involving many bodies of water and many landmasses is a relatively recent development. A casual look at the edges of North and South America, Europe, Africa, and the submerged range of mountains located in the center of the Atlantic Ocean (called the Mid-Atlantic Ridge) shows all of them to be roughly parallel. If you take a pair of scissors and cut out all of the landmasses along their continental shelves, you can fit them together like a jigsaw puzzle, as shown in figure 7.1.

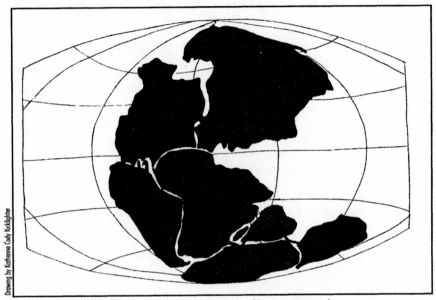

Drawing by Katherine Cody Kicklighter

Figure 7.1: Continents Fit Together like a Jigsaw Puzzle

In addition we find that rock and fossil types on opposing shorelines correlate exactly, indicating that the two continents were once joined. This jointure is also supported by satellite measurements taken from space revealing that the continents are still moving today. The process is called plate tectonics, and the movements are often referred to as continental drift.

The point is that historically all the continents started out as a single, large supercontinent that later segmented. In fact, there have been many supercontinents in earth's history, with the oldest one known as Rodinia. The last supercontinent was called Pangea, which is a Greek word meaning "all land." The surrounding ocean was called Panthalassa. Once again, the Bible is on target by accurately indicating that land first appeared as a large supercontinent, only to break up later and eventually become what we see today.

Sequence in Plant Life

> **Special Hebrew Words for Plants**
> deshe (Hebrew)—literal meaning: tender grass, one easily crushed or broken. e.g., lichens, mosses, and liverworts
> eseb (Hebrew)—understood by ancient Hebrews to refer to an herb that lacked a hard seed. e.g., ferns, horsetails, and conifers (gymnosperms)
> ets (Hebrew)—a tree (from its firmness); bearing fruit with the seed in it. e.g., aspen, birch, and oak (angiosperms)

The Bible then tells us about the sequence involved in the formation of plants. In verse 11 we are told that the first living thing was grass. The Hebrew here is *deshe,* and the word literally means tender grass. This is not the grass a person mows with a lawn mower. That word is *chatsir.* Tender grass is described as being easily broken and refers to algae, mosses, and liverworts.

The second plant material produced in the sequence is the herb from the word *eseb.* These ferns and conifers are to be distinguished from the "tree yielding seed after its kind, and the tree yielding fruit, whose seed was in itself." This latter use of the Hebrew word *ets* refers to an angiosperm—a tree with fruit and seed—not a fern or a grass. It seems that there are three kinds of plants given in the biblical sequence—the tender grass, the herb, and the flowering tree with fruit in itself. Undoubtedly, any student of botany reading this paragraph would recognize the order as the process of succession.

This sequence of events is something that God has created and used over and over in the history of our planet, and it is still taking place today. My brothers and I own a fishing camp in Canada. Many years ago, a terrible forest fire burned the area right down to bedrock, so that not a blade of grass or a crumb of organic material remained. Over the years, we have watched the process of recovery.

In the beginning, mosses and lichens began covering the rocks in some of the shaded places. These simple plants are like the "tender grass" described in the third creative day of Genesis. In one place, I recall, the moss grew so thick that I sank in deep when I walked on it, and when I lay down, it felt like a thick, soft mattress.

Eventually, we began to see a few ferns and horsetail and then some conifers (gymnosperms) start to grow in places where the mosses and lichens had accumulated enough organic material to enable the gymnosperms to grow. In just the last few years, we have seen aspen, oak, and birch trees starting to grow where the gymnosperms established a base for them. This succession is in perfect agreement with what happened in the primitive earth during creation, and it continues to occur today.

Sequence in Animal Life

The Bible's sequence of animal creation starting in verse 20 also corresponds remarkably with the evidence seen in the fossil record. Animal life is scientifically known to have begun in water. In the Genesis account, the Hebrew words used suggest that a wide range of swarming creatures began in the sea. The fossil record confirms this fact. Forty more animal phyla than exist today are contained in the earliest rocks—even animals with backbones.

We see additional examples of the sequential accuracy of the Bible by the order in which it introduces new life forms to us. According to verse 20, the first warm-blooded creatures were birds. In the fossil record, we see bird fossils, such as archaeopteryx, protoavis, and several similar finds in China, that authenticate the biblical statement. Mammals are described next in verse 24, with humans portrayed as being the last of God's creation in verse 27.

Thus the biblical sequence agrees with the fossil sequence, and since the Bible is not attempting to give us the actual time for these events, we should be impressed with its accuracy and reliability. It is interesting that, while evolutionary models come and go, from its beginning, the Bible has given us a model that still stands as credible.

In fact, discoveries are being made weekly that add to the Bible's credibility as an accurate source of information, describing events that only could be known to an intelligent designer of the universe, namely God. It has been said that if you do not believe that the universe was created by an intelligent designer, then you should wait a week, because the next new discovery may convince you otherwise.

These claims will be substantiated in the next few chapters as we accept God's invitation through Job to let the natural world tell us about the mighty hand of God in the creative process. First, we will "speak to the earth, and it will teach [us]" (Job 12:8). We will do this in detail by placing the Bible account of creation alongside the latest scientific research on cosmology and geology.

Chapter

8

LET THE
EARTH SPEAK

In the last chapter, we talked about letting the Bible speak, and we discussed the historical narrative style of Genesis 1. In so doing, we maintained that the general creation of the heavens and earth was included in the events described in Genesis 1:1.

The remaining verses of chapter 1 were applicable ultimately to the creation of Adam and Eve in the Garden of Eden. However, the sequence of that creation is one that God has used numerous times over—on an earthwide scale in preparing the earth for humans (Genesis 1:1) and on a local scale when some limited portion of the earth has had to recover from a severe natural disaster.

In this chapter, we are going to let the earth speak by examining the major events implied in Genesis 1:1 as revealed through the fossil record. Since we are mainly summarizing information from scientific and not religious material, we will follow the time periods used in current geology textbooks. Although these assigned time periods are not biblical (because the Bible does not tell us the age of the earth), they will give us a framework for correlating the evidence presented.

We will begin when our planet was first formed and end when animal life suddenly appeared in abundance 550 million years ago. By carefully studying geologic history, we will soon recognize a close parallel between what the earth tells us and what the Bible tells us about the order of creation.

COSMOLOGY IN THE GENESIS ACCOUNT

"In the beginning God created [Hebrew, *bara*] the heavens and the earth" (Genesis 1:1). From this first sentence in the Bible, we are told that there was a beginning to matter, the source of that matter was God, and the heavens were created before the earth. Whatever the early readers of Genesis might have visualized with these words, today it is clear that our concept of the expanding universe also fits the biblical description. The big bang that caused the universe to pop into existence from a singularity was truly a miracle by every definition of the word. There is no other known process by which the event can be characterized. Its miraculous nature is emphasized by the use of the Hebrew word *bara* for *created* in this verse.

In Genesis 1:1, the heavens take precedence over the earth. In the verses that follow, all things, even the sun, moon, and stars, are described relative to the effect they have on the planet earth. With the words of Genesis 1:2, "Now the earth was formless and empty," the Bible writer's perspective changes from God's vantage point outside our universe to that of an earthbound observer of God's next creative acts.

In order to let the earth speak to us about God's involvement in its formation and design, we need to listen briefly to the voices of secular historical geologists. If the details they glean by their study of earth science can be placed among the sequential categories of creation described in Genesis, then both the Bible and science will assure us "that the hand of the LORD has done this" (Job 12:9). With this in mind, we will begin with the current scientific explanation for how our solar system came into existence.

Formation of the Sun

The leading theory of how our sun formed is called the Nebular Hypothesis (Tarbuck and Lutgens 1993, 10). When a massive star "dies," it collapses back upon itself and explodes, becoming what is called a nova. Geologists believe a nova occurred in our region of the galaxy approximately 5,000 mya (million years ago). Most of the huge cloud of hydrogen gas left over from the nova became our sun. The heavy, solid materials from the interior of the original star eventually consolidated into the rocky planets, among which our earth is included. Details describing exactly how the sun and the earth came to occupy their precise positions are not well understood at present, and the origin and position of the moon continue to be subjects of intense debate (Audouze and Israel 1988, 96).

Early in the formation of the solar system, the interstellar space between the earth and the sun was filled with a lot of dustlike particles.

Origin of the Solar System

The explanation for how our solar system formed leaves us with many mysterious coincidences. The precise size and position of the moon cause it to exactly cover the sun during an eclipse. The synchronous revolutions of the moon and the earth keep the same side of the moon always facing the earth. The perfect distance between the earth and the sun places the earth in a very restricted "habitable zone" where water can exist in all three of its forms—liquid, solid, and vapor.

These are just a few of many mysterious coincidences in our solar system. Trying to explain their formation by natural means is like trying to explain the formation of the presidential faces that decorate Mount Rushmore by natural processes.

As an alternative theory, could our solar system have come into existence in the same manner as the universe—from a singularity in a mini big bang? Dr. Stephen Hawking says there is no physical reason why a singularity could not happen at any time and at any place. Therefore, a supportable but not yet established explanation could be that the solar system formed in the same way as the universe itself began.

Light from the sun would not reach the earth until this space could be swept clean by means of a solar wind radiating out from the newly activated sun (Chernicoff and Venkatakrishnan 1995, 10).

Formation of the Earth

The earth at first was a ball of red-hot, semimolten material formed by accretion, which is the violent accumulation of heavy debris left over from the exploding star. At this time, the increasing gravity of the developing earth attracted numerous asteroids. Wherever these asteroids hit, they melted vast sections of the earth's surface. Included among the asteroids were comets made up mostly of water. This water was absorbed as superheated steam within the molten rocks.

Each time the earth was hit, its orbit, speed, and radius were affected, causing a constant changing of its position in space. Since the earth's location relative to the sun is crucial for life to exist (with only a 5% margin of error allowed), scientists comment on the happy coincidence that the earth finally situated itself exactly in this very narrow zone that supports life. For this reason, the area is called the "continuously habitable zone" (Condie and Slone 1998, 131). It is reported that this asteroid activity reached its peak about 4,500 mya.

Asteroids

A look at the moon's craters gives us some idea of the extent of asteroid bombardment on the primitive earth. Because the moon's surface is not affected by the same erosion, earthquakes, and volcanic activity that constantly alter the surface of our planet, its craters remain almost unchanged since their original formation.

Although we are no longer threatened by earth-orbit asteroids, occasionally an asteroid from what is called the main-belt asteroids located between Mars and Jupiter still can impact the earth and moon. Scientists believe a hit from one of these asteroids may have contributed to the extinction of the dinosaurs. Much later in A.D. 1178, a group of men in Kent, England, watched an asteroid collide with the moon, forming a 22-km crater now called Giordano Bruno (Condie and Slone 1998, 77).

Comets

Comets are, indeed, an interesting sight to see. When they pass by, their tails are always pointing away from the sun because the sun's energy discharge (solar wind) has blown them in that direction. Comets are like a dirty, dry ice and water snowball built around a small, solid nucleus.

With few exceptions, they are believed to have originated in the Oort Cloud, which surrounds our entire solar system. In 1950, Jan Oort concluded that the debris cloud was located about 50,000 times the distance from the sun to the earth away and contained about 1,000 billion comets. Its total mass was estimated to be about equal to that of the earth.

What makes comets suddenly leave their positions and plunge toward the sun? Astronomers speculate that there must be a mysterious Planet X out there somewhere beyond Pluto that disturbs their arrangement and causes them to take the plunge.

HISTORICAL GEOLOGY IN THE GENESIS ACCOUNT

First Event: Now the earth was formless and empty, darkness was over the surface of the deep, and the Spirit of God was hovering over the waters.

Atmospheric Temperature

As the earth began to cool, more factors for temperature regulation were needed than simply maintaining a proper distance from the sun. Here is where an extremely well-organized system of checks and balances operated to maintain a constant atmospheric temperature on the earth of between 0° and 100°C. In the beginning, when the earth's interior was exceptionally hot, the sun compensated by radiating only about 70% to 80% of its current output of energy. This radiation was also intercepted by interstellar dust. As the earth cooled, the sun's output rose and the dust began to clear, allowing the increased solar heat to precisely counterbalance what was lost (Lamb and Sington 1998, 230).

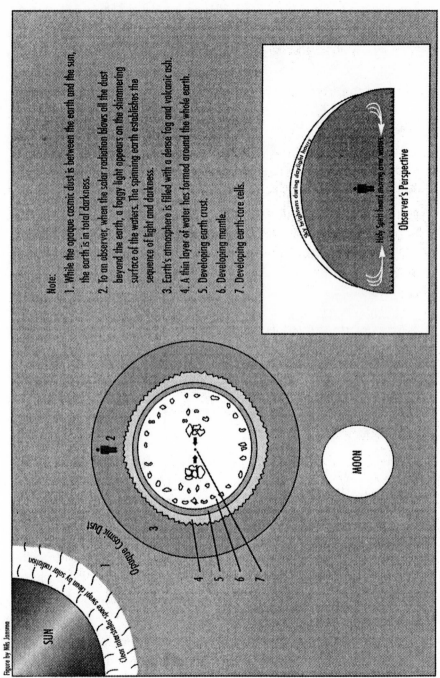

Note:

1. While the opaque cosmic dust is between the earth and the sun, the earth is in total darkness.

2. To an observer, when the solar radiation blows all the dust beyond the earth, a foggy light appears on the shimmering surface of the waters. The spinning earth establishes the sequence of light and darkness.

3. Earth's atmosphere is filled with a dense fog and volcanic ash.

4. A thin layer of water has formed around the whole earth.

5. Developing earth crust.

6. Developing mantle.

7. Developing earth-core cells.

Observer's Perspective

Sky brightens during daylight hours

Holy Spirit heard moving over waters

Opaque Cosmic Dust

Clear interstellar space swept clean by solar radiation

SUN

MOON

Figure by Nils Jansma

Figure 8.1: First Event

Surface Water

Besides a gradual inner cooling of the earth, the formation of surface water began an outer cooling process that helped to solidify the earth's crust. Water, so essential for life and so dependent upon a narrow temperature range, was present in the original mass components from which the earth was made. When the interior rocks reached their melting point, water vapor was released and migrated to the surface in geyser-type vents like Old Faithful in Yellowstone Park. Additional water vapor came from comets and asteroids that bombarded the earth during its formation (Lamb and Sington 1998, 220). Based upon measurements taken in 1999, this latter source of water vapor is not unusual because free water molecules exist in plentiful supply in interstellar space (Talcott 1999, 1–2).

As the earth's crust thickened, water vapor continued to be emitted from the earth's hot interior in large volumes. This activity soon produced a thin ocean of water that completely covered the earth. Large amounts of water vapor also remained in mist form, thickly enshrouding the earth, quite similar to conditions found on the planet Venus today.

This insulating barrier of water vapor, along with atmospheric carbon dioxide, conserved needed heat. It also acted as a protection from the sun's harmful ultraviolet rays, which would soon be shining directly upon the earth's upper cloud layer. Based upon these facts, it is very possible that an observer present on the earth about 4,200 mya would be in complete darkness and would hear the waters churning below as they were disrupted by occasional subsurface volcanic eruptions.

Light

Second Event: And God said, "Let there be light," and there was light. God saw that the light was good, and he separated the light from the darkness. God called the light "day" and the darkness he called "night."

As the space between the earth and the sun was swept clean of interstellar dust, the side of the rotating earth facing the sun became illuminated, while the opposite side was swathed in darkness. Because the earth's primary atmosphere was probably like a thick fog, an observer could easily sense the difference between day and night, but would not be able to see anything else. According to current evidence, production of water vapor in the atmosphere reached its peak about 3,600 mya.

Secondary Atmosphere

Third Event: And God said, "Let there be an expanse between the waters to separate water from water." So God made the expanse and separated the water under the expanse from the water above it. And it was so. God called the expanse "sky."

It is very unlikely that life would be able to survive in the initial foggy atmosphere of the proto earth. Fortunately, at this time rampant volcanic activity on earth released huge amounts of water vapor, along with carbon dioxide and nitrogen. These gases replaced the fog with what is called earth's secondary atmosphere. It consisted of a transparent expanse or zone covered by a layer of heavy clouds.

Here we see another beneficial series of checks and balances taking place. As the debris between the earth and the sun cleared and the fog dissipated, a compensating barrier of clouds formed. These high clouds shielded the earth from the sun's ultraviolet radiation and provided insulation to conserve heat on its surface. In the creation account, the transparent expanse or secondary atmosphere was called heaven or sky, depending upon the translation used.

Any loss of heat from the sun's rays reflecting off the clouds was balanced by a growing volume of carbon dioxide in earth's atmosphere that conveniently provided a warming "greenhouse effect." The time was ripe for the foundation materials of life to appear. In laboratory experiments, eighteen of the twenty known amino acids found in living organisms have been produced in this type of early atmosphere. These experiments show that such simple compounds could exist at this time

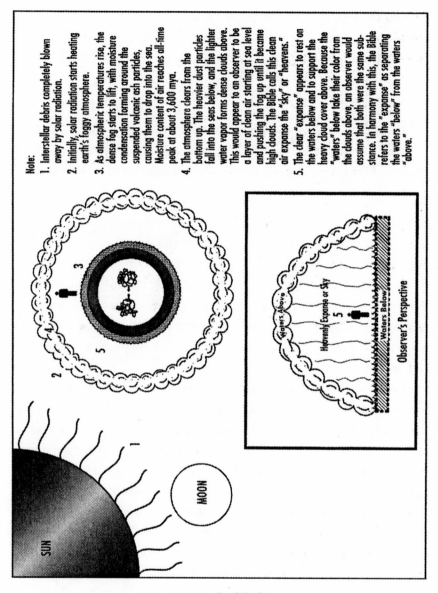

Note:

1. Interstellar debris completely blown away by solar radiation.

2. Initially, solar radiation starts heating earth's foggy atmosphere.

3. As atmospheric temperatures rise, the dense fog starts to lift, with moisture condensation forming around the suspended volcanic ash particles, causing them to drop into the sea. Moisture content of air reaches all-time peak at about 3,600 mya.

4. The atmosphere clears from the bottom up. The heavier dust particles fall into the seas below, and the lighter water vapor forms dense clouds above. This would appear to an observer to be a layer of clean air starting at sea level and pushing the fog up until it became high clouds. The Bible calls this clean air expanse the "sky" or "heavens."

5. The clear "expanse" appears to rest on the waters below and to support the waters above. Because the heavy cloud cover above would take their color from the clouds above, an observer would assume that both were the same substance. In harmony with this, the Bible refers to the "expanse" as separating the waters "below" from the waters "above."

Figure 8.2: Second and Third Events

without deteriorating. However, it should be understood that the more complicated production of information-carrying molecules such as DNA and RNA still remain far beyond the reach of laboratory simulation.

Supercontinents

Fourth Event: And God said, "Let the water under the sky be gathered to one place, and let dry ground appear." And it was so. God called the dry ground "land," and the gathered waters he called "seas."

The earth's surface had now cooled to life-supporting temperatures. Shortly after this, a remarkable phenomenon known as convection cells was set in motion within the earth's mantle. Hot convective currents within the magma (melted mantle rocks), like those seen in a pot of boiling water, began to churn and glide along the underside of the newly formed upper crust (lithosphere). As a result, complementary halves of the thin crustal shell began to move in opposite directions (Redfern 1980, 22), forming the earth's first oceanic spreading center.

Since these convective currents always operate in pairs and oppose one another, the two separating crustal hemispheres moved apart, causing them to collide and buckle on the opposite side of the earth. The collision would induce the heavier oceanic materials to buckle downward and the lighter continental materials to be scraped off and accumulate on top of the impact zone. These series of events would result in the continental crust material being separated and piled up, forming an underwater landmass. It is interesting to consider that, because the oceanic spreading center region on the opposite side of the earth would be uplifted significantly during this operation, the depth of the ocean in the vicinity of the forming continent would be unusually deep. As a consequence, the entire continent could form without ever protruding above water. However, when the two hemispheric convection cells within the earth's mantle segmented into multiple cells, the uplifted region would rapidly sink, causing the water covering the continent to quickly flow toward the basin created by the lowering of the ocean

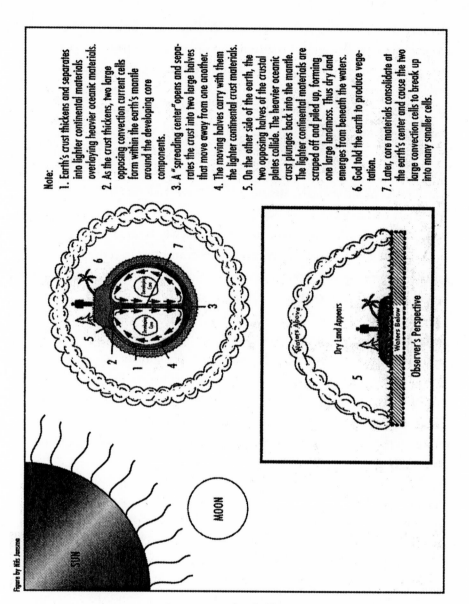

Note:

1. Earth's crust thickens and separates into lighter continental materials overlaying heavier oceanic materials.

2. As the crust thickens, two large opposing convection current cells form within the earth's mantle around the developing core components.

3. A "spreading center" opens and separates the crust into two large halves that move away from one another.

4. The moving halves carry with them the lighter continental crust materials.

5. On the other side of the earth, the two opposing halves of the crustal plates collide. The heavier oceanic crust plunges back into the mantle. The lighter continental materials are scraped off and piled up, forming one large landmass. Thus dry land emerges from beneath the waters.

6. God fold the earth to produce vegetation.

7. Later, core materials consolidate at the earth's center and cause the two large convection cells to break up into many smaller cells.

Figure 8.3: Fourth and Fifth Events

floor. Remarkably, this is the same way in which the Bible describes the appearance of land. We are not told that dry land rose from the ocean's depths, but rather that the waters flowed off the land and were gathered into "one place" (Genesis 1:9).

An observer situated just above the earth's surface would be able to see a single landmass, a supercontinent, slowly appear as the waters retreated off its surface. The geologic record shows that between 2,800 and 2,600 mya, the initial continental building process was the most accelerated in all of earth's history (Clondie and Slone 1998, 111).

After the appearance of that first supercontinent, more convection cells formed within the earth, causing the newly formed continent to break up. The resulting smaller continents continued to move over the earth's surface in a repeating pattern of colliding, forming another single landmass, and then breaking up again.

Scientists believe a supercontinent they named Rodinia existed when life suddenly appeared in abundance around 550 mya. As mentioned in chapter 7, if we place our present-day continents in a jigsaw puzzle configuration, they seem to fit what geologists believe was the last of these consolidated landmasses called Pangea. All of this movement and collision activity, along with weathering processes taking place on the surface of the earth, served to form the needed topsoil for the creation of plant life which took place next.

First Plant Life

Fifth Event: Then God said, "Let the land produce vegetation (Hebrew, *deshe*): seed-bearing plants (Hebrew, *eseb*) and trees (Hebrew, *ets*) on the land that bear fruit with seed in it, according to their various kinds." And it was so. The land produced vegetation: plants bearing seed according to their kinds and trees bearing fruit with seed in it according to their kinds.

Trace fossils of living cells have been found in ancient Hadean rocks that date back to about 3,800 to 3,600 mya. Though scientists describe these cells as being simple, in fact they were very complex.

They contained highly structured DNA and RNA molecules that made cellular division possible, along with the ability to manufacture numerous essential amino acids. An extremely sophisticated membrane had to form—one which not only prevented the intrusion of harmful substances but also allowed food nutrients to pass through without substantial difficulty.

Surprisingly, there is evidence that such cells appeared very soon after the earth's crust had solidified and the oceans had formed. Though they were bacteria, these cells looked like blue-green algae. Because of their complexity, their quick emergence defies credible explanation from an atheistic viewpoint. This is probably one of many reasons why Dr. Francis Crick, the codiscoverer of the DNA molecule, suggested that life came from outer space. He recognized that the time available for such complex cellular life forms to evolve naturally was not nearly long enough.

It should also be noted that the Bible account indicates that both dry land and plants appeared together. The sequence of plant life in the fossil record finds the algaelike plants (Hebrew, *deshe*) appearing first, followed by spore-bearing or external seed-bearing plants (Hebrew *eseb*) like ferns, horsetail, and gymnosperms (conifers), which dominated the earth during the time of the dinosaurs. Angiosperms (Hebrew *ets*) or trees that bear fruit necessary to sustain human life appeared much later.

Precambrian Era

Sixth Event: And God said, "Let there be lights in the expanse of the sky to separate the day from the night, and let them serve as signs to mark seasons and days and years, and let them be lights in the expanse of the sky to give light on the earth." And it was so. God made two great lights—the greater light to govern the day and the lesser light to govern the night. He also made the stars. God set them in the expanse of the sky to give light on the earth, to govern the day and the night, and to separate light from darkness.

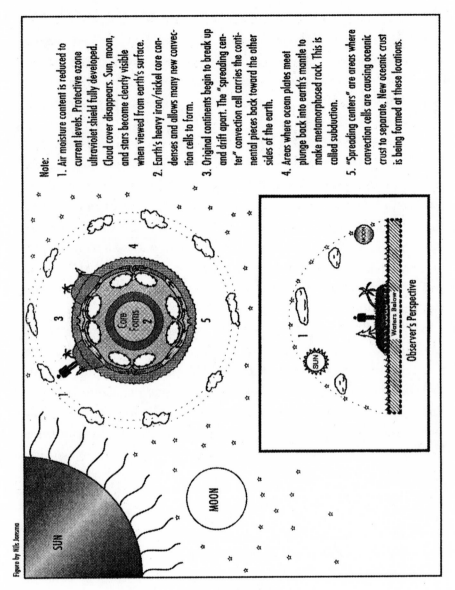

Figure 8.4: Sixth Event

The time from 4,550 mya to about 550 mya is collectively known as the Precambrian era and accounts for about 87% of the geologic time scale (Tarbuck and Lutgens 1993, 11). All during this incredibly long period of time, there was little opportunity for life to increase in complexity because of the limits placed upon it by the developing environment.

Before multicelled organisms could survive, the oxygen content of the ancient atmosphere needed to reach almost 7% of its current levels (Condie and Slone 1998, 125). An ozone layer had to form in the upper atmosphere to protect future life on land from ultraviolet radiation once the protective cloud cover disappeared. Continents had to be reshaped and covered with a usable layer of topsoil to support the more complex plant life that was scheduled to arise in the future. The ocean's water also needed to be enriched with dissolved oxygen so fish could survive.

Anaerobic Cells

The introduction of plantlike bacterial cells early in earth's history was the beginning of these preparations. The very first cells were one-celled, anaerobic (need no oxygen) prokaryotes (no enclosed nucleus) that reproduced simply by dividing themselves in half. They would start cleansing the atmosphere and oceans of harmful components by a process called fermentation (Curtis and Barnes 1989, 206). These plantlike bacterial cells also helped to break down the composition of surface rock, which is a necessary first step in soil formation.

Aerobic Cells

With the emergence of photosynthetic life forms about 3,600 mya to 3,000 mya, the production of oxygen began. This process was accelerated still more by the progressive clearing of both the upper and lower atmospheres. At about 2,100 mya, we find evidence that the amount of atmospheric oxygen began to increase dramatically (Lamb and Sington 1998, 181). (See appendix 9.) As it reached about 60% of its current levels, the first aerobic (oxygen breathing) eukaryotic cells (with an enclosed nucleus) appeared in the fossil record.

Balanced Atmosphere

It is likely that now the ozone layer was almost completely developed, replacing the disappearing cloud cover. An observer on the surface of the earth at this time would probably see the sun, moon, and stars appear occasionally through a broken cloud layer. From this point of view, it would be as if these heavenly bodies had been newly created because they were distinctly visible for the first time. To be able to establish "signs, seasons, days, and years," ancient people would have to have a reasonably clear view of the sun, moon, and stars. It is no accident that the Genesis account tells us that these divisions of time (which are so important to humans and to some migrating animals) were not possible until the sun, moon, and stars were clearly visible.

By about 900 mya, all the delicate balances of gases in the atmosphere necessary for life in abundance had been attained. Describing the tenuous role of carbon dioxide in a perfectly balanced atmosphere, Lamb and Sington say, "So we have in effect a complex system made up of temperature-sensitive chemical reactions and full of checks and balances, which seems to have subtracted or added carbon dioxide to the atmosphere in just the right way to maintain roughly constant surface temperatures" (1998, 233). (See appendix 10.)

This balance of carbon dioxide in the atmosphere is only one of the many incredible coincidences described in geology texts regarding the formation of our solar system and the earth. To the believer in God, these "coincidences" are evidence of a Master Designer who precisely and successfully engineered each complex system.

As we have seen, the Bible paints in broad brush strokes what geology fills in with details. The order is amazing considering how long ago the Book of Genesis was written. Yet we should not miss the major points of this discussion. The Genesis account is good for our instruction and edification by telling us who created and why. The fossil record satisfies our natural curiosity by progressively revealing to us many of the fascinating details about the handiwork of God that the Bible's abbreviated account omits. Therefore, both the Bible and the fossil record should be allowed to stand as testimonies to the power and wisdom of the living and working God of the universe.

So far, we have followed historical geology to a time when the earth and the atmosphere have been prepared to support independent living creatures. Now the Bible says God created in abundance, and the oceans, skies, and land swarmed with living creatures all producing after their kinds. In keeping with Job's invitation, it is time to ask the animals to teach us about how and when God intervened in their creation. We will do this by continuing to place the fossil record alongside the brief account in Genesis.

ASK THE ANIMALS

But ask the animals, and they will teach you, or the birds of the air, and they will tell you; or speak to the earth, and it will teach you, or let the fish of the sea inform you. Which of all these does not know that the hand of the LORD has done this? In his hand is the life of every creature and the breath of all mankind. (Job 12:7–10)

In this chapter, we are continuing to highlight the sequence of events in the geologic record. As a result, we will follow the same format regarding time periods as we did in chapter 8. When the animals speak to us from the fossil record, they tell us about how God progressively created life. Their remains show that various types of animals existed over long periods of time, during which they helped to prepare the earth for eventual use by humans. Often after an animal had completed its apparent task, it went into extinction and was replaced by a more advanced and/or complex creature.

Many times, massive, worldwide extinctions took place, followed by the sudden emergence of whole new populations over relatively short periods of geologic time. Since there are no believable evolutionary explanations offered for such quick recoveries, they testify to the progressive nature of God's creative work over time.

So far, our discussion of historical geology has been like the first stage of the agave (pronounced a GAH vee) or century plant. This unusual plant, found in the southwestern United States and Mexico, grows very slowly over many years. Suddenly, almost overnight, it produces a rapidly growing flower stalk that shoots up as high as 40 feet before it briefly blossoms and dies.

To watch its growth with time-lapse photography, a person would see a prolonged period of preparation time. During this long, slow period, a root system would become established and thick, fibrous leaves would grow and arrange themselves into tight rosettes. Then in a burst of activity, the plant would appear to come alive as the flower spike emerged and bloomed.

CAMBRIAN PERIOD (550 TO 505 MYA)

Like the first stage of the century plant, for most of earth's history (87% or about four billion years), the record in the rocks shows preparation time while the earth's surface, seas, and atmosphere were slowly changing to support life. Now we are about to witness a growth spurt, seemingly overnight in geologic time, wherein an astounding number of distinctive animal types come into existence. Such an abundance of life occurred in the oceans at the beginning of what is called the Cambrian period.

Stephen Jay Gould, a renowned author and evolutionist, describes the event as follows: "This 'Cambrian explosion' marks the advent (at least into direct evidence) of virtually all major groups of modern animals—and all within the minuscule span, geologically speaking, of a few million years" (1989, 24).

In harmony with the geologic evidence, the Bible also describes an explosion of life forms beginning in the sea.

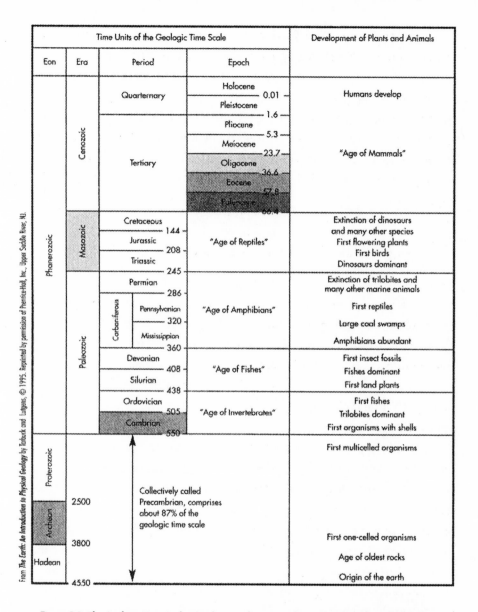

Figure 9.1: The Geologic Time Scale. Numbers on the time scale represent time in millions of years before the present. These dates were added long after the time scale had been established using relative dating techniques. The Precambrian accounts for more than 87% of geologic time. (Data from Geological Society of America)

Seventh Event: And God said, "Let the water teem with living creatures, and let birds fly above the earth across the expanse of the sky." So God created the great creatures of the sea and every living and moving thing with which the water teems, according to their kinds, and every winged bird according to its kind. And God saw that it was good. God blessed them and said, "Be fruitful and increase in number and fill the water in the seas, and let the birds increase on the earth."

When the Bible says, "Let the water *teem* with living creatures," the fossil record shows this is exactly what happened. As proof, we look to the Burgess Shale and the Chengjiang fossils.

Recent Fossil Finds

In 1909, Charles Walcott, recognized by some as America's greatest paleontologist, discovered a veritable treasure trove of fossils high in the Canadian Rockies. The mountainous area in eastern British Columbia was once near the equator and under water. Approximately 530 mya, it appears that swift ocean undercurrents transported hundreds of thousands of organisms out of a lagoon to the base of an undersea limestone cliff.

The life forms were buried deep in anaerobic (no oxygen) clay when the cliff collapsed, beautifully preserving them in exquisite detail. Normally, only the hard body parts of life forms are fossilized, leaving the scientist to guess at what the soft, inner workings of the creatures were like. In the Burgess Shale, however, soft bodied organisms, like worms and sponges, are incredibly preserved. Not only can delicate structures such as muscles and membranes be observed and studied, but even the last meals eaten by some of the creatures are visible within their guts.

The discovery of these fossils gave scientists a unique window into the past, and they were astounded by what they saw. Most Precambrian life had consisted of simple, single-celled organisms. It was not until a very short time before the Cambrian that any traces of multicellular creatures occurred, and these were fluffy organisms known as Ediacara fauna, along with trace fossils of worm holes. No actual worms have ever been found. Proof for their existence came in the form of grooves and burrows left on the seafloor, suggesting they were very simple creatures.

The Ediacara fauna were soft, coral-like animals with no heart, no brain, and no means of forming a skeleton, muscles, or a circulatory system. They spent their entire lives either floating in currents or lying on the ocean bottom (Monastersky 1993, 3). Since there is at present serious doubt that Ediacara fauna were related to any modern life form (Gould 1989, 312), the worms are left as the only apparent ancestor to the vast array of complex animals found in the Burgess Shale.

It is little wonder, then, that scientists were amazed. Suddenly, geologically speaking, only 15 to 20 million years after the beginning of the Cambrian, the oceans were teeming with more than 70 body designs (phyla). Today, there are only about 30 or so of these unique body types left. According to Gould, "The Burgess Shale includes a range of disparity in anatomical design never again equaled, and not matched today by all the creatures in all the world's oceans" (1989, 208).

Exploding onto the world scene like life's big bang were sophisticated creatures possessing legs for walking, paddles for swimming, and compound eyes for seeing—eyes so remarkably designed they are comparable to those found in modern-day insects (Levi-Setti 1993, 32, 54). Circulatory, respiratory, and digestive systems were all in place, functioning in jointed bodies with hard exoskeletons, some of which were cleverly engineered to enroll or curl up as a defense tactic.

How could life have evolved so profoundly from a Precambrian worm in just 15 to 20 million years? If that question was difficult to answer during the 75 years that the Burgess Shale was unique, it became a true conundrum (mystery) with the unearthing of the Chengjiang fossils in 1984. That was the year when paleontologist Hou Xianguang discovered a fossil site in China containing the same variety of life forms in the same perfectly preserved condition as those in the Burgess Shale. One significant difference, however, with the Chengjiang fossils was their age. They were dated 10 to 15 million years *older* than the Burgess Shale, placing them virtually at the beginning of the Cambrian period. Now evolutionists no longer have even 15 to 20 million years for complex life to develop. They have no time at all from a geologic perspective. That is why life's big bang remains such a big mystery.

When we combine this unexpected explosion of complex life with a drastically reduced time period for its evolution and with modern genetic research considerations, we get a much different picture of life's history than Darwin had. We see an earth covered with primitive algae and bacteria for billions of years suddenly come alive without any advanced warning. We find the fossil record unexpectedly revealing exquisitely designed, complex sea creatures whose unique body parts have no earlier transitional forms. Among the most spectacular structures that appeared in the Cambrian fossils were "the new types, numbers, and arrangements of appendages: a blizzard of arms, legs, swimming paddles, mandibles, antennae, and more" (Pendick 1998, 28).

The Distal-less Gene

In the past, scientists believed that animals developed these appendages by somehow inventing new genes as the need arose, requiring millions of years of separate evolutionary transformations for each new body part to form. However, Grace Panganiban, in association with Dr. Sean Carroll and fellow researchers at the University of Wisconsin, made an amazing discovery that would not only explain the sudden appearance of complex appendages in the Cambrian explosion, but would also provide believers in God with another important proof for the existence of a Creator.

It appears that the same limb-building gene called Distal-less found in all six branches of our modern animal kingdom can be traced back to the Precambrian worm mentioned earlier. The gene carries a basic program for appendages of all kinds and needs only minor modifications to grow a variety of limbs outward from the body wall. As the article in *Earth* magazine states,

> According to the purple specks that marked a gene Panganiban had pursued doggedly for three years, the Cambrian explosion hap-

pened in large part because primitive animals—namely that elusive Precambrian worm—bequeathed a fully stocked toolkit of limb-building genes to their Cambrian descendants. Using that set of genes in different ways, animals could re-engineer themselves with what amounted to minor tinkering. (Pendick 1998, 28)

The discovery of this Distal-less gene and others like it negates the major tenet of evolutionary theory that, as demands arose, designs followed. This gene is an example of modular programming with advanced planning, "like a subroutine in a computer program" (Brownlee 1997, 3). Only an intelligent designer would be able to anticipate future demands by engineering a versatile tool kit that could be used over and over again with only "minor tinkering" to meet a variety of environmental needs.

This gene described as a "tool kit" explains why many unrelated animals have similar body parts, such as the wings of birds and those of flies. Obviously, a common winged ancestor is not available as a supposed evolutionary explanation. Similar body parts are called either "analogous" or "homologous" structures and are said to be the result of "convergent" or "parallel" evolution. The argument is that the same environmental demands caused different life forms to separately evolve comparable survival characteristics.

Such a claim, though, soon becomes stretched beyond acceptable limits. For example, at present atheistic evolution cannot satisfactorily explain the development over time of the complexities of a compound eye in even one species. To assert that the same processes also occurred independently of each other in separate environments with other species makes the probabilities impossible. However, we can see that a modular tool kit gene seems to be the way God has equipped a variety of animals with the ability to quickly adapt to the same type of environment using body components that look almost alike.

Another significant area in the Darwinian model of evolution seriously affected by the fossil finds of the twentieth century is illustrated in figure 9.2. If organisms evolved over millions of years from simple to complex, why did they not follow the cone-shaped pattern shown in figure 9.2, by gradually growing in numbers and complexity?

Instead, the record shows that just the opposite occurred. Figure 9.3 illustrates the Christmas tree pattern described by Gould (1989, 301). In this pattern, the waters suddenly teemed with living creatures that had no apparent predecessors. Yet they possessed body forms that were greater in variety and equal in complexity to any living in modern times. From that amazing beginning, they went on to *decrease* over millions of years to the approximately thirty major groups or phyla existing today.

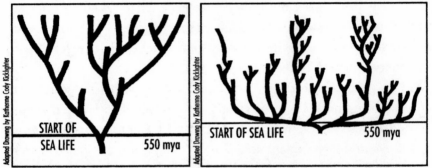

From *Wonderful Life: The Burgess Shale and the Nature of History* by Stephen Jay Gould Copyright ©1989 by Stephen Jay Gould Used by permission of W. W. Norton & Company, Inc

Figure 9.2: The False but Still Conventional Iconography of the Cone of Increasing Diversity

Figure 9.3: The Revised Model of Diversification and Decimation, Suggested by the Proper Reconstruction of the Burgess Shale

Geologic Events

Although the Cambrian period is best known for the sudden appearance of complex life forms as we have discussed, it was also a time period of significant geologic events. For example, three well-known formations were deposited that were later exposed when the Grand Canyon formed. To the east of what is now the Grand Canyon, a large mountainous landmass called the Transcontinental Arch extended north and south across the United States from Canada to the Gulf of Mexico.

As the sea level rose slowly, it eroded material off the Arch and deposited it as a near-shore sand we call the Tapeats Sandstone. The Bright Angel Shale, which contains fossils of trilobites, was the result of an offshore deposit of clay. On top of this is a deeper, oceanic layer called the Muav Limestone. All of these formations can be clearly seen when one travels down the Colorado River through the Grand Canyon.

Trilobites, crablike creatures with a compound eye, remained quite numerous during the Cambrian period, even though their populations were negatively impacted by five major extinctions. Each time the earth has experienced an extinction—and there have been many of them—the recovery time for the animals has been extremely rapid. Without acknowledging the intervention of a supernatural source of power and design, there is no satisfactory explanation as to how these recoveries could have occurred.

For many Christians and many evolutionists, the Cambrian is the most exciting period in the geologic time scale for the aforementioned reasons. Yet the periods following the Cambrian contain characteristic life forms whose existence and decimation were dramatically choreographed by the continued preparation of earth for human habitation.

The following brief overview of each historic period will give us an idea of what was happening on earth to produce the landmasses and natural resources that were in place when humans first appeared. It will also familiarize us with the sequence of life exposed to our view in the fossil record worldwide. We will be impressed with how inadequate a purely natural evolutionary explanation is for what appears to be an instantaneous reappearance of life after each catastrophic extinction.

The conclusion of almost every geologic period was marked by a devastating catastrophe, and the Cambrian was no exception. Possibly a climate change (no one knows for certain) left only 5% of the trilobites to survive into the next period, the Ordovician.

ORDOVICIAN PERIOD (505 TO 438 MYA)

From the Ordovician period, we find evidence of the first fossilized fish and land plants. The plants, which were only a few millimeters high and similar to modern liverworts, superseded the bacterial land plants that had been slowly degrading the rock over the past two billion years (Condie and Slone 1998, 206, 255).

The Ordovician period also saw a massive volcanic eruption at the Blackriver-Trenton boundary in North America. It was 500 times greater than that of Mount St. Helens in 1980 and resulted in another large-scale extinction of many sea animal species. The extensive ash beds it left have been dated back 456 million years.

Using this date as a reference, researchers have calculated that the nine surviving species in the area of the eruption increased to approximately 65 species within 100,000 years. That would be a rate of one new species every 1,500 years. According to present knowledge, such a rapid rate of change cannot be explained by natural causes.

The third most devastating extinction recorded in geologic history concluded the Ordovician period. A vast ice age began, which dropped sea levels approximately 600 to 1,000 feet and wiped out all the tideland species worldwide.

Mountaintop Fossils

As evidence for the biblical flood of Noah's day, some have pointed to the discovery of shells on mountaintops as proof that the flood waters covered the highest mountains. This claim could possibly be true if the shells were lying loose on the ground and represented an environment that existed long enough during the flood for generations of shells to accumulate.

However, there are a number of problems with this viewpoint. Shells found on mountaintops are mostly saltwater shells, not the freshwater shells one would expect to find if a flood had deposited them. During the flood, all the saltwater shell creatures would have died and been left on the bottom of the ocean. Only freshwater shell creatures could have risen with the waters to the tops of mountains. They would also have to be in flood debris, all mixed up with large and small animals. In general, the shells we observe are not a jumbled mixture, but, in most cases, are very uniform and show gradual accumulation.

Additionally, shells found in the mountains, such as those in the Burgess Shale, are not loose, but embedded in the rocks as fossils. This fossilization indicates that they have been transformed by heat and/or great pressure and then uplifted to their present height, all of which would have taken a long time.

SILURIAN PERIOD (438 TO 408 MYA)

While no new major groups of invertebrate animals appeared during the Silurian period, gigantic reef systems formed around inland seas on the North American continent. These reefs became the source of oil deposits, so crucial for the technological advancement of human civilization millions of years later. The same can be said for deposits of iron and other valuable ores that began their formation during this Silurian period.

Our knowledge of the natural conditions that allow water-dissolved minerals to solidify into concentrated ore beds has helped us locate and mine these minerals for modern use. This fact alone is strong evidence that these events actually occurred in the way and order in which historical geology describes them. To the believer in God, the formation of natural resources like coal and oil was providential and a part of God's plan to provide for the anticipated energy needs of his ultimate creation, humans.

Jawless fish are seen in the fossil record about the middle part of the Silurian period. They are quickly followed by the first jawed fish. Toward the end of the Silurian, vascular land plants appear. The structural ducts in their stems for transporting nutrients and water allowed them to grow taller than their predecessors.

DEVONIAN PERIOD (408 TO 360 MYA)

The Devonian period is called the age of the fish because, by its conclusion, there were almost as many different types of fish in existence as there are today. Plants and vertebrate animals made spectacular appearances as well. Forests and swamps covered vast areas and provided the environment necessary for the formation of coal. True forests were in existence by the end of the Devonian, with shrubs and tall trees all living together.

Fossil spiders and insects are also connected with this period, although they are not listed in the Genesis account of creation. Since many insects form a symbiotic relationship with plants, it is possible they were included along with the creation of plant life.

Two major extinctions during the Devonian decimated the fish populations. One was an ocean water extinction believed to be caused by a small asteroid impact, and the last extinction (cause unknown) was restricted to freshwater fish.

CARBONIFEROUS PERIOD (360 TO 286 MYA)

A coal-forming cycle begins when tropical swamps covered with giant trees and lush plants become buried by a rising sea (called a transgression). As the sea rises, the rotting vegetation is compressed by layers of sand and clay deposits. When the sea level reaches a peak and then lowers (called a regression), another swamp grows and the cycle is completed. The Carboniferous period (which is divided into the Mississippian and Pennsylvanian periods in the United States) is uniquely marked by numerous cycles of this type, called cyclothems. Sixty completed cyclothems have been identified in the state of Illinois alone.

A graph of sea level fluctuations during this period looks like a fine-tooth saw, extending over 65 million years. Although the causes of these cycles continue to puzzle geologists, the believer in God sees the entire process of coal formation as specifically designed for the future benefit of humans.

Along with coal beds, marine limestones were also being deposited in the Mississippi Valley because a shallow sea covered most of the United States at this time. In the Grand Canyon region, the 450-to-700-foot-deep Redwall Limestone was slowly accumulating. The limestone and other rock strata of this period show an increase in the number of amphibian life forms.

At the end of the Devonian, amphibians were mostly water dwellers feeding on fish. By the conclusion of the Carboniferous, fossils of land-dwelling, insect-feeding amphibians have also been found. Additionally, about this time, the first flying insects appeared. Some were giants by our standards, such as dragonflies with 28-inch wingspans.

PERMIAN PERIOD (286 TO 245 MYA)

The first of many true land animals appear in the fossil record beginning with the Permian period. The Bible, too, asserts that God created land animals after sea creatures.

> Eighth Event: And God said, "Let the land produce living creatures according to their kinds: livestock, creatures that move along the ground, and wild animals, each according to its kind." And it was so. God made the wild animals according to their kinds, the livestock according to their kinds, and all the creatures that move along the ground according to their kinds. And God saw that it was good.

Among the first land animals inhabiting the earth was a fish-eating reptile similar to a modern crocodile, called a mesosaurus. Fossils of the mesosaurus are found in early Permian beds located in both Brazil and South Africa. The only way these animals could appear in identical Permian deposits in both places would be if the continents of South America and Africa were joined when these beds were laid down. This record of the mesosaurus is one of many proofs for the existence of the last supercontinent, Pangea, which was almost fully assembled by this time.

The Permian period ended with the largest extinction in geologic history. Recent findings indicate that the event took place over a very short period of time (around 10,000 years), rather than over the 10-to-15-million-year period estimated earlier (Kerr 1998, 1007; Bowring et al. 1998, 1039).

Whatever caused the extinction, there is evidence that "super-plumes" occurred around the same time. These mysterious plumes, composed of molten rock (magma), rose up from within the earth like enormous bubbles. They erupted at plate ridges where the extruding molten rock began separating the plates and causing landmasses to move away from each other. This is just one process that started the breakup of Pangea about 250 mya (Lamb and Sington 1998, 194).

TRIASSIC PERIOD (245 TO 208 MYA)

Toward the end of the Triassic, dinosaurs began to appear in ever-increasing numbers. Their remains are found on most continents today because although Pangea was already starting to fragment in places, the areas where the dinosaurs roamed were still contiguous.

Studies indicate that dinosaurs traveled in herds, nested in groups, and laid eggs. They apparently tended their young and fed them in the nest until they were at least three feet long (Condie and Slone 1998, 343). Most illustrations of dinosaurs show them walking with their tails dragging along the ground. However, recent research on their skeletons has determined that they normally walked with their backbone and tail in a horizontal position. Their fossilized tracks reveal that typical walking speeds were about 5 miles per hour, while the fastest runners could travel at about 25 miles per hour.

The first flying reptiles appeared in the late Triassic. This period ended with the fourth largest extinction in geologic history, which affected land animals more than sea creatures. The cause still remains a mystery.

JURASSIC PERIOD (208 TO 144 MYA)

Ever since the movie *Jurassic Park* became so popular, the majority of people associate dinosaurs with the Jurassic period in geologic history. In fact, dinosaurs dominate all three of the periods between 245 and 65 mya. During the late Jurassic, land dinosaurs grew very numerous.

This period was also marked by the appearance of small insect-eating mammals, crocodiles, turtles, and frogs. Birds find their way into the fossil record by late Jurassic. So far, only eight specimens of the first creature classified as a bird, called archaeopteryx, have been found. Most of them have been discovered in lagoonal deposits located in Bavaria in southern Germany that date back to about 150 mya.

Originally scientists claimed that birds descended from dinosaurs, but new arguments relating to what could be called their hands and fingers, along with significant differences in their respiratory systems, seem to suggest otherwise (Siegel 1997, 1–2; Boyle 1999, 1–3).

CRETACEOUS PERIOD (144 TO 65 MYA)

The Cretaceous period was noted for its unusual weather conditions. All ocean temperatures were warm, and sea levels rose 900 feet above present levels, causing significant shallow flooding of the North American continent. An extensive inland sea from the Arctic to the Gulf of Mexico split North America in half.

Warming Trend

As a result of the warm temperatures and high sea levels, coral reefs developed all around the world, and extensive tropical forests grew in what are now the polar regions. Conditions such as these explain why we find redwood deposits in drill cores from the north slopes of Alaska and why Michigan's state rock is the Petosky Stone, a tropical coral that will not grow in water colder than 68°F.

The World's Greatest Fossilist

A remarkable woman named Mary Anning (1799–1847) discovered the first fossil Plesiosaur. Mary was born in Lyme Regis, England, a town situated just east of limestone cliffs dating back to the early Jurassic period. She and her brother Joseph were the only survivors of ten children and were required to help support their mother after their father died. Even though Mary was only eleven years old at the time, she managed to make money by digging for fossils in the nearby cliffs and selling them as "curiosities," which they were called then.

Mary's reputation as a fossilist grew to such an extent that she became the source for the well-known tongue-twister, "She sells seashells by the seashore." She is often pictured with her loyal dog who helped her dig fossils and who then guarded them until she could return with people to assist her in carrying them home. Mary's dog served faithfully until one day, while doing his job as usual, he was killed in a rockslide.

In spite of several major handicaps—a childhood in poverty, a lack of formal education, and her gender—Mary earned the respect of the scientific community and in 1837 received the title "The Greatest Fossilist the World Ever Knew."

When shallow seas compress the remains of creatures like phyto-plankton (possibly killed by a change in water temperatures), an ideal environment is provided for the production of oil. Not surprisingly, then, the largest oil production in geologic history occurred at this time, with rates five times greater than any other period before or after.

The apparent cause for the widespread increase in temperature during the Cretaceous period has to do with the breaking up of the supercontinent Pangea. Seafloor spreading, which set the continents in motion, also increased the frequency of volcanic eruptions. Since carbon dioxide gas is a large component of volcanic gases, a greenhouse effect probably developed, increasing global temperatures.

Sea levels would also rise as a direct result of continental move-ment. When Africa split away from South America about 120 mya due to a possible superplume rising from within the earth, continental drift speeds increased and midocean ridges were lifted in the process. This pushing up of the Pacific ridge resulted in extensive flooding of North America (Lamb and Sington 1998, 196).

Plants and Insects

The warm, carbon-dioxide-rich atmosphere was just right for the development of plants. It could have been anticipated, then, that this period saw the first flowering plants. Along with the emergence of flowering plants around 120 mya came an abundance of pollinating insects. Many insects were found to be in a symbiotic relationship with specific plants, which aided in the growth and expansion of both life forms (Condie and Slone 1998, 367). Soon after plants and insects arrived, insectivore mammals and a great variety of insect-eating birds followed.

From 75 to 67 mya, about 35 dinosaur genera seem to have disap-peared, possibly due to a gradual decrease in seawater temperature from 68° to 65.5°F (Condie and Slone 1998, 372). The prevailing theory is that just a minor drop in water temperature would produce even more severe repercussions on land. As a result, those dinosaurs that were cold-blooded would become sluggish and unable to survive. Therefore, by the end of the Cretaceous, the dinosaur population was already decreasing.

Asteroid Collisions

The Cretaceous period ended with the now-famous asteroid impact believed to have caused the mass extinction of the remaining dinosaurs about 64.7 mya. The geologic feature marking this extinction is called the K/T Boundary (Cretaceous/Tertiary Boundary).

It is currently believed that most of the catastrophes of the past were probably related to significant changes in the earth's average temperature, changes that may have taken place over extended periods of time. The K/T extinction, however, was much more spectacular. It involved a worldwide disaster that occurred over a very short period of time.

Three extinction models have been proposed involving comets, volcanoes, and asteroids. At present the asteroid model is supported by the best evidence. In 1980, physicist Luis Alverez and his son, geologist Walter Alverez, proposed that an asteroid 6 miles in diameter impacted the earth and left its mark by depositing a thin layer of distinctive clay over almost all of the earth's surface (Dalrymple et al. 1993).

They theorize that the asteroid made a 112-mile-wide crater in the Gulf of Mexico near Chisxulub in Yucatan, Mexico. The crater is 19 miles deep. The impact turned huge quantities of sediments and crustal materials into a fine dust that eventually settled out as a thin layer of clay. The clay contains droplets of molten glass (called tektites) and significant traces of the extremely rare element iridium. Both of these substances are associated with meteor and/or asteroid bombardment.

In fact, current evidence indicates that there were at least two separate asteroid impacts, one immediately following the other. Twin craters of Clearwater Lakes in Canada show that multiple impacts have occurred in the past (Hickman et al. 1997, 177). Drastic changes in the atmosphere and then in water temperature resulting from such asteroid collisions would begin a chain reaction of temperature extremes, acid rain, forest fires, storm surge waves, and tsunami waves. These conditions, in turn, would lead to the extinction of some marine organisms and all land animals weighing more than 50 pounds.

AGE OF MAMMALS (65 MYA TO PRESENT)

Following the famous K/T Boundary extinction, the Age of Mammals begins and continues to the present. The time period is divided up into seven epochs listed in figure 9.4.

The first four epochs covered a time of great mountain-building activity. Pangea had broken up, and the continents were well on their way toward their present locations. India collided with Eurasia about 60 mya and began to form the Himalayas. As the epochs progressed, the Andes, the Rockies, and the Alps formed from a combination of continental collisions and internal uplift.

As has been typical, the K/T extinction was followed by considerable animal diversification, which took only about 1 million years of

Epochs	Begins	Ends
Paleocene	65.0 mya	57.8 mya
Eocene	57.8 mya	36.6 mya
Oligocene	36.6 mya	23.7 mya
Miocene	23.7 mya	5.3 mya
Pliocene	5.3 mya	1.6 mya
Pleistocene	1.6 mya	10,000 years ago
Holocene	10,000 years ago	Present

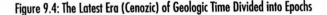

Figure 9.4: The Latest Era (Cenozic) of Geologic Time Divided into Epochs

recovery time (Lamb and Sington 1998, 199). Most of the ancestors to the animals we know today appear in the fossil record at this time. The recovering climate warmed and brought more rain. Plants thrived because dinosaurs were no longer in existence to eat and destroy them.

Between 50 and 20 mya, marine mammals such as whales, sea cows, seals, and sea lions came onto the scene (Condie and Slone 1998, 414). At the same time, land mammals were still generally small in size, averaging about 55 pounds. By about 30 mya, the mesohippus, a collie-dog-sized, horselike animal, became typical of the medium-sized mammals appearing in the record. Larger animals were characteristic of middle Miocene (18 mya), when the first elephants seem to have migrated to North America.

The larger, grazing animals needed grass for survival. Therefore, prior to their appearance, definite seasonal climate cycles began, similar to the ones we experience today. Instead of forests at the poles, massive sheets of ice formed. Between 30 and 20 mya, the lower latitudes became dryer and produced savanna-like grasslands. These grasslands were uniquely suited for the newly emerging grazing animals whose teeth were perfectly shaped for eating the grass (Condie and Slone 1998, 414).

By the end of the Miocene (5.3 mya), most of the animal types we recognize today were present. As we leave the Miocene and enter the Pliocene epoch, we are introduced to the first Hominids. These are animals that are members of the Primates order. This order includes the genus *Homo*, of which modern human beings are the only extant (living) members.

PUNCTUATED EQUILIBRIUM

Our examination of the fossil record during the prehistoric time covered in this chapter has revealed a certain pattern of change over the years. Mass extinctions appear to be followed by rapid recoveries of both the environment and life. Then long periods of time pass with very little change before the next extinction begins the process all over again. Scientists have been able to recognize this pattern only recently due to increased sophistication and accuracy in their dating and research methods.

Before Darwin's time, both religion and science in the Judeo-Christian world agreed that the earth was created in the not-too-distant past. They believed that its mountains and valleys were shaped by direct catastrophic acts of God, catastrophic acts that no longer occur naturally. After Darwin introduced his theory of evolution, the question of time took on a new dimension. The catastrophe theory was based upon a young-earth concept, whereas evolution was based upon an old earth. Catastrophism was quickly replaced by the theory of uniformitarianism, which states that the "present is the key to the past." In other words, scientists believed that evolution progressed slowly, with many small, discrete changes occurring over great periods of time.

Though this view had been offered as a possibility before, Darwin identified the means by which these changes would take place. Since Darwin was familiar with "selective" breeding practices, he simply redefined that process using, instead, the term "natural selection." Although it was not necessarily Darwin's intention, many of his supporters took God out of the picture and left it entirely up to nature to do the selecting.

As is often the case, old ideas resurface with new discoveries. Catastrophism is a good example. The years since Darwin have not proven the doctrine of uniformitarianism to be correct, after all. Instead, current theories recognize the role that catastrophes have played in shaping the earth and its inhabitants.

Extinctions, such as the one believed to have been responsible for the demise of the dinosaurs, are now considered to be the primary causes for evolution. The uniform periods between the extinctions are called "stases," or long periods of no change. According to the theory of punctuated equilibrium, a disaster may occur that results in the loss of many animal species. This event provides the opportunity for evolution to rapidly fill in the ecological niches of the deceased animals with newer and more complex creatures better suited to meet the challenges of the new postextinction environment.

Cactus Model

Even though punctuated equilibrium seems to be a more accurate explanation for the fossil record than its predecessor, uniformitarianism, both theories fail when based upon purely natural processes as the only means of change. Neither can adequately explain the sudden appearance of complex life forms in the Cambrian explosion. Figures 9.5 and 9.6 show the problems inherent in both of these theories.

Evolutionary Models

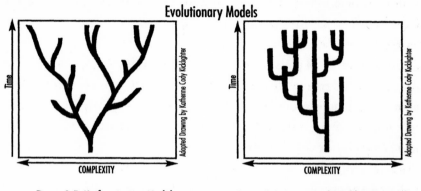

Figure 9.5: Uniformitarian Model   Figure 9.6: Punctuated Equilibrium Model

The tree of evolution shown in figure 9.5 has been used in the past by the Chicago Field Museum of Natural History to illustrate uniformitarianism. It represents the process of change from one life form to another described by Richard Dawkins as a series of "gradual, cumulative, step-by-step transformations from simpler things, from primordial objects sufficiently simple to have come into being by chance" (1987, 14). These gradual changes require long time periods, time not available considering the rapidity of the Cambrian explosion.

Since the acceptance of punctuated equilibrium, however, the tree illustration has been modified to look more like a cactus. Unlike a tree with Y branches extending up at an angle from the trunk denoting a gradual change into a new species, a cactus has branches resembling the letter L. Change takes place rapidly along the horizontal leg, followed by long periods of stasis or no change represented by the vertical leg of the L. (See figure 9.6.)

When both of these models are compared with the fossil record, several significant problems emerge that are difficult to solve with a purely natural evolutionary explanation. Regarding the tree of evolution, the oldest and simplest forms of life should be found at the trunk of the tree and the more complex and recent forms of life should be located in the top branches. Yet the extremely complex trilobite, with its equivalent to a modern compound eye, its hard exoskeleton, and its ability to defensively enroll itself, appeared at the beginning of the Cambrian period, the root of the tree, not the top where simple-to-complex evolution would place it.

This reversal of placement for complexity is repeated over and over again with the tree model, rendering the concept of uniformitarianism unacceptable in the face of the evidence. As a result, scientists are currently considering a forest hypothesis to represent the many different and separate lines of apparent evolution starting at the Cambrian. In the forest model, each tree begins independently, but the changes in the tree eventually lead to a diverse population of animals that are uniquely linked. (See figure 9.7.)

A major problem with this latter theory involves the time restrictions already discussed for the evolution of life. If sufficient time is not available for even one "tree" to have evolved the incredible complexity of a trilobite, how could an entire forest of equally complex yet diverse life forms have evolved simultaneously without direct intervention by an intelligent designer like God?

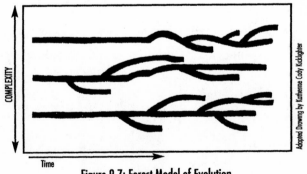

Figure 9.7: Forest Model of Evolution

Biblical "Kinds"

A solution to the above problems is to evaluate all the models of evolution by comparing them to the Genesis account of creation. In so doing, we find that all the confusion caused by atheistic evolution disappears. Genesis states that God created life forms in the seas, air, and land to reproduce "after their kind." The word *kind* in Hebrew (*min*) is a broad term defined later in the New Testament (1 Corinthians 15:39) to mean four separate forms of "flesh"—the flesh of fish, birds, beasts, and humans.

These biblical "kinds" correspond more closely with our modern taxonomical category of class rather than species, as shown in figure 9.8. This chart uses the robin as an example of the classification system in use today. The robin is one of 9,700 known species of birds that are all of the same class, Aves.

In view of this definition, the questions arise, Did God separately create every one of the 9,700-plus species of birds, or did he design birds with the ability to adapt to many different environmental settings? Genesis 2:3 speaks of God both creating (Hebrew, *bara*, meaning to make miraculously out of nothing) and making (Hebrew, *asah*, meaning to mold or shape something already created).

Level	Bird (Robin)	Fish	Beast	Human
Kingdom	Animalia	Animalia	Animalia	Animalia
Phylum	Chordata	Chordata	Chordata	Chordata
Class	**Aves**	**Pisces**	**Mammalia**	**Mammalia**
Order	Passeriformes			Primates
Family	Turdidae			Hominidae
Genus	Turdus			Homo
Species	migratorious			sapiens

Figure 9.8: Assumed Biblical Taxonomy of Life

Since both words are used to describe God's creative acts, it appears that he may have equipped animal DNA with the ability to microevolve within the general bounds of an animal's class, which the Bible refers to as *kind*. In other words, the Bible and the fossil record would be in precise agreement if God programmed the DNA molecule to produce a wide variety of life forms within each animal class. When the need for change became too great, God would produce a new and different kind of animal by creatively "tinkering" with its genetic "tool kit." This exciting, relatively new concept is known as "basic type biology" (Hartwig-Scherer 1998, 215).

If this hypothesis is correct, then, to the consternation of the evolutionary community, we should find evidence for both gradual and rapid changes taking place within the fossil record. This very conclusion is summarized well in the book *Understanding Human Evolution*, which says:

> Although there is considerable disagreement among paleontologists, evidence for both gradual evolutionary change and for the punctuated equilibrium model can be gleaned from the fossil record. There is very heated debate on this point. It should not surprise us, however, that evidence seems to exist for both evolutionary models, and we shall encounter this problem at other points in this book. (Poirier and McKee 1999, 34)

Again, we should ask ourselves, Is it just another coincidence that the Bible specifically says that God both "created" and "made" all the living things around us?

In this chapter, we have let the animals speak, and they have told us that God appears to have progressively created a large variety of plants and animals over a long period of time in preparing the earth for use by humans. While the sequence of these occurrences is generally outlined by the six creative days discussed in Genesis 1, it is my personal opinion that the actual events described were all accomplished within the time period covered by the expression, "In the beginning God created the heavens and the earth" (Genesis 1:1).

In the following chapter, we will review the evidence directly leading up to the creation of humans in the image of God. Some of this evidence may raise challenging questions about our traditional interpretations of the Bible. However, if the Bible is to remain the inerrant word of God, we must be willing to reconsider past interpretations in the light of new and heretofore unknown realities.

WHAT
IS MAN?

So God created man in his own image, in the image of God he created him; male and female he created them. (Genesis 1:27)

The LORD God formed the man from the dust of the ground and breathed into his nostrils the breath of life, and the man became a living being. (Genesis 2:7)

In these two succinct verses, Genesis describes the unique position of humans in God's arrangement. Humans alone are created in the image of God, and only humans receive the breath of life directly from God. Humans are not unique, however, in the formation of their bodies, because they share the dust of the ground with the animals (Genesis 2:19).

For thousands of years, believers in the Genesis account of creation have not been as concerned about the literal meaning of these words as we are today. Some may have occasionally wondered, Does being made in the image of God mean that we look like God physically? Does being made from the dust of the ground mean that we are made of literal dust, or does it mean that our physical bodies are made of elements taken from the earth? Did God form Adam as a sculptor would form a human shape from clay and then miraculously transform the clay figure into flesh and blood?

Today, however, these questions become more significant in light of scientific discoveries made over the past hundred years. The Darwinian theory of evolution has raised challenging questions about the very definition of *man*. Ancient bones and partial skeletons have been unearthed and pieced together to give a picture of humanlike creatures roaming the earth long before the creation of Adam. These creatures are called Hominids.

INTERPRETING THE EVIDENCE

When we combine these discoveries with improved dating techniques, Christians are finding it increasingly more difficult to summarily dismiss all the recent evidence as fictitious and unreliable. On the other hand, to blindly accept every claim made by paleoanthropologists regarding the "evolution of man" would be to ignore the sometimes scanty nature of their findings. Blind acceptance can also result in a failure to recognize hidden political agendas, which have been known to influence the interpretation of fossil finds. So before we define "man" and compare our definition with the series of creatures we see depicted in biology textbooks, we should first consider some of the problems inherent in identifying a so-called missing link between humans and animals.

Reconstructing Forms

To begin with, suppose you were to find the skeleton shown in figure 10.1 completely assembled, without any missing bones. What kind of a reconstruction could you make of the animal from which the skeleton came? Could you identify the detail shown in figure 10.2? Certainly, you could tell about how big the animal was, something about how it stood and moved, and perhaps what it ate and how it managed to survive.

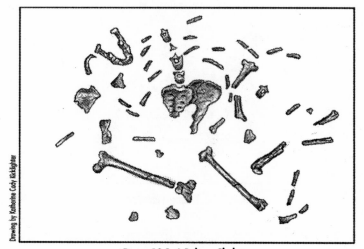

Figure 10.1: A Baboon Skeleton

Figure 10.2: An Artist's Concept of Pliopithecus

However, the size of the nose, the amount of head and body hair, the shape and size of the ears would all have to be reconstructed by guesswork. Surely, no one finding a skeleton of a proboscis monkey as shown in figure 10.3 would guess that it possessed such a large nose.

As far as head and body hair is concerned, the tendency is to show less of it so a proposed missing link would look more like a human. Yet

Figure 10.3: Proboscis Monkey

since many of the creatures depicted lived in cold climates and since there is no evidence that they wore clothes, the likelihood that they had a covering of insulating body hair is very high. Calling attention to these distinctions is important, because much of the evidence presented to support evolution as a proven "fact" has been established by the kinds of reconstructions we have just discussed.

On some occasions, scientists have presented extensive reconstructions based upon only one tooth. Sometimes these imaginative renditions have held up under further scrutiny. Other times they have not, as in the case of the Nebraskan man. This "man" was reconstructed upon the basis of a single tooth, which later turned out to be a molar from a giant wart hog (Goldschmidt 1940, 84–89). Although the scientific community has been honest in acknowledging its mistake regarding the Nebraskan man, the example is particularly noteworthy when we consider that its original proposed existence was used dramatically in court to support the theory of evolution in the now famous Scopes monkey trial held in 1925.

Since time and further research can either verify or dismiss imaginative representations of fossil finds, obviously all reconstructed forms are not automatically genuine proof of man's apparent evolution. Caution, therefore, should be exercised when we are asked to accept other, more radical claims about the evolution of humans based upon very recent finds. It takes time to conduct a proper investigation. Prehistoric events must be inferred indirectly from archeological excava-tions, where the available evidence relating to prehistoric people is rare and often fragmented.

Establishing Reliable Dates

There is also the problem of establishing reliable dates for some fossils, because modern dating methods do not give good results for the critical period ranging from 50,000 to 500,000 years ago. As a result, less reliable relative dating methods may be used to cover this time period. So when we see conflicting interpretations founded upon such questionable evidence, it is wise to withhold acceptance until more proof becomes available. Drawing hard and fast conclusions based on insufficient evidence is not in accord with the scientific method.

We also need to be reminded that economics can influence interpretations of evidence. The business of finding old fossils is very competitive. A great deal of grant money for research frequently depends upon the age of the bones unearthed. The older, the better. Though it does not happen often, occasionally there have been serious disputes regarding the ages and classifications of fossils. The disputes appear to be motivated more by economic or personal factors than by the actual evidence involved (Tattersall 1995, 230), as the book *Bones of Contention* well illustrates (Lewin 1987, 195). Consequently, archeological sites that are assigned unusually old dates should be questioned until more information becomes available.·

Distinguishing between Lumpers and Splitters

Disputes about the classification of fossils are not always due to a race for commercial funding. Whether an illustration of the evolution of man shows a series of intermediate life forms connecting two different species or simply shows a gap between them very often depends upon the philosophy of the classifier. Some are "lumpers" and others are "splitters."

Definition of Race

Louis Leakey was a leader in the splitter camp. Every time he found a part of a primate in the stratum he was studying, he gave it a new name. Those of the lumper camp, however, lumped many of these new forms into already existing groups. They suggested that the numerous fossils Leakey had found were merely different races of the same species of animal.

At this point, it might be helpful to explain what is meant by the term "race." A race is a group of individuals possessing a physical characteristic chosen by the observer as a basis for identification. For example, a teacher could decide to segregate students into three racial groups according to the size of the their earlobes, whether they are long, intermediate, or short.

Some who think skin color is the only determining factor for racial prejudice might object to this rather peculiar use of the word. We prefer skin color as a criterion for separating the races because we choose to do so. As a matter of convenience, we need an obvious, prejudicial characteristic that is readily identifiable. Skin color is obvious and is identifiable at fifty yards. Electing to examine an earlobe to distinguish between those we will accept from those we will not could be awkward, to say the least, and would probably be much harder to sell socially.

Example of Racial Variations

How do racial variations come about in real life? The earlobe illustration can answer that question. Earlobe size has been a function of social custom at various times in the past. A certain group may have felt that people with long earlobes were witches and needed to be executed to protect society. As a result, eventually everyone remaining alive would have short earlobes because according to the rules of heredity, children would generally look like their parents.

Conversely, in another culture, long earlobes may have been a sign of beauty or virility. A person with such a distinguished characteristic could hang jewelry on the earlobes and be more attractive than average. This would mean that such people would probably marry sooner, have more children, and thus increase the number of people in the community with long earlobes. Subsequently, two races (based upon earlobes) would come into existence by a very natural process. The intermediate earlobe would be formed, perhaps, by interracial marriages between the other two earlobe types.

Application to Microevolution

If we understand this definition of racial differences, we can appreciate the problem inherent in a lineup of humanlike animals illustrating how man is supposed to have gradually changed over a long period of time. Do the changes in form represent separate species that required macroevolution? Or are they simply racial variations within the same species, meaning that only microevolution has been taking place?

For example, the average size of a male Japanese skull prior to World War II was just over 900 cubic centimeters, whereas today the average size is 1,400 cubic centimeters Since brain size is proportional to body size and modern Japanese males are significantly taller today, the increase in brain size can be attributed simply to improved nutrition.

If splitters were to unearth skulls with such differences in size as the ones just described, they could easily assume that two separate species of creatures were represented. On that basis, they could go on to erroneously use them as examples of several "missing links" between apes and humans. Lumpers, on the other hand, would see the increase in brain size as merely a racial variation of the same species, a change well within the limits set by natural adaptation and not, therefore, an example of macroevolution at all.

For this reason, we should use caution when weighing the evidence for newfound links in the so-called evolutionary chain. Being cautious, however, does not mean automatic rejection. We do not want to imply that all research done in tracing hominid-like creatures through the fossil record is erroneous.

Quite the contrary, the argument that the human body may have evolved and the search for evidence to validate that claim are examples of how we are able to advance in knowledge and technology. Without proposing theories, right or wrong, and searching for data to substantiate them, we would still be living in the Dark Ages.

We have mentioned these problems to show that it would be deceptive to state as a fact that humans are *solely* a product of evolution when it is obvious that grave difficulties are inherent in that position. Nevertheless, an honest consideration of the research on evolution has caused many Christians to discover how God may have used microevolution as a part of his creative process.

DEFINING *MAN* BIBLICALLY

As we consider what the fossil record reveals to us about the so-called history of man, we encounter hominid-like creatures that are believed to have fashioned crude stone tools. The Bible student may wonder how these creatures fit into the Bible's description of Adam as the first man God created. Here is where we need to define what *man* is according to the Bible and then compare the Bible's description with the anthropological definition of *man*.

We find that in Genesis 1:27 and 2:7, quoted at the beginning of this chapter, a distinction is made between the way God created animals and the way he created humans. Both were made from the dust of the ground, but God made the first human in his own image and personally breathed life into him.

When the Bible uses the phrase "image of God," should that be taken to mean that humans look like God physically? Obviously not, or else we would all look identical, and God would have a physical body just like ours. Such a view would conflict with other descriptions of the Creator found in the Bible. In chapter 5 of this book, we discussed the Bible's claim that God is not flesh and blood (Matthew

16:17 KJV), God is spirit (John 4:24), and God does not have physical limitations as we do (Luke 1:3; Jeremiah 23:24). Therefore, the image of God must refer not to the physical but to the spiritual nature of humans, because spiritually we do all "look" alike.

Possession of a Soul

Such a definition enables us to see what humans really are. We are those beings who possess souls uniquely created in the image of God. We possess intellect, personality, and the ability and inclination to worship. We can be taught to reason, to feel guilt, to be sympathetic, to forgive, and to create works of art and music. All these characteristics are embodied in the concept of "culture," and it is the cultural aspects of our existence that set us apart from the animals and clearly identify us as human.

Even the most intelligent animal cannot reflect the image of God. Chimpanzees do not write protest songs or paint creative expressions of their beliefs. I have an adopted son with a measured Stanford-Binet Intelligence Quotient (IQ) of about 55. There are many porpoises and chimpanzees who are said to have intelligence quotients somewhat higher than his.

Contrast with Animals

Nevertheless, has a porpoise or chimpanzee ever expressed himself in art or music that made any sense at all? Extensive programs of instruction designed to teach these animals to do so have not had favorable results. An animal is capable of drawing nothing beyond crudely executed circles and lines randomly oriented. My son Tim, on the other hand, draws pictures showing personal sensitivity and expression. He also composes his own songs. Obviously, he does not do these things because of his intelligence. It is his spiritual makeup that makes these uniquely human traits possible.

Is it possible for a creature's environment to account for all these characteristics? If a chimpanzee were brought up in the same environment as my son, would that make a difference? A psychology professor named Dr. Kellogue of Indiana University conducted an experiment to test this hypothesis. Later another scientist duplicated his experiment with similar results.

When Dr. Kellogue's wife brought their three-day-old son home from the hospital, Dr. Kellogue brought a three-day-old chimp home from the zoo. The human and chimp infants were raised in identical environments and given equal stimulation, love, and education. Dr. Kellogue's hypothesis was that the chimpanzee would do all the things his son would do, but on a lower level because of lower intelligence. At the conclusion of his experiment, however, Dr. Kellogue's chimp had failed to create any works of art or music or, for that matter, to demonstrate any uniquely human characteristics.

Even one of the most famous of the intelligent chimpanzees, Washoe, was not able to demonstrate anything approaching human intelligence. Washoe's trainers claimed she had mastered many elements of American Sign Language, but critics have successfully argued that her humanlike actions were primarily the result of subtle clues she inadvertently received from her handlers, along with their often generous interpretation of irrelevant gestures as being words.

Figure 10.4: Tim's Drawing

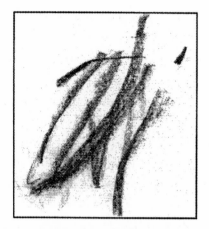

Figure 10.5: An Artist's Rendition of a Chimpanzee Drawing

Thorndike has shown that pigeons given equivalent amounts of time can be conditioned to make seemingly intelligent responses as well (1978). Mark Caldwell reports, "The history of science is littered with animals that seemed to be displaying extraordinary brain power but were just responding to unconscious prompts from their owners and trainers" (2000, 73).

Humans alone possess the unique characteristics of independent, creative intelligence because they are created in the image of God. There is no workable explanation for how these intellectual abilities could have been acquired naturally, and no animal has ever been observed to manifest true human traits, even under the most favorable conditions.

The inherent desire to worship a Supreme Being is additional evidence of humanity's created nature. No matter how primitive or advanced a person might be, even if geographically isolated from traditional influences, he will eventually engage in religious practices involving supernatural powers. No animal does this consciously, regardless of how high its IQ is. Yet my mentally retarded son, even with his low IQ, leads us in prayer, talks about God, and participates in worship.

Humans also differ from animals in their capacity to feel guilt and sympathy and in their willingness to forgive others. Sometimes we associate these qualities of guilt and forgiveness with animals, especially with our pets because we tend to anthropomorphize them (assign human feelings to them).

However much we would like them to be more like us, there is no visible evidence that a dog feels sorry for the neighbor's cat when running it up a tree, regardless of how many times this might happen. True forgiveness, while rare in adult humans, is nonexistent in animals.

When my daughter picked out a pet kitten at the humane society, I was forced, unfortunately, to pull it roughly out of a cage containing other kittens and cats. For the next eight years, every time that cat saw me, it instinctively hissed and spat, even though I fed it, petted it, and repeatedly tried to play with it. Humans can act that way, too, but the capacity to forgive and forget is also there. Animals do not possess these singularly human characteristics at all.

Instinct and Conditioning

Often what may appear to be a humanlike response can be attributed to instinct and what we call "conditioning." Instinctive commands are "hard wired" into the creature's brain and form subconscious mental pathways, often equipping the creature to perform astounding feats, such as a spider's ability to spin a complicated web. The animal or insect is not conscious of what it is doing any more than we are conscious of making our hearts beat faster when we are frightened.

Conditioning an animal to repeat instinctive behaviors is based upon the research of Russian physiologist Ivan Pavlov, wherein a trainer rewards the animal over and over again until a desired pattern of behavior emerges. Eventually, the behavior becomes ingrained in the animal's brain because of the response-reward training program.

A very interesting project showing the remarkable potential for conditioned, instinctive behavior has to do with parrots. Animal behaviorist Irene Pepperberg, who has researched animal intelligence for more than twenty years, has demonstrated that parrots can be taught to perform tricks and speak human phrases that are beyond anything they would do in their natural environment. One of the most mysterious of their talents involves the letters *b* and *p*, which we form with our lips. Nobody knows yet how a lipless parrot can form these sounds, let alone how it can so successfully imitate human speech in general (Caldwell 2000, 74).

So an animal can be trained to sound and look as if it has human characteristics, but it cannot be trained to feel the personal emotions that produce them naturally. A parrot imitates human speech, but it does not originate the thoughts behind the words.

Capacity for Language

Here is where the most significant components of a human soul made in the image of God become obvious, namely in the phenomenon of consciousness and the capacity for language. Consciousness is a metaphysical or spiritual state. Despite numerous efforts, a conscious center located somewhere in the brain has never been identified. That is because unconscious brain matter cannot produce physical consciousness any more than a computer, no matter how complex, could ever become conscious as we are (Tattersall 1998, 190–197). The state of consciousness comes from God, whether genetically or directly.

Consciousness also involves having a sense of "self" that is impossible without the capacity for language. In order to have personal memories, we must have language in which to encode them. This is more than just mental pictures. It is actual self-talk, conversations with ourselves that we remember and use to interpret our mental pictures. In order to have higher-order thought processes to subjectively qualify and quantify what is seen, heard, or felt, we need language to express those thoughts to ourselves and to others.

Despite many decades of investigation, the biological bases for consciousness and language remain a mystery. This is significant to those who believe in Divine creation because some experts in the field now theorize that the ability to use a syntactical language may have emerged rapidly as the result of a "single genetic event" (Clark 1993, 172).

Creature without a Soul

This distinction between human and instinctual behavior is important in dealing with some of the hard-to-answer questions associated with the so-called history of man. The fossil evidence strongly suggests that long before God created Adam and Eve, he created a number of other humanlike animals that, as we have said, have been classified as hominids. These creatures had smaller brains that were apparently preprogrammed by instinct to perform a number of needed survival skills, but the creatures did not display any of the unique char-

---

The Difference between Macro- and Microculture

The word culture has a variety of definitions, depending upon the dictionary consulted. More modern dictionaries exclusively associate culture with human behavior. However, older dictionaries broadly define culture as being "any learned behavior that is not inherited by instinct." Within this broad definition, many animals qualify as being cultural because their parents teach them certain survival behaviors. Unless the reader knows this difference, confusion can result when culture is associated with the behavior of an animal, such as a chimpanzee.

In this discussion, we will view culture the same way we view evolution. Just as micro- and macroevolution reflect differences between small and large changes in physical attributes, so micro- and macro-acculturation (the acquisition of culture) would reflect similar differences between simple (small) and complex (large) cultural behavior changes.

Many animals display micro- or simple acculturation when culture is defined as any "behavior that is socially taught, rather than instinctive" (Scott, Foresman Advanced Dictionary, 1993). However, only humans display macro-acculturation, defined as being "the totality of socially transmitted behavior patterns, arts, beliefs, institutions, and all other products of human work and thought. These patterns, traits, and products [are] considered with respects to a particular category, such as a field, subject, or mode of expression; [for example] religious culture in the Middle Ages; musical culture; oral culture" (American Heritage Talking Dictionary; Copyright 1997, The Learning Company, Inc.).

acteristics that reflect a spiritual makeup. This is a fact that is not disputed by science.

An instinctive animal like this would live from day to day by means of its preprogrammed routines and remember new things (store additional information) for survival purposes only. It would not remember daily events contextually. Even today, it is observed that "monkeys employ rulelike strategies for promoting the welfare of a group, including maintaining peace, observing boundaries, and sharing food. And they abide by these rules without necessarily understanding them" (Hauser 2000, 55). This is an example of microculture.

Stone Tools

The expression, "Monkey see, monkey do," arises because monkeys are recognized as being capable of mimetic behaviors (mimicking) without knowing what they are doing or why. While some paleoanthropologists see the making of tools as being a purely human ability, others disagree.

Colin Renfrew of the McDonald Institute for Archaeological Research in Cambridge, England, states:

> An alternative view [to human toolmakers] is that the Lower and Middle Paleolithic do indeed represent a "mimetic" phase, and that the production of well-defined tool forms does not require any very sophisticated conceptualizing power. Moreover such conceptualization as was needed need not have been language dependent. (1998, 177–178)

The early prehuman toolmakers were nothing more than instinctual animals with a wide range of built-in skills that were transmitted through mimicry, without the necessity of human intelligence.

A brief look at the stone "tools" used by these animals supports this view. Normally, when we hear the term "stone tools" or "stone tool industry," we picture a tool pouch loaded with a neat array of rock tools, possibly resembling Native American arrowheads or knife blades that are excellently crafted and obviously the work of skilled specialists.

This is not the case, however, with the stone tools associated with early hominid fossils.

The hominid tools were crude and, in their original setting, would be hard to distinguish from naturally broken rocks. In fact, when the science of classifying stone tools was first introduced, a trialsome period followed when many naturally broken rocks were ambitiously categorized as being tools (Tattersall 1998, 128). Many of the specimens that are classified as "hand axes" are nothing more than two hand-sized stones that were struck together to produce a single-sided, sharp edge. Such altered rocks and their flakes are frequently found scattered randomly around a site. If a natural cause for the damaged rocks cannot be envisioned, then it is assumed that a hominid did the work, whether any evidence of a hominid is found there or not. Of the tens of thousands of broken stones classified as being over one million years old, fewer than a dozen have been objectively assigned an actual use (Jones et al. 1992, 328).

When hominids did use these tools, there is no indication that they treated them any differently than ordinary rocks. Apparently, when the animals needed something to cut with, they looked around until they found a suitable sharp stone flake. If one was not available, they may have banged two rocks together until one chipped off.

The chipped-off flakes may have been used as crude blades held between the first two fingers. When the creature finished using it, the blade was dropped without particular notice. So, pragmatically, we might not even think of these as real tools in the modern sense. They were just convenient items that were used when needed and abandoned when not. (See figure 10.6 for an illustration of how stone tools have changed over time.)

Yet despite this uncertainty about the tool's formation and use, the hominids believed to have made them are referred to as being human and classified as *Homo*. In many cases, this classification is deceptive because the creatures were no more human than trained chimpanzees. Today groups of chimpanzees are known to accumulate tool-like debris

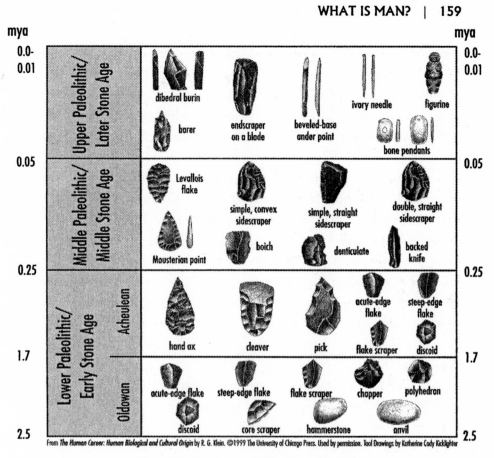

Figure 10.6: How Stone Tools Have Changed over Time

at their sites similar to the stone "hammers" found on ancient hominid sites (Jones et al. 1992, 326).

Based upon this evidence, we can conclude that if a hominid did not demonstrate image-of-God characteristics, it would be an animal. Such an animal could never be classified as being a person as we understand the word.

DEFINING *MAN* ANTHROPOLOGICALLY

Making this distinction is important because when asking for a scientific definition of *man*, a person is likely to get a variety of responses, depending upon the specialty of the scientist queried. The definition has particular relevance because of the popularization of physical anthropology in books such as *National Geographic* and/or the *Time-Life* series on the evolution of man. Through these publications, the names Leakey, Johnson, White, Dubois, and Goodall have become well known in the United States. The research of these scientists has led to what can be called the "caveman complex," which asserts that man's evolutionary descent from tree-dwelling apes has been proven as scientific fact.

The supposed evolutionary progress of man has been depicted as a line of advancing body shapes starting from a small lemur and ending with modern man. Because pictures and exhibits like these are found in many museums and schools, the message is that the lineup is based upon discovered evidence in the fossil record. In the past, those who believed in the biblical account of creation have shown that the evidence does not support such a simplistic view. It appears now that the facts are finally winning out. Hublin, paraphrasing a portion of a book by anthropologist Richard G. Klein, says, "The once-popular fresco showing a single file of marching Hominids becoming ever more vertical, tall and hairless now appears to be a fiction" (2000, 263).

Though the author writes from an evolutionist's perspective, his honesty allows us to be encouraged by his findings. To investigate the matter further, we need to decide what the words *man* and *human* really mean when applied to hominid fossils.

Physical Attributes vs. Soul

In figure 10.7, we see a list of physical attributes that anthropologists tell us are unique to humans. They contend that if an animal possesses any of these traits, it may be physically and intellectually related to man. Such a creature is then often referred to in scientific circles as being "unconditionally human." A more accurate description would be "hominid-like animal," or better yet, "bipedal primate" (erect-standing, highest-order mammal).

After reviewing these human characteristics, it should be apparent that this approach to defining man has almost nothing in common with the biblical definition discussed earlier or with relevant facts. Based upon what we have reviewed about consciousness, is it possible

1. A cranial capacity of 900 to 2300 cubic centimeters.

2. 50% more nerve cells in the visual center than other animals.

3. A rounded skull with a vertical forehead.

4. Moderate supraorbital ridges.

5. Rounded instead of pointed occipital.

6. A lack of muscle ridge.

7. A vertical forehead.

8. An arched dental pattern.

9. A second molar behind the canine.

10. A 2-1-2-3 tooth pattern.

11. A skeleton adapted for upright locomotion.

12. A total dependence on learning for survival.

13. A totally opposable thumb.

14. An extreme organization of the brain.

15. The longest childhood dependency period.

Figure 10.7: Physical Attributes Said to Be Unique to Humans

that a hominid-like animal might possess all fifteen of these characteristics and yet still not have a soul? Remember, without a soul such a creature would have no self-consciousness and, therefore, would not be a person.

In tacit support of this possibility, it is now becoming apparent to leaders in the field of paleoanthropology that hominid-like bodies came into existence thousands of years before any truly "modern behavioral patterns" associated with human activity were discernible in the fossil record (Tattersall 1998, 175). Klein concurs when he states, "Together, the fossil and archeological records suggest that the modern physical form evolved before the modern capacity for culture" (1999, 572).

Realizing this should quickly make it obvious that the starting point for the argument over the origin of man depends upon which definition of *human* a person is willing to accept. Literally, a caveman, biblically speaking, is a man with a soul who lives in a cave, nothing more and nothing less.

Hominids vs. Prehistoric People

The typical scientific prehistoric caveman is more accurately defined as a cave hominid. A search in any good encyclopedia will show an outline of the descent of "man" under the heading "Prehistoric People." This sequence is assumed to cover a time period from 60 million years to about 5,500 years ago when writing suddenly appeared. Starting with writing, we entered into what is called "historic" times, because we can now refer to written records as an aid in determining past events.

To avoid unnecessary confusion, we should qualify the term "prehistoric people." Most reference sources do not distinguish between animals and people, even though over 99.8% of the prehistoric period deals only with animals. To eliminate this problem, we will reserve such terms as *people* and *human* to refer only to descendants of Adam created in the image of God.

All other humanlike creatures will be recognized as being animals and called either by their taxonomic names or by their general family name, Hominidae. A hominid, simply put, is a higher order mammal that has a basically similar skeleton to that of a human. The three other distinguishing features of hominids have to do with the size of brain and teeth and the flatness of face. Most animal faces are not flat. Animals have snouts that project out from their faces (prognathism), leaving them chinless.

Modern apes are not considered to be hominids. In scientific circles, it is clearly recognized that they are not part of the so-called human family tree. Apes do not walk erect. They are recognized as being knuckle walkers, since they generally use their hands or fists somewhat like a four-footed animal when walking. They are in the family Pongidae.

Where does all this leave us? So far we have reviewed the differences between the biblical and the anthropological definitions of *man*.

We have also considered the difficulties involved when interpreting the fossil evidence regarding many of the hominid creatures unearthed in the last two hundred years. At this time then, we are ready to complete our journey through the fossil record and through Genesis 1, both of which conclude with the appearance of humans made in the image of God.

LET HUMANS
SPEAK

In his [God's] hand is the life of every creature and the breath of all mankind. (Job 12:10)

THE CREATING OF HUMANS

As has been shown in chapter 10, it is apparent from a study of the fossil record that humanlike hominids have existed for a long time in the past. Because of this, Christians are faced with several questions. How can the fossil record and the Genesis account of creation be harmonized regarding the creation of humans? Did God possibly use a different method to create the human body than he did to create the human soul? Does an examination of human and chimpanzee DNA give us any clues?

In chapter 7, we discussed the significance of why the Bible says that God both created (*bara*) and formed (*yatsar*) man. This fact strongly implies that God *created* the human spirit *ex nihilo*, which means "out of nothing." (Genesis 1:27) He then combined this newly created spirit (breath) with a body which was *formed* from the "dust of the ground," and man became a living soul (Genesis 2:7 KJV). This same distinction between spirit, body, and soul is made in other biblical texts as well (Ecclesiastes 3:18–21; 12:6–7; 1 Thessalonians 5:23).

Is the statement regarding Adam's body being made from the "dust of the ground" to be taken literally? Of course not. How do we know this? We can examine the human body and see that it is not made of dust or dirt or any other earthlike, organic compound. We are flesh and blood. No doubt, some may say that the word *dust* or *clay* was not meant to be taken literally, but was actually used to represent some or all of the elements within the earth's dust or soil. This interpretation may be valid.

However, the point to be made is that how God chose to create man's body is not clearly stated in the Bible. Instead, God spoke metaphorically of forming or making a clay image or doll and then breathing the spirit of life into it. This metaphor somewhat parallels the children's story of Pinocchio, who was transformed from a wooden puppet into a real, living boy. Just as with children today, the ancient reader was not likely to question the miraculous power God used to make such a transformation possible.

Animals and the "Dust of the Ground"

The Bible also says that in a similar fashion, God formed animals out of the "ground" (Genesis 2:19). The picture we are given is of God making a series of clay animal images and then somehow transforming them into living creatures. Again, current evidence shows that being made out of the ground is not a literal statement because, biologically, humans and animals are very similar in that both are made of flesh and blood. This is an important fact to remember. Since the Bible says that the bodies of both man and animals were made in a similar fashion by being formed out of the ground, then if we want to find out how God may have formed Adam's body, we can examine the fossil record to see how he may have chosen to "form" many of the animals.

Microevolution and Direct Creation

The evidence implies that God started out with simple animal forms and progressively made them more complex over time, which is an example of God's "making" (*asah*) and not "creating" (*bara*). Families of animals were allowed to exist for as long as they were needed. The different species of animals within these families were equipped genetically to adapt to a variety of environmental conditions and were thus able to change along with the changing earth. We have referred to this adaptive capability as "microevolution."

For example, when available oxygen was low, anaerobic (not requiring oxygen) organisms thrived. As earth's biosphere developed, animals were modified accordingly. When conditions changed beyond an animal's adaptive capability, the fossil record indicates it was quickly replaced with a similar but more complex animal that would survive as a new family of species. In harmony with this model, scientists have discovered that there are "developmental constraints" that limit how much change an organism can undergo through normal adaptation (Dalton 2000, 125).

We believe these sudden increases in complexity were a demonstration of God's Spirit in action. It was not due to random chance mutations modified by natural selection, as evolutionists would have us believe. Instead, God appears to have performed genetic surgery on the perishing, obsolete animals, causing them to quickly produce offspring that were better suited physically to survive in the future. These types of changes were probably not radical because the obsolete animals would have trouble raising radically different offspring.

How might these rapid genetic changes have been made? The Bible does not say specifically, but we have a vivid example involving Jesus that shows such changes could be made by God whenever he chooses. Jesus' birth was an example of changes being made to his virgin mother's genes. Mary could not have had a male child without receiving a Y chromosome from somewhere outside her body. Genetically, a normal woman does not have any male Y chromosomes. We do not know how God actually performed the necessary operation to artificially inseminate Mary, but in answer to her question regarding this very issue, the angel Gabriel said, "The Holy Spirit will come upon you, and the power of the Most High will overshadow you" (Luke 1:35).

Along with the many times we see rapid genetic changes taking place in the fossil record, there are also times when totally new families of creatures seem to pop into existence. Such sudden appearances would be examples of unique "creation" (bara), as demonstrated by the Cambrian explosion considered in chapter 9. The Bible supports this understanding, because Genesis 1:21 is one of the few scriptures that says God did not "make" but directly "created" (bara) all the early sea creatures.

In this regard, we discussed in chapter 9 why modern evolutionists have been forced to revise their original uniformitarian (slow change) theory. The majority of them are replacing it with the punctuated equilibrium (fast change) theory in an attempt to explain these relatively rapid transformations that are often evident in the fossil record (Tattersall 1998, 182).

The scriptural examples cited of the direct creation of the sea creatures and the genetic changes made to allow for the birth of Jesus show how God could have both created new animal forms in the beginning and made physical changes over time as the need would arise. Therefore, based upon this brief review, the fossil record seems to indicate that the biblical term "formed from the ground" could mean either a genetic modification of a previously existing animal or a direct creation of an entirely new animal.

If this is true for animals, can it also be true for man, biologically speaking? How closely are the fleshly bodies of modern humans related genetically to other animal primates? Scripturally speaking, there should be no objection to this question because the Bible says that humans were created physically in the same way animals were created (Ecclesiastes 3:19–20).

Whether God chose to create man instantly (*ex nihilo*) or whether he chose to modify the genes of a preexisting creature in no way detracts from the miraculous event, just as Jesus' birth through the virgin Mary did not detract from the miraculous entry of God's son into the world of man. The correlation in this regard is relevant, because the sinless Jesus is universally recognized as being genetically superior to his mother through the power of the Holy Spirit. Jesus' unblemished body was no less perfect for sacrificial purposes just because he was born through an imperfect, carnal woman.

The Human Genome Initiative

A quick way of finding out where man stands genetically is to review the latest findings from the growing volume of evidence being developed as a part of the "Human Genome Initiative." The human genome is the heritable DNA transferred at conception that directs the cell's maintenance and development activities. It is located in the nucleus of every human cell. The Human Genome Initiative is an ongoing program started in the United States in 1990. Its ultimate goal is to identify every gene in the human body and to determine its chromosomal location (locus), its precise chemical structure, and its function.

As of November 17, 1999, one billion of the three billion nucleotides (gene building blocks) that make up the human genome had been successfully identified in sequence (Dickson and Macilwain 1999, 331). Since this time, greater progress than expected has been made.

It is now also believed that the original estimate of 80,000 genes in the human body may be too low. The figure has been revised upward to a number close to 140,000 genes. This additional complexity makes the likelihood of a natural evolution of the human genome even more improbable.

Modern Humans and Chimpanzees

Investigations similar to this are also being conducted to determine if there is a genetic similarity between modern humans and chimpanzees or apes. The procedure used to determine if a similarity exists is fairly routine and considered reliable. If two DNAs are closely related, they can be subjected to a process called DNA hybridization. As discussed in chapter 4, the DNA molecule is a complementary stranded helix that looks like a twisted ladder. When DNA hybridization takes place, the molecule is heated in a solution until its strands separate.

These separated strands are complements of one another and will recombine if the solution temperature is lowered. If separated DNA coding strands of the same protein are taken from two different animals and mixed together, they will also recombine wherever they can, forming a new but different double stranded chain. When the properties of this newly formed DNA are compared to the properties of either of the original DNAs, a measure of their dissimilarity can be determined. Doing this type of experiment on the same protein genes from two human donors may yield a similarity difference of up to 0.1%, which is apparently what it takes to genetically distinguish one race from another.

Using the DNA hybridization method, it has been determined that, overall, chimpanzee DNA is at least 98% similar to human DNA. More impressively, when specific human and chimpanzee protein sequencing is compared, it differs only by about 0.3% (Poirier and McKee 1999, 51).

In other words, for every 1,000 nucleotide base pairs examined, only three of the human pairs are found to be different from the chimpanzee's. This is truly remarkable when compared to the difference between the human races, which is one base pair per thousand, as stated above (Jones 1993, 34). Biologically speaking, then, only a small difference in a creature's gene structure can make a big difference in appearance and actions.

Therefore, it should not surprise us to find that humans and chimpanzees are very closely related genetically (Poirier and McKee 1999, 50, 51). This is understandable because chimps look a lot like humans in a variety of ways. In 1968, a study by Edward Tyson found that chimpanzees and apes, in general, resemble humans in forty-seven aspects, while resembling lower monkeys in only thirty-four. So apes resemble humans more than monkeys from outward appearances (Tattersall 1995, 4). I remember how surprised I was to learn in my anthropology class that only humans and apes share what is called a y-5 molar tooth design. So apparently, the more living things look alike, the more their DNA will be alike.

These facts do not mean that there is an evolutionary connection between chimps and man. It only shows that it would not take much DNA modification to convert one creature's body into the other creature's body, if the ability and resources were available to do it. In this regard, we are only speaking biologically.

Even if a chimpanzee could be converted into a human biologically, we would still have to deal with the man's soul and spirit—metaphysical components that have been made in the "image of God." In fact, in the Bible, God is referred to as the "Father of our spirits" (Hebrews 12:9). So when God personally breathed the spirit of life into Adam's body, the mysterious "image of God" transformation that clearly distinguishes man from the animals occurred.

To avoid misunderstandings, we want to emphasize that God could have instantaneously created all the animals we have discussed. God can do whatever he wants to do. Herein, we are merely reviewing current evidence to see if it is possible to harmonize the Bible and science regarding how God may have accomplished his creative objectives. In this respect, it is not a coincidence that we conclude our historical journey with our focus centering on humankind. According to the fossil record and the Bible, humans were the last to emerge (not counting domestic animals). It should be clear by now that the earth and everything associated with it was created specifically for humans (Isaiah 45:18).

CLASSIFICATION OF FOSSILS
Overview

A quick review of the definition of taxonomy will help us understand the terms used to distinguish the various fossil finds said to be related to the so-called development of humans. Taxonomy, you may recall, refers to the science, laws, or principles of classification. Our modern system, begun by Carolus Linnaeus in the latter 1700s, assigns all living creatures to various classification groups in such a way that any animal can be uniquely identified by only two or three names. It reminds us of our own family system that uses first, middle, and last names for identification.

This taxonomic naming procedure is governed by the International Rules of Zoological Nomenclature. It requires that every animal have at least two names designating its genus and species (Jones et al. 1992, 18). For example, humans are called *Homo sapiens*. Notice that the first name is capitalized and the second is not. *Homo* is taken from Latin and means "human being or man." *Sapiens* means "wise."

We find that the naming procedure and the associated assumptions are probably major causes for the confusion involving the prehistory of man. As discussed in chapter 9, the problem arises because the biblical word *kind* is far broader in scope than that encompassed by the Linnaeus method of identification.

Much of the confusion persists because the numerous theories of hominid history are closely related to how the various animal species are categorized scientifically. For this reason, we should recognize that this classification scheme is for identification purposes only and does not indicate a proven relationship or ancestry.

However, when scientists apply the system today, we find that evolutionary assumptions are used as an underlying guide. This practice sometimes results in the reclassification of animals based upon new speculations and theories. For example, the tree shrew was changed from an "insectivore" to a "primate" to fit the current theories of primate evolution.

Normally, the system seeks to divide every living thing into seven specific groups or taxa, namely kingdom, phylum, class, order, family, genus, and species. We can trace some of the theories of human descent by examining the fossils designated as being in the family of Hominidae. To do this, we will conduct a brief review of the so-called human family tree as it has been hypothesized.

Hominids

Hominid fossils are composed primarily of teeth and lower jaw bones, followed by the upper part of the skull or cranium. These are usually fragmented and so may be in many, many pieces. Each separate piece is called a fossil "specimen." Often the specimens must be reassembled like a jigsaw puzzle. If enough of the skull is recovered and reassembled, the brain size can be estimated. Whether the animal walked on two or four feet is very difficult to determine.

Primarily, erectness is established by examining the lower opening into the skull called the "foramen magnum." If a skull fragment does not include this feature, erectness cannot be determined with certainty. While thigh bones are occasionally retrieved, feet, hands, pelvis, and spinal parts are rare. Sometimes a single tooth may be all that is found of an individual hominid, while at other times, an individual may be represented by numerous bones and/or hundreds of fragments.

Here is where we encounter some of the problems discussed earlier in chapter 10, particularly when splitters and lumpers enter the scene. When it comes to interpreting the fossil evidence regarding hominids, some scientists who are splitters want to separate groups of similar creatures and say that they represent different species leading up to modern humans.

However, it is my opinion that lumping groups together is in closer harmony with the biblical account and will be supported more firmly by the scientific community as new information comes to light. With this in mind, the following broad categories of apes, hominids, and humans are listed in the chronological order in which they make their appearance in the fossil record.

Prehominid Apes

It is theorized that archaic Primates (higher order mammals, including humans, apes, monkeys, and lemurs) of unknown origin living about 60 mya evolved into true Primates, which emerged about 56 mya. From here we go through Adapids (40 mya), to Early Catarrhines (35 mya), until we get to Proconsul (21 mya).

One of the principal Proconsul fossil finds is from Africa and consists of many fragmentary skeletons. These animals have been dated from 23 to 15 mya. Proconsul had monkeylike hands and feet, but it was not built for hanging in trees. It probably moved slowly and walked on all fours along branches and on the ground.

Most of these species of animals were sexually dimorphic, meaning that the males were much larger than the females. This is a trait often found in animals. There are even disputes today regarding whether some fossil finds represent two discrete species based on size difference or whether they are male and female of the same species.

Australopithecines (First Hominids)

In Africa, a gap exists between 13.5 and 5 mya in which no fossils are found relevant to the hominid family line. Then the record comes alive again about 4 mya with the earliest Australopithecine (southern ape) fossils. There are five to seven recognized species.

No complete skeleton of this hominid has been found to date. In 1974, a partial skeleton, humorously named *Lucy* from a Beatles song, was unearthed and assigned an age of 3.2 mya and classified as *Australopithecus afarensis* (A. afarensis). The early species of these animals were about four to five feet tall and probably moved much like modern baboons, with a little more emphasis on upright walking.

One reason these animals probably did not walk exactly like a modern human has to do with the shape of the pelvis. Lucy's pelvis is not identical to ours, as shown in figure 11.1. In this figure, we find depicted three pelvises, one of which is human. A casual glance will show that all three are significantly different.

It is partly on the basis of similarities and differences like these that evolutionists believe this hominid is a human ancestor. However, since there is not nearly enough time for random chance evolution to realistically account for the differences between chimpanzees and Australopithecines, they were apparently both created miraculously by God. How God chose to make the changes is not important. The

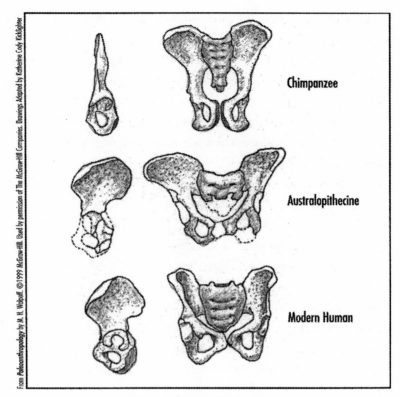

From *Paleoanthropology* by M. H. Wolpoff. © 1999 McGraw-Hill. Used by permission of The McGraw-Hill Companies. Drawings Adapted by Katherine Cody Kiddigthere

Chimpanzee

Australopithecine

Modern Human

Figure 11.1: Human Pelvis Significantly Different

important point is that changes in the fossil record are seen to exist, and we should honestly acknowledge them.

Homo habilis

Homo habilis (human + skillful, sometimes known as "handyman") is the first animal whose remains were believed to be associated with tools, dating back approximately 2 mya. However, there is some controversy here also. It is reported that the tool-like rocks were identified before any actual fossil bones were found. *Habilis* was prenamed in anticipation of finding a toolmaking animal, even though what they finally found appeared to be an A. *africanus,* a long-lost cousin to Lucy (Tattersall 1998, 127). *Habilis* also had long arms like a tree-dwelling ape (Cavalli-Sforza and Cavalli-Sforza 1995, 42). Here is a prime example of the misleading classification *Homo* given to a creature that is clearly not human.

The difficulty when considering this subject historically is that new fossil finds or reinterpretations of old finds make the previous assumptions quickly obsolete. Human evolutionary theories comprise a dynamic and changing area of science. Therefore, we should not draw hard and fast conclusions when the most current information seems to be unreasonable.

I frequently hear teenagers say something like, "If we didn't evolve from a baboon, how come my buddy here looks so much like one?" Without delving into the motivations associated with this irrelevant question, it is important to recognize that there are similarities in the physical appearances of humans and some animals. These similarities do not conflict with the biblical concept that man is a spiritual being. The Bible does not discuss how we have changed physically, where the races came from, or how we have been forced to adapt to a changing world. What the Bible does describe is the much more relevant concern about what really distinguishes us as creatures created in God's image.

Homo Erectus, Neanderthal, *Homo Sapiens*

There has not been and never will be a fossil found with "Adam" or "Made by God" engraved on the bones. What we do know is that an anthropologically unique primate lived all over the world that was called *Homo erectus* (erect man). Since that time, other classifications have been given to fossil finds, such as Neanderthal and *Homo sapiens*.

Unlike splitters who would separate these into a line of increasingly more complex creatures until the appearance of modern humans, I believe *Homo erectus* was the first human made in the image of God. All others since then were simply racial variations of the "erect man." In other words, if an anthropoligist were to find the remains of Adam and Eve, I believe that he or she would likely classify them as *Homo erectus*. Those following *Homo erectus* are equally human but with different physical characteristics. Most have been named after the area in which their remains were found—Rhodesian man, Peking man, and Swanscomb man, to name a few.

Adam and Eve

Based upon both the biblical and geological records, it is not possible to determine precisely how and when Adam and Eve were created. As we have already indicated, it is our opinion that this time period is described in the Bible starting at Genesis 1:2 and extending to Genesis 2:25. These verses specifically describe the creation of the first humans and their immediate surroundings. The sequence of these events is patterned after the sequence of the original creation of the earth itself, which is generally described in Genesis 1:1 by the words, "In the beginning God created the heavens and the earth." The verses following describe events with Hebrew words that relate specifically to man, his crops, and his animals.

We start with a place of desolation no doubt caused by some local natural disaster. Just as a forest recovers after a fire, God restored this area in preparation for his human creation. There is no specific evidence to determine whether these creation events listed in Genesis 1:2–31 happened over an extended period of time or occurred within six, literal, 24-hour days.

This uncertainty in time is due to a lack of fossil evidence that would allow for a more precise determination. It is likely that future discoveries will clarify matters considerably. Therefore, while it may be our opinion that Adam, Eve, and the vegetation area around the Garden of Eden, along with its peaceful animals, were likely created miraculously in six, consecutive, 24-hour days, it also could have taken longer.

Within this context, it would appear that Adam and Eve began as primitive people who existed in a world suited to their physical make-up. To be primitive does not mean to be unintelligent. In paradise, they had no compelling needs. They were gatherers, vegetarians, and secure in having all their necessities provided.

After leaving paradise, they had to get their food by means of hard labor, and even then, they could not depend upon reaping rewards for that labor. If they and their offspring were to survive, physical adaptations no doubt had to be made. As the environment changed and as humans migrated throughout the world, their needs changed. A cold climate does not require the same bodily attributes as does a warm climate.

When we make the statement that it is not possible to determine precisely when Adam and Eve were created, a person might object and point to the chronologies of the descendants of Adam and Eve listed in Genesis 5 and 11. Do they not limit the creation of Adam and Eve to about 6,000 years ago?

Biblical Chronologies

The time periods listed in Genesis are often based upon Ussher's chronology mentioned briefly in chapter 6 of this book. When James Ussher calculated the year 4,004 B.C. for the creation of the earth and six days later for the creation of Adam, he made these four assumptions, among others:

1. There are no undated verses in the biblical account.

2. There are no missing people in the biblical genealogies.

3. The purpose of the genealogies was chronological, so they are all written in chronological order.

4. No historical period is missing from the Bible.

Any dating method that attempts to use the Bible as a basis will have to apply these assumptions, and yet all of them appear to be incorrect. First, there are many undated verses and events in the Bible. A good example is Genesis 1:1, as we have already discussed.

Second, since biblical genealogies are given to confirm a specific line of descent and not necessarily to calculate time or establish chronology, complete listings are not always recorded. When Matthew 1:1 says, "A record of the genealogy of Jesus Christ the son of David, the son of Abraham," it is obviously omitting many generations between Jesus, David, and Abraham. Ezra 7:3 lists "Azariah the son of

Meraioth," yet 1 Chronicles 6:6–10 adds the names of six more fathers and sons between the two.

Well-known supporters of a young-earth perspective and authors of *The Genesis Flood*, Whitcomb and Morris also recognize the problems inherent in Ussher's chronology. After discussing the parallel construction of both genealogies in Genesis 5 and 11, Whitcomb and Morris conclude, "Since, therefore, so many pedagogical purposes are evident in these two genealogies that have nothing to do with the actual length of the overall period, it is unnecessary to press them into a rigid chronological system" (1961/1998, 477).

The authors then go on to discuss why they believe the gaps in the genealogies could not amount to more than several thousand years, thus placing the age of the earth somewhere between 6,000 and 10,000 years. The point here is that there are obvious gaps in biblical chronology. The length of the gaps is very much subject to interpretation and precludes any reliable estimation of a biblical age for the earth. That is why those who have presumptuously used these chronologies as a basis for predicting the end of the world have always failed.

Finally, Ussher's fourth assumption that no historical period is missing from the Bible is also inaccurate. The years omitted between the Old and New Testaments is just one such missing block of time. Therefore, if we recognize these chronological limitations when interpreting the Genesis account, we should begin to see that the timeless sequence of events in the Bible agrees with the geologic record.

The Flood of Noah's Day

Between chapters 5 and 11, which contain the genealogies, we find the Bible's description of a worldwide flood in the days of Noah. The traditional biblical interpretation of the Flood is that it was global and covered all of the existing mountains. While it would not be a problem for God to bring about a flood of these proportions miraculously, it has been difficult to prove scientifically.

However, this problem should not be an issue since there are numerous events in the Bible that we accept by faith alone without the need for scientific proof. Among these would be the plagues used against Egypt (Exodus 7–11), the parting of the Red Sea (Exodus 14–15), the sun and moon standing still in Joshua's day (Joshua 10:13), raising people from the dead (2 Kings 4:34; John 11:43–44; Matthew 28:6), and even calming raging storms (Mark 4:39). So when it comes to corroborating a recent worldwide catastrophic flood, we should not be discouraged by an apparent lack of geologic evidence.

On the other hand, if the biblical Flood is interpreted as being limited to the world of mankind living along with Noah, we find credible geological evidence for its support. At the conclusion of the last ice age, the oceans were several hundred feet lower than they are today. Under such circumstances, a vast area of land called the continental shelf region would have been exposed, an area that today lies underwater.

The world's population of that time could have been living exclusively within this continental shelf zone. Communities would have bordered the oceans where the climate would be conducive to human survival and where fishing and the sea would provide an abundant food supply. It is conceivable that God caused a rapid, earthwide melting of the continental ice sheets to occur, which raised the oceans accordingly. Such an act would have been a unique event in the history of man, one that God promised never to repeat (Genesis 9:11).

Indicating that rising water played a significant role in the flooding process, Genesis 7:11 says, "The fountains of the great deep burst open, and the floodgates of the sky were opened" (NAS). Normally, rising water follows a period of intense rainfall. Nevertheless, the biblical record says that the rainfall followed the rising water.

In the geologic record, there is evidence of warming pulses occurring at the end of the last ice age. These warming pulses might have caused such a rapid melt-off. These events could have happened in such a way that the people living in these coastal regions were caught unawares. However, because Noah was warned in advance, he, his family, and his animals had time to prepare their escape by following God's instructions to build an ark.

We have not discovered the remains of these communities today because they are located hundreds of feet underwater. However, we have found underwater caves along the coast of the Mediterranean Sea filled with artwork, showing that humans were active in the area when the water was much lower than it is today.

In fact, after a major study of the Black Sea region, it has been determined that a similar flood occurred there about 7,600 years ago. The Black Sea was hundreds of feet lower than it is today, with people living in the exposed regions of the seabed. Over a very short period of time, the seawater rose and became salty, replacing the fresh water originally there.

This incident is described in *Noah's Flood*, where authors William Ryan and Walter Pitman calculate that "ten cubic miles of water poured through [the Bosporus Strait ancient river channel] each day, [which is] two hundred times what flows over Niagara Falls, enough to cover Manhattan Island each day to a depth of over half a mile" (1998, 234).

We are not saying that this is the event that the Bible describes as being Noah's flood. We only use it to illustrate how a similar event probably caused earthwide flooding to occur when the continental ice glaciers were much larger.

Based upon our understanding that the Garden of Eden dealt with man's world, it is likely that God had Noah save all the domestic plants and animals given to Adam to name and to use (Genesis 2:9, 19–20). This view also harmonizes with the geologic record, because both domestic animals and plants seem to have suddenly appeared in the area we associate with Noah's immediate descendants.

Because of the curse placed upon the land by God (Genesis 3:17–19), these plants and animals did not become a significant part of the geologic record until after the Flood when the population increased and began to spread out in unprecedented numbers. This time period also marks the beginning of large-scale farming, which harmonizes with God's promise to remove the curse from the land (Genesis 8:21).

With the conclusion of the Flood of Noah's day, we, too, conclude our journey through the "record of the rocks." Along the way, the Bible has shown itself to be a reliable guide. It alone gives an accurate sequence of events when describing prehistoric times. Though other ancient sources may have provided incomplete, fantastic stories about these same events, they have been long lost in the ruins of the past. Those that have been discovered and translated have proven to be only inaccurate paraphrases of the Genesis narrative. The Bible alone has been miraculously preserved intact, readily available for anyone wanting to read a tried-and-true history of the earth and its inhabitants.

Chapter

12

GOD'S PERMISSION
OF EVIL

A discussion of reasons to believe in God would not be complete without addressing one of the biggest barriers to the acceptance of an omnipotent Creator—the existence and continued thriving of evil in this world. Understandably, an atheist might argue that even if scientific evidence points toward the existence of God, the injustice, suffering, and pain of this life deny both his power and his love.

Yet in the midst of all this injustice and pain, Christians are able to maintain faith in a God of love. How is this possible? What does the Bible reveal about evil and about the kind of God who would permit it?

THE LAW OF PARITY

First, we should recognize that the mere existence of evil does not necessarily mean there is no loving God. The coexistence of good and evil is in harmony with a basic concept in science and philosophy called the law of parity. This law states that for a physical process or form there is a mirror image. For example, an application of the law of parity caused Dr. Carl Anderson in 1932 to look for a particle that would be the mirror image of the negatively charged electron. He hypothesized that a positively charged particle with properties identical to the electron in every way, but opposite, should exist. Based on this law, Dr. Anderson did indeed discover a positively charged electron that, when it touches a normal electron, results in total annihilation.

Dr. Anderson's Nobel Prize-winning discovery of antimatter brings up another possible application of the law of parity, namely that equal amounts of matter and antimatter should exist in space. Could it be, then, that there are galaxies, solar systems, planets, and even some forms of life out there made of positrons, antiprotons, and antineutrons, identical to us in every way but fundamentally opposite? If true, we can imagine a tragic love story involving the matter boy and the antimatter girl whose passion drives them to indulge in one fleeting but fatal kiss, resulting in an enormous nuclear reaction that consumes them both.

Bringing the subject back to reality, we see that the law of parity in the natural world can often result in equal but opposite forces. In the case of matter and antimatter, we are dealing with concrete, measurable particles that physically support the law of parity.

THE PRINCIPLE OF PARITY

In the philosophical world, however, parity becomes more like a principle that logically requires an abstract concept such as good to have its antithesis in the concept of evil. How can we appreciate the value of being good if we have no comprehension of the negative effects associated with badness? If there is a potential for good, there will also be the potential for the opposite of good, or evil. How did God create good? He provided an arrangement wherein living creatures could live forever without experiencing painful adversity.

How, then, did evil come into existence? In chapter 7, we discussed the difference between God's direct creation (Hebrew, *bara*) and his indirect creation or making of matter (Hebrew, *asah*). In the case of evil, God's direct creation of goodness allowed for evil to be made by any free-will creature who chose to do so. Therefore, evil was made, not created.

Since evil as a mere concept is powerless, it would need to be personified to cause problems. For example, a pornographic book laid on a shelf unread does nothing. Only if someone reads the book and acts upon the information does evil possess any power. So, too, the evil resulting from the existence of good possessed no power until it became personified in a being desiring to oppose God's goodness and love. With this explanation in mind, we can understand how a free-will creature described in the Bible as Satan could exist independently of God's objectives and become the source of evil without God's help or approval (James 1:13). Knowing this, though, is not completely satisfying. It leaves open the question about what kind of relationship Satan has with God. What are our options?

The Concept of Dualism

Some might argue that the principle of parity implies a dualism between God and Satan. If this were true, then Satan would possess all of God's powers in a mirror-image sense. He would be a spiritual being who had always existed and who could oppose God with equal power. He would be able to exist in all places at the same time and could continuously nurture his own selfish interests by miraculously performing evil deeds. Like God, he could create matter from nothing, which, in his case, would probably be the antimatter described earlier.

As far as the Bible is concerned, however, Satan does not have the power necessary to support this concept of dualism. He is described as a spiritual being capable of doing some miraculous things beyond our comprehension, such as his ability to torment Job, but he is not portrayed as the evil equivalent of God. In Job 1 and 2 and in other places throughout the Bible, God effectively limits Satan. Additionally, there is no doubt according to Scripture that God will win out over Satan in the end.

The Description of a Fallen Angel

A preferred alternative to the duality argument is that Satan, the personification of evil, is simply a fallen angel. The Bible describes angels as spiritual beings who have specific assignments of responsibility in God's dimension or what we call heaven (Hebrews 1:14; Luke 1:19). As "sons of God," they were joyful witnesses when God created our universe (Job 38:7). At one point in the past, the angel referred to as Satan made evil come into tangible existence by revolting against God. As a result, God chose to separate this rebel angel from the rest of his realm by exiling him to the vicinity of the earth, along with those angels who chose to rebel with him.

The following verses support this view:

> For if God did not spare angels when they sinned, but sent them to hell, putting them into gloomy dungeons to be held for judgment... (2 Peter 2:4)

> And the angels who did not keep their positions of authority but abandoned their own home—these he has kept in darkness, bound with everlasting chains for judgment on the great Day. (Jude 6)

The above references lend credence to Satan's position as a fallen angel because God clearly exercises superior power over Satan and his agents. So the principle of parity explains why the possibility for evil should exist, and the Bible describes the one who chose to personify it.

We might still wonder, though, what caused Satan to revolt in the first place? Does his fall mean that when humans finally reach heaven, they will still potentially be able to fall victim to evil? Will the practicing of evil never end?

THE NECESSITY OF FREE WILL

To answer these questions, we need to acknowledge the place of free will in God's arrangement. When the Bible speaks of angels "sinning," it appears that God made them with enough free will to choose to be either good or bad. This does not say that God created the evil deeds they perform as a result of their choices any more than God directly causes tragedy in human affairs today. Rather, it means that God only allowed the potential for the expression of evil to exist.

Why would God create intelligent beings with the free will to love or hate? Why would he not just make them so that they could do only good? The answer is that true love is impossible unless there is a choice. If my wife were forced to love me and had no other choice, I could never be really confident of her love. Sexual relations between a man and a woman without choice is called rape and is universally recognized as having nothing to do with love. Real love has to involve a choice. If God's objectives were to include mutual love, then there had to be a choice available for the angels and for us.

By giving his angels the choice to be good or evil, God opened up a potential for revolt. Satan, whose name means "opposer," chose to lead such a revolt and to become the manifestation of evil. In the judgment, those obedient to God will be with him and will experience all the joys associated with love and goodness, whereas the temptation to choose evil will be completely eliminated when the devil and his forces are immobilized forever (Hebrews 2:14–15). At present, Satan apparently rejoices because he is free to show his power by winning over many men and women to support his cause. However, he is also cognizant of his final end, and for this reason, he and his cohorts "believe and tremble" (James 2:19 KJV).

GOD'S PURPOSE IN CREATING HUMANS

The next logical question in this discussion has to do with God's purpose in creating humans. Why did he create us when he knew that our free will could lead us into so much tragedy and pain? What role do we play in the final outcome of God's purpose?

Perhaps we can gain some insight into these questions by reviewing an everyday example. Suppose I have an idea for a machine that I believe is so good that I choose to invest my life's savings to develop it. What would I do to test the idea before committing my resources in such a way?

First, I would create a model of my idea in a lower dimension, such as drawing a plan of the machine on a two-dimensional sheet of paper. We call this drawing a plan or blueprint. Next, I would allow my plan to be examined by a number of critics. I should be prepared to defend my idea, using all my talents to help make it survive any test. If my idea were a good one, it would withstand the test, and then I would have confidence that it would be a worthwhile investment. If the idea were bad, though, it would not pass and probably should be abandoned.

The following biblical passages indicate that our existence and our actions are indeed being observed and tested by critics in heavenly places:

> For our struggle is not against flesh and blood, but against the rulers, against the authorities, against the powers of this dark world and against the spiritual forces of evil in the heavenly realms. (Ephesians 6:12)

> His [God's] intent was that now, through the church, the manifold wisdom of God should be made known to the rulers and authorities in the heavenly realms. (Ephesians 3:10)

> "Simon, Simon, Satan has asked to sift you as wheat. But I have prayed for you, Simon, that your faith may not fail." (Luke 22:31–32)

God could destroy Satan just as I could shoot the critic of my idea with a gun, but would that give onlookers (spiritual forces in high places) any confidence in either the creation or the Creator? Or would eliminating critics simply support the evil contention that "might makes right?" We are told in the Bible that humans are created a little lower than the angels (Psalm 8:5; Job 1–2). We are also told that after we die, we will become as angels (Mark 12:25). Therefore, humans appear to be the preliminary stage for achieving God's purpose, which is to share his existence eternally with perfect beings created in his image.

Job's Example

While we may not fully understand all of God's plans, we can see, to a limited extent in the Book of Job, how God handles some of the issues regarding our existence. In Job 1:8–12, good and evil are personified in God and Satan as they exchange challenges. God holds up Job as an example to show that because Satan's tools of evil do not work on everyone, Satan is not in total control of the earth. Satan accuses God of making Job's existence so comfortable that God has essentially bribed Job into being good. God responds by telling Satan that he will reduce his protection of Job and allow Satan to do anything except harm him bodily.

It is important to point out here that God does not personally attack Job. God does not directly tempt anyone (James 1:13). Instead, he allows humans to deal with the problems necessarily inherent in the exercise of free will, knowing that these problems will only exist temporarily until the achievement of his final objective. At present, our pain is a source of much grief to both God and us.

Most of us are familiar with Job's success in enduring the initial trials and tribulations to which Satan subjected him. Faced with failure in this first attack, Satan confronts God again (Job 2:1–6). He concedes to a mild defeat but claims that if he can cause Job to suffer physical pain, evil will easily triumph.

In response, God allows Satan to afflict Job with severe illnesses. At first, Job reacts with tears, anger, and regret that he had been born. His reaction, in part, was due to ignorance of the cosmic challenge behind his suffering, a challenge that involved the universal issues of free will and of God's eternal, loving purpose for his human children.

We might read about Job and conclude that while God did not cause Job's suffering, he was indirectly cruel and unloving in allowing it to happen. Yet this experience, as bad as it was, eventually opened Job's eyes with regard to God's majesty and power. He was assured that the all-powerful Creator of heaven and earth was aware of his suffering and cared. Even though Job did not receive specific explanations for his misfortunes, he was satisfied that God was in charge and that, from Job's position in time and space, the answers were beyond human comprehension. Therefore, Job finally said to God, "I know that you can do all things; no plan of yours can be thwarted. You asked, 'Who is this that obscures my counsel without knowledge?' Surely I spoke of things I did not understand, things too wonderful for me to know. My ears had heard of you but now my eyes have seen you" (Job 42:2–3, 5).

God, in turn, rewarded Job for his faithfulness, just as he promises to reward us for ours.

Our Example

If we accept the account of Job as both factual and as a metaphor for the suffering of humanity, then each of us can replace Job's name with our own. We are all afflicted by Satan, this world, and the consequences of our free will. Therefore, we all need to decide how we should react to the struggle between good and evil. Yet maintaining faith in a God of love is easier for us than it was for Job.

We have the advantage of being aware of the universal issue involved in the attack on Job. We also know more about God's love for us because we have the record of the life and death of Jesus Christ to assure us that God cares. In Christ, even though we do not have all the answers, our need for justice is satisfied.

Christ became the archetypical figure for whom all humanity longs—the disguised king who lives as one of his subjects in order to become a more compassionate king; the general who eats, sleeps, and endures the deprivations of war side by side with his troops before he leads them into battle. In Christ, we see the God who willingly gave up all his advantages to live our life and feel our pain. As Dorothy Sayers expressed it:

For whatever reason God chose to make man as he is—limited and suffering and subject to sorrows and death—He had the honesty and courage to take His own medicine. Whatever game He is playing with His creation, He has kept His own rules and played fair.

He can exact nothing from man that He has not exacted from Himself. He has Himself gone through the whole of human experience, from the trivial irritations of family life and the cramping restrictions of hard work and lack of money to the worst horrors of pain and humiliation, defeat, despair, and death. When He was a man, He played the man. He was born in poverty and died in disgrace and thought it well worthwhile. (1969, 14)

Though, like Job, we do not have all the answers now, we can be assured that God sympathizes with our fears and will eventually reward our trust in him. He has promised us eternal life in a higher dimension free of suffering and pain in accord with his original plan (Revelation 21:4; Isaiah 25:8; Matthew 25:34). Yes, our pain is real, but when contrasted with eternity, our present life is incredibly short. A whole lifetime of pain can be likened to a trip to the dentist. We get a shot of novocaine or something similar before the dentist works on our teeth. Why? Because we are gladly willing to endure thirty seconds of the needle against what seems like an eternity of drilling. By comparison, how much will seventy-five years of pain and suffering mean in the context of an eternity in God's domain?

The choices we make now will have eternal significance. None of us can be neutral in this matter. If we choose evil, we will experience the consequences associated with that choice. If we choose good, the beauty of God will shine through us now in this world as well as in the world to come, when God's plan will be vindicated and evil will be a thing of the past.

Chapter

13

WHY CHOOSE THE BIBLE AS THE WORD OF GOD?

Throughout this book, we have associated the person of God with the God described to us in the Bible. He is the omnipotent, omniscient, and immortal Being, unbounded by time, who inhabits a dimension beyond our universe. He is the source of all the intelligent design and power required for the existence of our earth and for the web of life upon it. We have also shown how closely the Bible's account of creation has followed the sequence of events preserved in the fossil record.

For some people, these arguments are enough to convince them of the existence of God and of the authority of the Bible as his inspired Word. For others, however, the question arises about whether other deities and other sacred works, such as the Vedas, the Koran, and the writings of Confucius, are equal or superior to the Bible.

In my own case, when I finally left atheism and accepted the existence of God, I began a spiritual quest to determine who God was and what he expected of me. My reading included the Vedas, Upanishads, the Bhagavad-Gita, the Koran, Tripitaka, Avesta, Tao Te Ching, Angas, Upangas, Bab, Bahaullah, and even the Book of Mormon. Since becoming a Christian, I have reread some of these books, especially the Koran, to make more specific comparisons with the Bible.

All holy books are interesting and beautiful in their own way. The authors present attractive ideas and, through the application of common sense, agree on many of the basic issues. Therefore, the question becomes not whether these words are wise, well-written, or beautiful but whether they actually represent the word of the God who created the universe. When choosing a book for spiritual guidance, it must be complete and correct in all aspects; otherwise, it could never have any significant impact on a person's life or be depended upon to help in making important decisions.

What evidence do we have showing that the Bible alone is the only reliable source of pure truth? Why should it be used exclusively for spiritual guidance to the exclusion of all the other sources I have mentioned?

INTERNAL EVIDENCE
Simplicity and Clarity

Within the pages of the Bible, we find a simplicity and a clarity conspicuously missing from other contemporaneous works of literature. When I was assigned to read Homer's *Iliad* in high school, I found myself more confused than informed. I remember complaining to my English teacher about her selection of study material. Her response was that since the *Iliad* was written around 800 B.C., I should not expect it to make as much sense as something written more recently. At that time, people had a vastly different world-view, often a much more indirect way of reasoning, and a wordier style of expression than we use today. Thus, it is often very difficult for someone living now to readily grasp the literal meaning expressed by ancient writers.

On the other hand, notice the simplicity of the first statement in the Bible: "In the beginning, God created the heavens and the earth." As I have previously stated, I have a mentally retarded son who has an

IQ of about 55. He can read that passage and understand it. The scriptural passage we are talking about was probably written some 700 years before the date of the *Iliad*, yet it is easily understood today.

In addition to simplicity of style, the Bible contains remarkable clarity. A verse-by-verse comparison with the Vedas will convince the reader of how sharp a contrast there is between these two books. A Hindu friend of mine confided to me that although he held a Ph.D. and was an upper-caste Hindu, he could not understand the Vedas and neither could any of his peers. If you question the validity of that statement, I urge you to secure a copy and read it for yourself. You will soon discover that the Bible is unique in its clarity.

Confident Voice

Another characteristic of the Bible is the obvious confidence with which its writers spoke and wrote. In contrast, writers of other holy books often express personal insecurity by interjecting such qualifiers as "I swear this is true" or "I am positive this is right." Yet nowhere in the writings of the Bible or in the message of Jesus Christ do we encounter comparable adjurations. Rather, people said of Jesus, "No one ever spoke the way this man does" (John 7:46), "because he taught as one who had authority, and not as their teachers of the law" (Matthew 7:29).

On another occasion, Jesus specifically discouraged prodigious oaths by saying,

> But I tell you, Do not swear at all; either by heaven, for it is God's throne; or by the earth, for it is his footstool; or by Jerusalem, for it is the city of the Great King. And do not swear by your head, for you cannot make even one hair white or black. Simply let your "Yes" be "Yes," and your "No," "No"; anything beyond this comes from the evil one. (Matthew 5:34–37)

This simple, straightforward recommendation contrasts significantly with the Koran, where we see hundreds of expressions of insecurity, such as "By Allah, I swear this is true."

Brevity

When historians or storytellers write and politicians or preachers speak, they are seldom brief. Conversely, the Bible is simple and to the point, especially in the Old Testament Genesis account of creation and in the New Testament style of writing in general.

For instance, in any large library in this country, there are millions of volumes of scientific material dealing with the origin of the universe and life. Dr. Carl Sagan estimated that there may be as many as 40 million books written about this subject. All of these 40 million volumes of scientific material are implicitly summarized in the first 31 verses of the Bible.

Paradoxically, this straightforward simplicity is also one of the problems that some people have with the Genesis record. They expect to find the essential knowledge of all those 40 million volumes somehow stated explicitly within these 31 short verses. While such an excess of information might satisfy some modern-day critics, it certainly would have been of no benefit to the great majority of the readers of Genesis. So the way the Bible has managed to convey God's creation message with simple but scientifically sound word-images is nothing short of miraculous.

Additional examples of brevity abound in the Bible. The baptism of Jesus is adequately reported using only four verses. The transfiguration of Christ, which is certainly a momentous event, is covered in only five verses, excluding his journey up and down the mountain. Of the 12,000 days that Jesus Christ dwelt on the earth and of the 1,200 days of his active ministry, only about 34 total days are accounted for in the Bible.

I had a friend who studied biographical styles for his doctoral thesis. One biography of John F. Kennedy that he reviewed included 183 more days in Kennedy's life than he had lived! Not so in the Bible. All unnecessary data are omitted.

Although brevity is appealing to the reader, it sometimes imposed a challenge to the Bible writers. We can almost sense their frustration because it seems as if they were not allowed to write as much as they would have liked. John says things like "Even the world itself could not contain the books" that he would like to have written (John 21:25 KJV). This unusual economy of words is not typical of other religious books. Just the sheer size of the Vedas literally proves this point. In the Koran, we see numerous examples of unnecessary detail, such as how many times a day Mohammed brushed his teeth.

Fulfilled Prophecy

While the account of Jesus' ministry may have been brief, it was, nevertheless, complete enough to establish the Bible as the indisputable Word of God. Writing history in advance or prophesying with absolute accuracy is something only God can do. In harmony with this,

Prophecies Concerning the Messiah

1. Where he would be born (Micah 5:2; Matthew 2:1).
2. He would be preceded by a messenger (Isaiah 40:3; Matthew 3:3).
3. How he would enter Jerusalem (Zechariah 9:9; Matthew 21:4–11).
4. His friends would betray him (Psalm 41:9; Matthew 10:4).
5. He would be betrayed for thirty pieces of silver (Zechariah 11:12; Matthew 26:15).
6. How the betrayal money would be used (Zechariah 11:13b; Matthew 26:15; 27:7).
7. He would be silent before his accusers (Isaiah 53:7; Matthew 27:11–14).
8. His hands and feet would be pierced (Psalm 22:16; Matthew 27:35; John 20:25).
9. He would suffer and redeem us (Isaiah 53:5–6, 11–12; Romans 5:17–18).
10. He would be beaten and spit upon (Isaiah 50:6; Matthew 26:67).
11. He would be given gall and vinegar to drink (Psalm 69:21; Matthew 27:34).
12. His clothing would be divided by lots (Psalm 22:18; Matthew 27:35).
13. He would cry out (Psalm 22:1; Matthew 27:46).
14. Darkness would cover the land (Amos 8:9; Matthew 27:45).
15. He would be buried with the rich (Isaiah 53:9; Matthew 27:57–60).
16. He would be called God (Isaiah 9:6; John 20:28).

we find that Jesus' ministry was preceded by several hundred prophecies, which served to establish, beyond a reasonable doubt, that he was the true son of God.

Dr. Peter Stoner, Professor Emeritus of Science at Westmont College, decided to assign his graduate students the task of calculating what the odds would be for these events to have happened by chance. Using just the first eight of the prophecies listed in the shaded box titled "Prophecies Concerning the Messiah," he calculated that the odds would be 1 in 10^{17} (that is, 1 in 100,000,000,000,000,000). According to reliable sources, Dr. Stoner's calculations have been reviewed and verified by a committee of the American Scientific Affiliation, Goshen College, and by the Executive Council of that same group ("Prophecies Concerning the Messiah" 2000).

Since this figure greatly exceeds the number of people who have ever lived, it can be safe to assume that it would be impossible for these events to have happened by chance alone. Some may argue that Jesus intentionally set out to fulfill personal prophecies, which would slightly bias the odds in his favor. While that is possible in some instances, there is a significant number of predictions over which he had no control, such as his lineage, his birthplace, and his mother's circumstances, to name just a few. These more than offset those he could have deliberately fulfilled, clearly showing that the supernatural was involved.

Honesty

In addition to the features we have listed, freedom from whitewash is another important characteristic of the Bible. The normal procedure to follow when writing a book of praise about someone is to omit any negative comments. For example, after reading the biography of John F. Kennedy, I came away feeling that this man had lived a flawless life. In recent years, however, other writings have shown that President Kennedy had some serious weaknesses that were not exposed in the biography I read.

In the Bible, we do not see this kind of whitewash. When we read about Abraham, who is truly one of the great heroes of the Old

Testament, we also read about his weaknesses. We see him willing to allow his wife to become a part of a ruler's harem on two different occasions because Abraham did not really trust in God. Then we read about David, who is said to be a man after God's own heart, and his sins are not hidden from our view. We are informed that he not only committed adultery with the wife of one of his best soldiers, but he also became an accessory to murder in order to suppress the truth of his affair. This information is not flattering to David, and it certainly is not what a nation would want history to record about its greatest hero. Nonetheless, the story is there and is spelled out in all its appalling details.

Such honesty is proof of the Bible's inspiration. If the Bible had been solely the product of human effort, these sordid accounts would no doubt have been excluded. This type of candor cannot be attributed to the Koran. It contains a group of selected quotes by Mohammed written by his contemporaries. When assembling it, the compilers chose to include only the best and the wisest of Mohammed's sayings and to exclude everything else.

CHECKABILITY

By checkability, we refer to statements in the Bible that can be checked to see whether or not they are accurate. One feature of the Bible that makes it easily verifiable is the language in which it was written. Adding to its simplicity and clarity of style is the vernacular of the people who wrote it. Common, concrete nouns and clear, action verbs are easily translated into modern languages with no essential loss of meaning. For those words and phrases that are ambiguous, the reader does not have to be a Greek or Hebrew scholar to understand them. All key words can be found in Hebrew or Greek lexicons.

Even though translators of the original Hebrew, Aramaic, and Greek have been careful in their translations, human errors have crept in from time to time, as well as differences based upon the interpretations and opinions of the translators. Sometimes limited knowledge of the original languages has caused confusion, such as whether Jonah was swallowed by a whale or a big fish. Other times, numerical data are poorly interpreted, which may require a detailed study to explain an apparent variance in the account.

However, these errors and problems are minor and are of little significance. They do not negate the claim that the original manuscripts of the Bible were literally inspired by God and thus were error free. In other words, we are asserting that the Bible is the inerrant Word of God.

If this is true, then it will not contain gross errors reflecting the ignorance of the men who wrote it. While the Bible does not specifically address scientific issues, it should not be filled with many of the local superstitious fantasies characteristic of the day in which it was written. What we should find are statements that are too insightful and profound to be attributed to luck or to advanced knowledge on the part of some of its human authors. Let us examine a few of the more impressive examples that prove inspiration by God.

The Value of Blood

During George Washington's time and well after his death, the medical practice of bloodletting was carried on. Barbers made a part of their living by bleeding people. The reason for this practice, which was also done in Egypt during the time of Moses, was that doctors believed that disease originated in the blood. To get rid of the disease, one should get rid of the "bad blood." Bloodletting, then, was an essential part of virtually all medical treatment.

Today we realize the foolishness of this practice because over the past 200 years, we have come to understand that blood serves a very useful role in fighting disease. Ironically, humanity could have known the importance of blood 3,200 years ago simply by reading Leviticus 17:1–14. In this passage, Moses, though trained in Egypt and aware of bloodletting, clearly states that blood is necessary for life. Bloodletting was not a teaching of the Hebrew Torah, even though it was taught by the surrounding nations of that day. As a result, Moses' statement about the significance of blood predates modern medical science by about 3,000 years.

Human Reproduction

In ancient Roman mythology, two boys named Romulus and Remus were born out of the mud and later became the founders of the city of Rome. As we can see from this myth, the idea that women were not always necessary when it came to human reproduction has ancient roots. It was believed many centuries ago that males alone possessed the seed of life and females provided nothing more than an ideal environment for the growing seed.

There were civilizations that built their whole social structure and sometimes even their religious beliefs around this concept. The results were that women came to be looked upon as nothing more than a man's property and a measure of his wealth and prestige. A man who collected many wives was a man who was wealthy, for wealth was necessary to support a harem. In some cultural systems, when such a man died, his wives were buried with him, whether they were dead or not.

On the other hand, the biblical view of women is radically different. In Genesis 2:22–24, God indicated the importance of women and their very special relationship to men by creating the first woman, Eve, from Adam's rib. Much later, the apostle Paul highlighted the significance of this act by showing that although the first woman came from man, all other men have come from women through the birthing process. So there was no basis for men to feel superior to women from a creation point of view (1 Corinthians 11:11–12).

Even more important is the fact that in Genesis 3:15 (KJV), mention is made of a woman's seed, yet the first egg of a woman (her seed) was not visibly seen until around 1922. The promise made to Eve's seed clearly shows the correctness of the biblical concept of women and their role in the process of human reproduction.

Animal Reproduction

Sometimes a more careful reading of the text substantiates the checkability of the Bible. A case in point is the animal husbandry practiced by Jacob in the book of Genesis. Critics have argued that here the Bible is contaminated by archaic, local folklore. Contrary to this claim, we find that if an account happens to include a description of events that may be founded upon superstition and myth, the biblical text usually clarifies matters with a qualifying statement or explanation.

Genesis 30:37–43 describes how Jacob apparently tried to develop a breed of goats that had spotted or speckled bodies. Critics have used this text to show that Jacob believed he could cause an animal to be born with spots if the mother was shown a spotted object while she was mating. By his actions, it is very likely that Jacob did feel this way and did, in fact, believe that he was successful, because an unusually large number of spotted animals were born to his father-in-laws's flocks at this time.

But rather than endorsing a practice that today we know is false, the Bible shows that Jacob's success was not founded upon his own efforts at breeding goats. A careful reading of Genesis 31:10–12 reveals the actual reason why Jacob prospered: "In breeding season I once had a dream in which I looked up and saw that the male goats mating with the flock were streaked, speckled or spotted. The angel of God said to me in the dream, 'Jacob.' I answered, 'Here I am.' And he said, 'Look up and see that all the male goats mating with the flock are streaked, speckled or spotted.'"

Here we find that God miraculously increased the libido of the spotted males, which apparently resulted in only spotted offspring. Though initially God allowed Jacob to assume that his success was due to his own personal, unscientific efforts, we later learn that Jacob had nothing to do with it. God was entirely responsible. He was causing "*all the male goats mating with the flock*" to be spotted. Obviously, God inspired this explanation because it was based upon genetics and not upon the primitive breeding methods practiced by Jacob and his contemporaries. Thus we find that the details in this account provide evidence for the checkability of the Bible.

Bacterial Contamination

Moses has been referred to by some writers as the world's first microbiologist. This idea developed because of the wisdom seen in his writings relating to the fields of hygiene, diet, and quarantine. We must remember that even during most of the nineteenth century, knowledge about diseases was so vague that bacterial infection ran rampant. Doctors would perform an autopsy in a hospital morgue, and then, without washing their hands, they would perform surgery, deliver a baby, or conduct a hands-on examination of a patient. The death rate among women giving birth in these hospitals ranged from 25% to 30%.

When Dr. Ignaz Phillip Semmelweis, who was practicing in Vienna, Austria, tried to change this procedure in the 1840s, he was driven into seclusion by his colleagues, in spite of the fact that his insistence upon simple hand washing had been proven effective. In wards under his charge, the death rate of his patients averaged no more than 0.85 percent. Ironically, Semmelweis died of childbirth fever (puerperal fever), a disease he spent his entire professional life trying to eradicate. He apparently caught the disease from one of his infected patients.

Is it a coincidence that 3,200 years ago, a man who knew nothing about bacteria, infection, or any of our modern medical concepts gave us a system of hygiene that is still followed by doctors today? Let us examine some of the rules given by Moses to the Israelites that we now know to be bacteriologically sound.

Handling Dead Objects

In Numbers 19:5–22 and Leviticus 13–15, Moses commands that an individual touching a dead person or animal should be quarantined. Prescribed washings and the burning of the clothes of one who contacted a dead person are given in the same passages. Even a casual observer can see the wisdom behind these commands. Any animal or person who died of unknown causes is likely to have died of a communicable disease.

The prescribed washings, burnings, and isolations Moses required would help to avoid the epidemic normally spread by such a bacterial or viral agent. The beneficial effect of these procedures became obvious when those who did not follow God's commands frequently became sick. Eventually this led people to erroneously associate sickness in general with sinfulness, which is why Jesus' disciples asked him, "Rabbi, who sinned, this man or his parents, that he should be born blind?" (John 9:2 NAS).

Burying Wastes and Quarantine

In Europe during the Dark Ages, people threw their waste products out the window into the street. The stench and pollution problems were bad enough, but even more important were the infection and disease problems caused by such a careless waste-disposal system. Writers of the time record that flies, rats, and other disease-carrying organisms thrived in the garbage found in the streets. The black plague, encephalitis epidemics, and a variety of other scourges have been attributed to this waste-disposal practice.

These facts make us appreciate even more the words in Deuteronomy 23:12–14, where Moses commands the Israelites to bury their wastes. Additionally, a person having any kind of discharge from his or her body was isolated or quarantined from the rest of the people. Even such bodily functions as menstruation and ejaculation were put into this unclean category. While this may have seemed extreme to us in the past, now because of the AIDS virus, we can readily appreciate the importance of removing all possible sources of disease. Yet during the time of Moses and for 3,000 years afterward, the whole concept of unseen contamination was totally foreign to human thought. Clearly, Moses had supernatural help in deriving his medical directives.

Prohibiting Certain Foods

Methods for cooking food during the time of Moses were highly inadequate, to say the least. The wandering Israelite population did not possess efficient ovens, nor did they have any way of refrigerating their foods as we do today. It should be obvious, then, that certain types of foods that could contain hard-to-kill parasites, worms, and bacteria would need to be avoided. In Leviticus 11, we observe that Moses excluded those very items from the Israelites' diet by forbidding pork, the flesh of scavengers like vultures, and many other potentially dangerous food sources. He even forbade the eating of animal blood (Leviticus 17:12–14), which is still done by some cultures despite the bacteriological hazards involved.

We are just now understanding the reasons for many of these dietary restrictions, like the avoidance of eating fat (Leviticus 3:17; 7:23). Moses' uncanny accuracy in singling out so-called clean and unclean animals goes beyond any chance logic. It is another clear demonstration of the miraculous source of his writings.

We can now see that these health commands by God were an important way of protecting his chosen people from the likelihood of being decimated by infectious disease. This, of course, was absolutely necessary if they were to survive as a nation long enough to provide the right kind of godly community within which Jesus Christ, the Son of God, could be properly raised.

Astronomy

Understandably, in the past, the combination of primitive superstition and a limited observer's viewpoint of the heavens and earth resulted in some fantastic astronomical theories postulated by ancient civilizations. In Hindu writings, the earth is described as resting on the backs of four elephants. The elephants are standing on the back of a giant turtle who is swimming in a sea of milk (Branley and Wimmer 1970, 30–36). Earthquakes, tsunami (tidal) waves, and other upsets in the earth's equilibrium are brought about when an elephant sneezes or tries to scratch itself.

The Japanese taught in many of their religious traditions that the earth was suspended on the back of a giant catfish. Once again, the various cataclysmic events that took place upon the earth could be explained by movements of the fish. Even the scholarly Greek civilization at one point taught that the earth was suspended upon the back of a god named Atlas.

These beliefs stand in sharp contrast to a people who depended upon the one and only God for direction. Moses, who probably wrote Genesis, was trained in Egypt where the sun was worshipped as the god

Ra and where the Egyptians, like the surrounding nations, had elaborate observatories and descriptions of star configurations. Yet Moses' writings were entirely free from mythological fantasy as an explanation for the suspension of the earth.

Even though the Bible makes very few remarks about the mechanics of the earth's position in space, the poetic writer of Job makes the statement, "He suspends the earth over nothing" (Job 26:7). The profundity of this ancient statement may not be obvious to us in this technological day of space travel. But when we consider how much astronomy was known 4,000 years ago in Job's day, we should recognize that this statement is without precedent. It was made thousands of years before Isaac Newton was supposedly struck by an apple and proposed the now accepted universal law of gravitation. It was an equally long time before the law of action-reaction was understood or the nature of centrifugal force was perceived, along with its importance in keeping the earth from colliding with the sun or spinning uncontrollably off into outer space.

Therefore, it was only through inspiration by God that Job was able to make such an accurate statement about the suspension of the earth when other ancient scientists spoke in terms of giant elephants, catfish, and a Greek god's shoulders.

PHYSICAL SCIENCE

We have said a number of times that the Bible is not a book of science. For this reason, we want to emphasize that we are not suggesting that the men who wrote these facts intended to be stating ideas relating to science. However, if the Bible is the Word of God, then we would expect it to be accurate. Because of this, when a scientific fact is implied or shown by example, it should be consistent with what we know scientifically today. To prove this hypothesis, let us briefly consider some additional examples where scientific issues are implied. In doing this, we will be impressed with the uniqueness of the subject matter and the difficulty in attributing the wisdom behind the words to the human writer alone.

Scientific Principles

In 1856, Hubert Spencer outlined a new and significant framework for scientific research and writing that gave substance and direction to analytical work. He asserted that in order for a scientific report to be useful, it must include all the relevant elements of the problem, such as time, force, action or direction, and weight or matter. In this regard, it is interesting to note that the Bible was the first report ever to contain all these vital elements as recognized by Spencer. Notice that Genesis 1:1 says, "In the beginning [time] God [force] created [action] the heavens and the earth [matter]." It seems that the biblical writer knew intuitively the best method of formatting a scientific report. Even though this is a minor point, it emphasizes the Bible's faithfulness to details.

Shipbuilding

It is scripturally significant that the first reinforced concrete ship ever launched had the dimensions 300 x 50 x 30 feet (DeHoff 1959, 53). Modern hydraulic architects have learned that a certain ratio between length, width, and height produces greater seaworthiness than other dimension ratios. These discoveries have come about through a long history of trial-and-error experiments. Even in our modern day of marine engineering and oceanographic technology, the basic size ratio of all ships considered to produce maximum seaworthiness is 30 x 5 x 3.

In Genesis 6:15, we read a 3,200-year-old narrative of God-given instructions to a man who was building a boat that had to be the epitome of seaworthiness. The dimensions of this boat were to be 300 x 50 x 30 cubits (30 x 5 x 3 ratio). Not only were the dimension ratios given accurately, but the ship also had design features that were not incorporated into sailing ships until relatively recent times.

The thin plank hull of Noah's ark was pitched (sealing pitch) instead of being made out of lightweight, bulky materials that could be depended upon to stay afloat by themselves. This was a novel technique for that day and time. It was pitched both inside and out to produce a watertight structure, another feature that was not introduced until much later in history. The below-deck area was compartmentalized into a sort of stateroom division now found on modern ocean liners. This design gives the vessel greater structural integrity.

In the ancient past, materials such as low density logs and marsh reeds were used because of their buoyancy. Noah's ark introduced the water-displacement concept, wherein a watertight box or hull made of strong, dense materials will readily float if it weighs less than the water it displaces. This idea was unique for that day, and it causes us to marvel at another "happy coincidence," scientifically speaking.

Geography/History/Archaeology

When we consider that at least forty different men were involved in writing the Bible over thousands of years, its accuracy geographically, historically, and archaeologically is amazing. When the Bible says a certain man went up or down from a certain place going to another place, geographic references have been correct in every testable case. The Bible is also accurate historically. Archaeologists and historians recognize that the Bible furnishes tremendous insights into the history of the period in which it was written. Even those records in the Bible thought to be in error (such as the existence of the Hittite nation that critics disclaimed for many years to be a biblical myth) have been shown by archaeologists to be true. It is not surprising that the official publication of the Harvard University Archaeological Studies Department is called *The Biblical Archaeologist*. In its very interesting monthly reports, it testifies again and again to the accuracy of biblical accounts.

MORALITY

Today a humanistic society, strongly influenced by evolutionary concepts, is trying to promote selfishness in the guise of "freedom." The message is "Do anything you want to. Since this life is all you have, there is no reason to live by an outdated moral code. Get what you can and enjoy it." Friedrich Nietzsche, a famous German philosopher, is reputed to have said, "There is no reason why the stronger and smarter should continue to be constrained by a 'value' that is obviously not in their interest."

As Individuals

In stark contrast with this self-centered philosophy, Jesus tells us how to live successfully by showing concern for others and by controlling our minds and thoughts. In Matthew chapters 5 and 6, not only are we told not to commit adultery, but we are told to keep such thoughts out of our minds altogether. Not only are we told not to murder, but we are told not to hate either.

The Bible makes an encouraging promise in 1 Corinthians 10:13: "No temptation has seized you except what is common to man. And God is faithful; he will not let you be tempted beyond what you can bear. But when you are tempted, he will also provide a way out so that you can stand up under it."

Those Christians who have believed and lived according to this promise can testify to its fulfillment in their lives.

Within the Family

The Bible also tells us how to deal with our home life intelligently and rationally. In Mark 10:6–9, Jesus commands that all men should practice a monogamous marriage relationship—one husband, one wife—for life. In fact, Jesus alludes to Genesis 2:24, which indicates that this was God's will from the very beginning. The alternative to this command is polygamy (multiple wives) and polyandry (multiple husbands). If you are a woman, do you really believe you can have the kind of relationship you want in life with a man who is also married to other women? Or if you are a man, do you really believe you can have what you want out of a marriage if you have to share your wife with other men? There is no question about the practicality and wisdom of the marriage requirements given in the Bible. This arrangement was intended to give children both a father and a mother devoted to raising them in a secure, loving family environment. Wherever this system has been followed, coupled with godly works, it has resulted in happy, well-adjusted individuals.

Within the Community

Assuming that our home life is in order, how are we to deal with people outside the home? The Bible tells us that we are to love other people, to be willing to symbolically turn the other cheek to them in times of conflict, and not to return evil for evil. In Matthew 5:41, the writer tells us that if a person is compelled to go one mile, he should go two miles.

In Roman times, it was law that a Roman soldier could require any Jewish citizen to carry his load for up to one mile, which was exactly 1,000 paces. However, the involuntary draftee was not required to go one pace beyond the legislated distance. It must have made a favorable impression on a Roman soldier when a Christian would volunteer to carry the load for 2,000 paces.

Implicit in this command from God were several requirements for sound mental health. A person who is forgiving, loving, polite, and free from prejudice is a well-adjusted, successful citizen. Jesus not only recommended this moral way of life, he lived it himself. He proved many times that neither he nor his Father are prejudiced (Acts 10:34–35).

Although Samaritans were shunned and despised by the Jews, Jesus had direct fellowship with several Samaritans, including one woman of questionable reputation. In both passages (Luke 10:30 and John 4:3–24), the Samaritans are viewed in a very positive light by Jesus and the Bible writer. In John 4, Jesus deals directly with the Samaritan woman, and she expresses surprise at this. Thus by example and command, Jesus teaches us tolerance and love and appreciation, no matter what our racial or social or economic circumstance.

What is the alternative to this godly system given to us in the Bible? We would have a system where there is little, if any, motivation toward true unselfishness. Such a system inevitably produces prejudice, bigotry, and anarchy. The Bible does not simply recommend, it motivates people to perform good works. For this reason, the Bible's instructions on how to get along with other people cannot be improved upon. One time when asked what he thought about Christianity in general, Carl Sandburg responded by saying, somewhat wryly, that he did not know—he had never seen it tried yet. Unfortunately, there are many people today who have not seen Christianity tried, even in the lives of some of those who claim to be Christians.

THE AUTHOR

Finally, perhaps the most important reason to choose the Bible as the Word of God has to do with its author. When we examine the other religions in the world, we find that all of the responsibility for establishing a relationship with God falls upon the seeker—humanity must reach up to God. God does not help at all in these religious systems. It is up to each individual to reach the goal—whether the goal is Nirvana or Brahma or whatever it might be. If a person is not capable of reaching the goal using his own strength and merit, then he may have to make repeated attempts by being reincarnated over and over again.

Notice the contrast in the Bible when the angel Gabriel told Mary her son would be called Immanuel, "which means, 'God with us'" (Matthew 1:23). In the last book of the New Testament, the resurrected Jesus says, "Here I am. I stand at the door and knock. If anyone hears my voice and opens the door, I will come in and eat with him, and he with me" (Revelation 3:20).

In John 10:14–18, the relationship of a shepherd with his sheep is given to characterize a personal God, not wanting any of us to be lost, but wanting all of us to be saved and live eternally with him (1 Timothy 2:3–4; 2 Peter 3:9). This reward is so awe-inspiring that it cannot be expressed in words. We are told that there will not be any more pain or suffering or agony (Revelation 21:3–4; 1 Corinthians 15:50–58). Our bodies will be changed to live in God's domain forever.

For those who diligently apply the Bible to their lives, there is a freedom from many of the serious problems plaguing this generation. Exhaustive studies have been done to see if being a Christian makes any difference in people's abilities to overcome drugs, alcohol, depression, mental illness, disease, and poverty. The National Institute for Health Care Research has found that Christianity has a statistically significant positive effect on people in general.

There are all sorts of people who demonstrate changed lives—freed from every problem imaginable. Testimony can be a risky road to truth because testimonies are often difficult to document from a scientific perspective. However, there are just too many cases to ignore where people have been turned from pursuing their own selfish schemes to living a life in pursuit of godly works.

So there are many reasons to choose the Bible as the inspired Word of God. We can have complete confidence in a book that is open to scrutiny in all areas of human life and consistently proves to be accurate —scientifically, socially, and religiously. The more we study the Bible, the more convinced we become that not only does God exist, but he personally encourages and rewards those who earnestly seek to know him better (Hebrews 11:6).

Chapter

14

CONCLUSION

The case for the existence of God does not hinge upon one piece of evidence or one particular concept or one logical approach. Instead, evidence for the existence of God can be found everywhere, from the formation of matter in the cosmos to the intricacies of the human cell. Even in this lengthy discussion, we have barely scratched the surface of the handiwork of God. New discoveries come to light on a daily basis.

In this book, we have shown that it is logical and reasonable to believe that the carefully designed creation we see about us is the product of a personal God. This belief contrasts sharply with accepting the notion that the cosmos came out of mindless nothing in a series of fortuitous accidents.

In Romans 1:19–20, the concept of design is offered as a proof for God's existence. The statement is made that even the unseen things of God can be clearly understood through what he has made and created. We have demonstrated in a variety of ways—both at the intuitive level and with some mathematical analysis—that the creation could not have occurred by chance but must be the result of intelligent design. We have found that this design argument applies to every relevant scientific discipline. If there is design, then there must be a designer or planner responsible for it all.

In this regard, we are living at a very exciting period in human history. For the first time, we have peered into the living cell and have seen a complexity of design unparalleled in anything humans have ever made or dreamed of making. This complexity, appearing so early in earth's history, has left no time for a purely natural evolution of life. If such a discovery has forced some scientists to theorize that life must have come to earth from outer space, we laud that conclusion and add to it by naming the source of life and power and design—the great God of the universe.

We are also living at a time when we have "seen" the Cambrian explosion of life in the Burgess Shale and the Chengjiang fossils. Here again, the length of time available for such a diversity of complex body parts and systems to come about by natural selection, mutation, and genetic drift alone is far too short to account for "life's big bang." But the Bible describes this sudden appearance of life in earth's oceans when it says, "And God said, 'Let the water teem with living creatures'" (Genesis 1:20).

In our opinion, these two events alone—the emergence of the living cell and the Cambrian explosion—have essentially invalidated the Godless theory of evolution. Therefore, we believe the question confronting scientists today is not, "Does God exist?" but rather, "How and when did God intervene in his progressive creation to produce the complex web of life we observe all around us?" As we keep abreast of the many new discoveries coming to light almost daily on this subject, we echo the words of Henry F. Schaefer, quantum chemist and five-time nominee for the Nobel Prize: "The significance and joy in my science comes in those occasional moments of discovering something new and saying to myself, 'So that's how God did it.' My goal is to understand a little corner of God's plan" (Sheler and Schrof 1991, 7).

Our goal in writing this book has been to do the same—to reveal just a small measure of God's creative power. In so doing, we have consistently turned to the Bible as his inspired Word. In the fields of medicine, astronomy, physical science, geology, and virtually every other discipline, the Bible makes statements that surpass the educational limitations of its authors. To quickly reject these statements as being due to luck or chance is not satisfying because there are just too many "chance" occurrences to account for.

For example, it is incomprehensible that a man writing 3,200 years ago could make accurate medical observations only now proven true through the use of highly sophisticated scientific equipment. The sequence of creation found in Genesis 1 is also more than coincidental. Fossil evidence has required scientists to revise their theories of evolution to agree with the Genesis account of creation. The theory of punctuated equilibrium is a compromise on the part of evolutionists in recognition of the fact that changes take place in the fossil record much faster than predicted by the evolutionary theory of uniformitarianism.

Some of the supposed contradictions between science and the Bible appear because of bad science, such as accepting the evolution of man from early primates as factual when there are valid academic arguments against the concept. Other contradictions appear because of bad theology, such as accepting the suggestions of men that the Bible can be used as a clock to establish the absolute time periods for various events in earth's history.

However, both the Bible and science agree that humans are conspicuously different from the animals that preceded them. The unique cultural endowments of humans establish them as being created in the image of God, clearly proving that we are not the product of chance but of intelligent design.

The charge that there is insufficient evidence for God's existence is plainly misleading. The problem is that many people today demand absolute proof in areas where absolute proof is not possible, unless God decides to reveal himself directly. Why is it that we humans demand far more proof when it comes to God than we do in other areas of our lives?

There is a leap of faith in nearly everything we seriously depend upon. Every Christian realizes that there are many questions relative to

God, his origin, his plan, and his methods that cannot be answered completely or, in many cases, even comprehended. Nevertheless, our leap of faith need not be a blind one. Indeed, God does not require such a mindless commitment but rather asks us to leap based upon rational, understandable evidence that he has provided in abundance.

To deny God, a man or woman must ignore a great deal of favorable evidence, as we have shown. The social consequences of such denials are obvious. Realizing this, it may be that you already see the importance of acknowledging that God exists and that he cares for you (Hebrews 11:6). This will allow you to personally experience his working in your life. However, this cannot happen until you give yourself to him unconditionally.

With this in mind, we urge you to review the arguments in this book to see if they will help you to intelligently make your own leap of faith. You can do this with the assurance that both God and Jesus Christ can and will work through you for the rest of your life on this earth and into eternity.

When we discuss concepts dealing with how God may have performed his acts of creation, we are bound to raise questions in the minds of our readers. For that reason, we invite you to ask us these questions by writing to us. We would welcome the opportunity to clarify ideas or to refer you to other sources of information. To contact the authors, write:

John Clayton
1555 Echo Valley Drive
Niles, MI 49120
E-mail: jncdge@aol.com

We do not have all the answers, but we have studied this material extensively. Therefore, we welcome the opportunity to be of assistance to you and to learn from you as well.

CALCULATED ODDS FOR BEING
SUITABLY LOCATED IN OUR GALAXY

To calculate the probabilities of having a solar system located in one of the inhabitable doughnuts, we will compare the volume of the total galaxy with the volume of the doughnuts.

If we assume the galaxy to be 100,000 light-years (l.y.) in diameter and of an average thickness of four l.y., we would have a cylinder whose volume could be calculated. Such a calculation would reveal the volume of the galaxy to be 3.14×10^{10} cubic l.y.

Measurements of the magnetic field of our galaxy show that small changes from our solar system's position would produce radical magnetic changes fatal to our existence. A similar calculation shows gravitational variances to be even more critical.

If we approximate these estimates, we could hypothesize a "safe" doughnut size shown in figure A1.1. By subtracting a volume of the inner cylinder from the outer, we can establish a doughnut volume of approximately 1.04×10^8, which we double since there are two possible doughnuts. The ratio of 2.08×10^8 to the galaxy volume of 3.14×10^{10} gives us a probability of roughly 1 in 150 on being located at the proper place in the galaxy to have a solar system like our own.

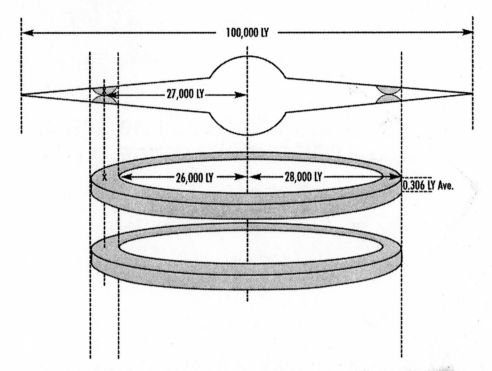

Figure A1.1: Approximate Doughnut-Shaped Area in a Spiral Galaxy Where a Solar System Could Exist

MORE ON UNIVERSAL CONSTANTS

THE GRAVITATIONAL CONSTANT

Newton's universal law of gravity states that the force of gravity is proportional to the product of the masses divided by the square of the distance between the two masses. If we wanted to find out how much gravitational force there is between the earth and the moon, we could multiply the mass of the earth by the mass of the moon and divide by the distance from the earth to the moon squared.

In order for this to work, however, we have to include the gravitational constant. This is a proportionality constant that makes the equation work. I can say cents = dollars, but unless I put the proportionality constant into the equation, it is not a true statement. Cents = 100(cents/dollar) times dollars is a true statement.

In the same way, Newton's universal law has a gravitational constant of 6.67×10^{-11}. This value for gravity works experimentally and in theory. It allows matter to exist and is vital to many areas of science. Einstein's improvements in defining gravity have not invalidated our understanding of its effects or changed the value of the gravitational constant.

THE ELECTRICAL CONSTANT

A similar type of discussion applies to electrical forces. In figure A2.1 we have the equation for electrical interaction between charged particles. Notice that the electrical equation is similar in form to the gravity equation with a constant that is huge compared to the gravitational constant. All electrical repulsive and attractive forces between charges are described by this equation.

$$\text{Cents} = 100 \left(\frac{\text{cents}}{\$}\right) \times \$$$

$$\text{Gravitational Force} = 6.67 \times 10^{-11} \left(\frac{N \cdot m^2}{kg^2}\right) \times \frac{M_1 M_2}{X^2}$$

$$\text{Electrical Force} = 9 \times 10^9 \left(\frac{kg \cdot m^3}{s^2 \cdot C^2}\right) \times \frac{Q_1 Q_2}{X^2}$$

Figure A2.1: Example Equations Involving Constants

The list in figure A2.2 gives some of the more commonly used constants. If it is supposed that the cosmos began by an explosion or inflation or any totally nonintelligent chance process, how could all of these constants have arrived at the precise values that allow water and carbon and life to exist?

When a material changes state from liquid to a solid, a liquid to a gas, or a solid to a gas, additional energy is required to make the transition. This again is a design feature that is very important to our survival. If this extra energy, called the heat of fusion in the change from ice to water, were not required, all the ice in the world would immediately convert to water the instant the air temperature reached 33°F.

Constant	Value
Speed of Light in Vacuum	2.99792458×10^8 m/s
Gravitational Constant	$6.6726(5) \times 10^{-11}$ N • m²/kg²
Avogadro's Number	$6.022045(31) \times 10^{23}$ mol⁻¹
Gas Constant	$8.31441(26)$ J/mol • K
Boltzmann's Constant	$1.380662(44) \times 10^{-23}$ J/K
Stefan-Boltzmann Constant	$5.67032(71) \times 10^{-8}$ W/m² • K⁴
Permittivity of Free Space	8.99×10^9 kg • m³/s² • C²
Permeability of Free Space	$4\pi \times 10^{-7}$ T • m/A
Planck's Constant	$6.626176(36) \times 10^{-34}$ J • s

Figure A2.2: Necessary Universal Constants

The flood produced by such an event would be cataclysmic. The physical reason this additional energy is needed involves the "locking" together of oppositely charged atoms in the freezing of the material.

In water, for example, the attractions between molecules in the solid state might look like the illustration below. The shaded areas show places where polar bonds are forming to lock the water molecules into a definite crystal lattice.

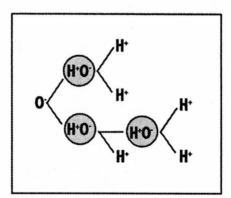

Figure A2.3: Example of Polar Bonds

STRING
THEORY

Another subject discussed by Stephen Hawking in his book *A Brief History of Time* relates to what is called "string theory" (1988, 159–162). This subject is very complicated and can only be briefly highlighted here. String theory addresses the difference between Einstein's general theory of relativity and quantum mechanics, which are fundamentally incompatible. Quantum mechanics explains the relationship between particles closer together than the Planck length of 1 million billion billion billionth of a centimeter (10^{-33}), leaving general relativity to deal with the larger distances. For this reason, string theory has been called the "Theory of Everything (TOE)."

We mention string theory because at least eleven spacial dimensions are required to make it work. Being familiar with the four dimensions of height, length, width, and time, we may find it hard to imagine an additional seven. However, though extra dimensions cannot be visualized, they are readily described mathematically and are believed to exist physically. If, in fact, it does take an extra seven dimensions to explain the existence of the universe, where are they today? Since these seven dimensions are needed only to unify the four fundamental forces at distances less than 10^{-33} centimeters, it is believed that they stopped growing at this level of expansion during the big bang.

Today, strings are accepted as being, in one way or another, the elementary particle-like components of all matter, having various shapes like one- or two-dimensional filaments that vibrate within all dimensions of superspace at the same time. It is the different modes of vibration that give strings their identifying properties (Green 1999, 142–146).

These facts, if true, have profound implications. While we are personally limited to experiencing only four dimensions of space, all matter has higher dimensional components at the smallest scale of existence. Since God has the ability to access these extra dimensions, quantum mechanics and string theory give us a physical explanation for how God can control everything, including time itself.

HOW MANY STARS ARE THERE?

If we assume that the universe began with a big bang, then that explosion-like event took place at a particular point in time and space. If it took place 20 billion years ago (a much older figure than many astronomers believe), nothing in the cosmos could be older than that figure. The light from that explosion would have traveled to a point 20 billion light-years from the point of the explosion. (See figure A4.1.) If you could go out to point G in the figure, you could, in theory, see the big bang take place.

Let us now do some crude calculations to find out how many galaxies there are in space potentially available to us. If we assume that the big bang was a uniform explosion creating a uniform space, the cosmos would be a sphere. The volume of that sphere could be calculated by the formula $V = 4/3 \pi r^3$ from elementary math. That would be $4/3(\pi)(20 \text{ billion})^3$ which works out to be approximately 10^{30} cubic light-years.

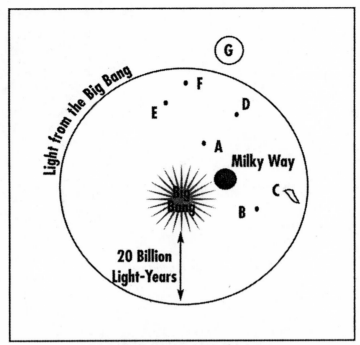

Figure A4.1: The "Big Bang" View of the Cosmos

In appendix 1, we calculated the volume of our galaxy to be 3.14 x 10^{10} cubic light-years. Notice that if there were no space at all between galaxies (and there is), the number of possible galaxies in space would be 10^{30} divided by 3.14 x 10^{10}, or roughly 10^{20} galaxies. If each of these galaxies contained 100 billion stars (and most contain fewer), the total number of stars would be 10^{20} x 10^{11} or roughly 10^{31}. The odds we have been describing are on the order of 1 in 10^{160}. For more complex proteins, these odds can quickly reduce to 1 in 10^{1000}. Based on either of these numbers, there are not nearly enough stars in the cosmos to allow chance to be a working factor in explaining the design we see.

THE VARIABLE NATURE OF TIME

In the equation, T_0 represents the time a person would experience if he or she were in a totally static condition, not moving through space at all. You may not realize it, but at this moment, you are traveling through space at about 600,000 miles per hour, because that is the speed of the earth through space. T then represents the time that we actually do experience and how long it is compared to static time. V is the speed the person or object is moving, and c is the speed of light in a vacuum, approximately 186,317 miles per second.

$$T = \frac{T_0}{\sqrt{1 - (V^2/c^2)}}$$

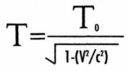

This equation, then, suggests that time is variable. Upon examining the equation, it becomes clear that, as one goes faster and faster (as

V increases), the value of T becomes larger and larger (time slows down). As V approaches c in magnitude, V^2/c^2 gets close to 1, and the denominator approaches zero, which makes the value of T become nearly infinite. In other words, each static second could become infinitely long by comparison. Now you know what happens when "time flies."

ROCK
CLASSIFICATIONS

In general, there are three types of rocks: igneous, sedimentary, and metamorphic. Igneous rocks (solid rocks) form naturally from magma or the hot semiliquid rock located below the earth's crust. By processes not completely understood and through volcanic activity, igneous rocks reach the surface in the form of granites and basalts. These rocks erode by a variety of means into sedimentary rocks.

Different conditions cause different types of sedimentary rocks to form. Rapid water deposits large boulders and gravels called conglomerates and breccias. Slower water deposits sands and silts called sandstone and siltstone.

Another sandstone formation that is spectacular but rare is formed by wind. Vast deserts are sometimes buried and transformed into sandstone by chemical interaction of sand with water and compressive forces. It is easy to identify this type of deposition by means of its characteristic 25-to-31-degree cross-bedding and its typically well-rounded, frosted quartz sand particles.

Quiet or still waters, such as those found in lakes and lagoons, deposit clays that become shales or mudstone. For quiet water environments, we can also add the formation of carbonate rocks. Carbonate rocks include limestone, which can form by chemical precipitation (solidification) in water containing a lot of dissolved carbonates (one carbon and three oxygen atoms). Under certain conditions, the carbonate combines with calcium to form limestone by solidifying in a way similar to that of rock sugar forming in the bottom of a jar of honey.

Sedimentary rocks, in turn, may slide under a continent (called subduction) or may be buried by miles of accumulated sediments. Both of these processes subject these deposits to intense heat and pressure. They are heated almost to their melting point and become like a super-thick jello. When finally cooled, they change into metamorphic rocks and retain certain characteristics of the original rock sediments from which they came. In this way, limestones are converted into marble and shales are converted into slates. Thus, all the common sedimentary rocks have similar metamorphosed (changed) rock equivalents.

Sedimentary rocks are the most common types one might normally encounter. They are common because they are the result of an ongoing process connected with a variety of environmental conditions, particularly with the weathering of mountains. For example, a stream starts in the mountains and transports the weathering rock materials down the hill. At the base of the hill, the larger particles drop out to form the conglomerates and the gravel beds. As the stream gradient flattens and becomes a river, the sands and silts drop out to form the finer sedimentary rocks. Finally, when the river reaches a lake or delta, the suspended clays slowly settle out. If the lake or lagoon warms up, under the right conditions, precipitate limestone will form.

This simple process becomes especially significant when it affects an entire continent. When sea levels lower or rise due to natural occurrences, such as ice-age cycles or continental building activity, events called transgressions and regressions occur. During a transgression, the sea slowly rises, depositing a specific pattern of sedimentary rocks in an ascending order. They are sandstones on the bottom, then shales, and carbonates on top. Just the opposite occurs when the sea level is falling, and it is simple to tell the difference. There is evidence that many parts of the continental United States have undergone numerous transgressive/regressive cycles during their formation.

The point is that, in this case, each type of rock sediment is associated with a different water environment. It is important, for instance, to realize the difference in the sedimentary rock deposits associated with transgressive/regressive cycles and those associated with a great flood. In the case of a flood, the sediments would be all mixed together originally, with all the heavy rocks falling out first, followed by the sands and silts, with the clays forming a final, thin layer over everything.

Appendix

7

DISCUSSION OF FLOOD GEOLOGY

ARGUMENTS FOR FLOOD GEOLOGY

Proponents of a young earth claim that the global flood described in Genesis 7 and 8 was responsible for the fossil record as we have it today. This flood, accompanied by earthquakes, volcanic eruptions, and powerful surge waves, is believed to have caused extensive erosion of soil and rock beds, burying plants and animals in the shifting mud and redepositing the soils elsewhere in stratified layers (Whitcomb and Morris 1961/1998, 123). The order of fossils in the rocks from simple to complex and from sea creatures to land animals is claimed to be the natural result of their flight to escape the flood.

In other words, the rising waters would have sorted out the life forms according to size and mobility. The smaller, less mobile creatures would occupy the lower layers of earth's rocks because they would have been the first to be buried. The larger, more mobile creatures would have run to higher ground only to be buried later. Whitcomb and Morris go on to state that the remaining humans and animals swept away at the very last "would not be buried but simply drowned and then carried about by the waters on or near the surface until finally decomposed by the elements" (1961/1998, 266).

According to this scenario, the flood would be totally responsible for the entire geologic column deposited since the Cambrian period estimated by scientists to have started some 550 million years ago. Likewise, the Grand Canyon would not have been caused by slow erosion cutting through solid rock over millions of years as the land gradually uplifted. Rather, it would have been formed by the rapid drainage of a series of lakes located to the east.

About two hundred years after the flood had laid down most of the deposits evident to an observer in the Grand Canyon today, natural earth and stone dams retaining these inland lakes would have broken, releasing a huge volume of water, mud, and boulders that would have quickly pulverized the newly formed rock into dust as it cut a canyon through the soft material on its westward course. A recent example of such rapid erosion took place at Mount St. Helens when a river of water and mud raced through 600 feet of recently placed volcanic ash and formed a deep canyon in that location. Therefore, it is reasoned that the same type of event could have rapidly formed the Grand Canyon (Brown et al. 1996).

These brief and very simplified explanations for the formation of the geologic record and the Grand Canyon are two examples of how proponents of creation science believe cataclysmic events by the hand of God shaped the world as we see it in less than 10,000 years.

ARGUMENTS AGAINST FLOOD GEOLOGY

Although young earth supporters Paul Nelson and John Mark Reynolds are excited about the potential for creation science research, they honestly admit that as a science "young earth creationism is generally underdeveloped" and that a recent paper presented on flood geology provides "a huge amount of room for future research" (1999,

98). This admission on their part can be substantiated by a few facts that show dramatically how far creation science must advance before it can be taken seriously from a scientific perspective.

The Geologic Record

At present, the claim that flood geology is responsible for the geologic record seems to be based more on faith than on solid evidence. For example, the order of animals fleeing from rising floodwaters would not result in the consistent, worldwide sequence of simple-to-complex life forms preserved in the earth. If trilobites, dinosaurs, and humans had lived contemporaneously for 2,000 to 4,000 years or more, then somewhere in the fossil record human and dinosaur bones would have been deposited together by natural processes before the flood occurred.

Somewhere in the lower layers of rock, even one small piece of pottery or other signs of human habitation from low-lying villages would have been buried with a trilobite or other primitive life form. And in the upheaval of mud by the raging torrents, branches and leaves from a Jurassic Cycad (a tree from the Jurassic period) or other extinct tree would have been unavoidably mixed in with branches and leaves from a more modern one. In fact, such combinations would likely be found over and over again (Robinson 1996, 3–5).

The reality is that, in centuries of research by tens of thousands of scientists, not one such combination has *ever* been found. Attempts to link humans and dinosaurs to the same time period, such as the Glen Rose, Texas, site, have all been proven to be erroneous (Morris 1986, 75; Kuban 1986).

What the fossil record often does show, however, is small, immobile creatures buried along with large, mobile animals, *all from the same geologic period*. It always finds deep-sea creatures entombed in deep-sea deposits and shallow, warm-water sea creatures in strata produced from warm, shallow seas. Churning, roiling floodwaters loaded with mud and silt and debris comprised of millions of different forms of plant and animal life would not lay down the type of sediments we see before us in the fossil record.

In addition, flood geology cannot account for hundreds of feet of windblown sandstone deposits that were once vast deserts before they were buried. They were clearly not deposited by floodwaters, yet flood geologists claim that the soils both above and below them were. The same problem exists with the numerous layers of volcanic rock that lie between two supposedly flood deposited layers.

The Grand Canyon

Entrenched Meander

One place where the flaws in flood geology become exceedingly obvious is in the Grand Canyon. If a massive amount of water rushing out of an inland lake formed the Grand Canyon in a matter of weeks or even months, the Colorado River should flow in a straight line, because its course would have been cut by a rapidly moving, high energy body of water whose projected course would be very difficult to change.

Instead, the Grand Canyon has a winding course called an entrenched meander (from the Latin *maendere*, "to wander"). It is not the shape of a valley quickly cut by large amounts of rushing water. A meandering river occurs where the land is so flat that the water cannot travel in a straight line. Rather, it follows a characteristic, back-and-forth weaving course of sinuous or winding curves.

After a meander course has been established and cut into the softer upper soils, if the land is uplifted slowly at about the same rate that the river cuts down into the harder rocks below, the river will cut deeply into the underlying rock without changing its meandering shape. The sides of the developing gorge will be vertical because of the internal strength of the rocks.

Experiments have shown that seasonal, high-volume floods carrying heavy rock sediments will cause meanders to be incised (cut) vertically once they are already formed. These are the very conditions that characterized the Colorado River before its waters were regulated by Glen Canyon Dam in 1963. So the Grand Canyon's entrenched meander shape indicates that it was not *initially* formed by rapidly rushing water.

Slope Stability

If a huge volume of water were to quickly cut a mile-deep trench through already flood-saturated soils to form the Grand Canyon, what would prevent the Canyon walls from caving in? Even shallow trenches on modern construction sites must be shored up to guard against collapse. The higher and more vertical the sides, the harder and stronger the soil or rock must be to resist slumping. If the Grand Canyon had been cut into recently deposited soils not more than 200 years old, they would not be internally strong enough to stand vertically. The resulting valley would have been shaped like a flattened V. As it is, in the Grand Canyon there is no evidence of numerous, massive mud slides and failed slopes filling in large sections.

The steep, vertical cliffs in the Grand Canyon have not collapsed because they were composed of hard rock when the river began its course of slow erosion. As discussed in chapter 6, relatively loose soils such as sand, clay, and lime ooze become rock over thousands of years as chemically rich water flows through them, causing reactions to take place that slowly cement the particles of soil together. The Grand Canyon exposes hundreds of feet of distinct layers of rock, including 450 feet of Redwall Limestone in some areas.

Flood geology cannot account for this rock. Floodwaters do not deposit a 450-foot-thick chunk of limestone. If the limestone had still been in its original state of ooze (even after a mere 200 years of drying out), it would have collapsed completely. If it had been solid rock when the canyon formed, then the flood could not have been its source.

Lava Dams

A final, insurmountable problem with flood geology in the Grand Canyon has to do with lava dams. In the past, a single volcano spewed out so much lava that it formed a dam across the river more than 800 feet high, forming a huge lake that extended all the way back through the Canyon and up into Utah. Geologists calculate that there were at least twelve major lava dams formed in the Grand Canyon during the last million years.

They also calculate that it took between 10,000 and 20,000 years for the river to successively erode away each dam. Therefore, it has been estimated that it would have taken about 180,000 years for the water to wear away just the lava flows, not to mention the rest of the Canyon.

Flood geology cannot accurately account for the erosion of these lava dams. Since the lava appears on top of the rocks, volcanic eruptions must have taken place after the flood. Yet 4,000 to 8,000 years from the time of the flood is not enough time for even one lava flow to erode, much less twelve. As a result, flood geologists compare the erosion rate of lava in the Grand Canyon to the lava on Mount St. Helens where a large volume of rushing water rapidly cut through the lava there.

Actually, there is no comparison, and to make one is deceptive. Mount St. Helens's ash-lava consists of material soft enough for mud slides and swiftly flowing water to cut through in a very short time. In contrast, lava in the Grand Canyon is so hard and dense that an observer can see areas where the river was unable to cut a path directly through it. Instead, the river was forced around the lava by slowly eroding away the rock lying next to it, rerouting the river and leaving the lava dam in place.

CONCLUSION

By presenting these counterarguments to flood geology, we are not saying that the biblical flood of Noah's day did not occur. (See chapter 11 under the heading "Flood of Noah's Day.") We are simply saying that there is a need for more research in the area of flood geology before credible claims can be made. So far, the scientific community in general has good cause to oppose this theory as a viable alternative to the geologic record that has been carefully established over the last two centuries. Although young-earth creationists remain optimistic about the future, Vern Poythress makes the following comment after critiquing an essay on young-earth creationism by Nelson and Reynolds: "But people have been working on young earth flood theories since at least the eighteenth century, and, if anything, the situation has become much more difficult for them with advances in astronomy and geology (including radioactive dating and plate tectonics)" (1999, 94).

Whatever the future holds regarding new discoveries in science, Christians must be willing to weigh the evidence fairly and adjust their understanding to maintain the delicate balance that exists between good science and good religion.

HEBREW WORDS AND DEFINITIONS IN GENESIS 1:1–31; 2:1–3

Understanding the Hebrew definitions of some of the key words in the Genesis creation account is helpful to our discussion. Following is the biblical account with key Hebrew words placed above the text. The English word or words to which each Hebrew word corresponds are underlined. Following the biblical text is an alphabetical list of the Hebrew words and their definitions. Finally, there is a list of the animals mentioned in the biblical account, their Hebrew name and definition, and the verses in which they are mentioned.

BIBLICAL TEXT (KJV)

    reshith   *elohim bara*   *shamayim*   *erets*

1:1) In the <u>beginning</u> <u>God</u> <u>created</u> the <u>heaven</u> and the <u>earth</u>.

    erets   *tohu*   *bohu*   *choshek*

2) And the <u>earth</u> was without <u>form</u>, and <u>void</u>; and <u>darkness</u> was

panim　　　*tehom*　　　　　*ruach*　　*rachaph*

upon the <u>face</u> of the <u>deep</u>. And the <u>Spirit of God</u> <u>moved</u>

panim　　*mayim*　　　*elohim*

upon the <u>face</u> of the <u>waters</u>. 3) And <u>God</u> said, Let there be

or　　　　　　*or*　　　　*elohim*　　　*or*

<u>light</u>: and there was <u>light</u>. 4) And <u>God</u> saw the <u>light</u>, that it

tob　　　*elohim badal*　　*or*　　　　　*choshek*

was <u>good</u>: and <u>God</u> <u>divided</u> the <u>light</u> from the <u>darkness</u>.

elohim　　　　*or yom*　　　*choshek*

5) And <u>God</u> called the <u>light</u> <u>Day</u>, and the <u>darkness</u> he called

layelah, layil　　*ereb*　　　　*boqer*

　<u>Night</u>. And the <u>evening</u> and the <u>morning</u> were the

echad yom　　*elohim*　　　　　　　*raqia*

<u>first</u>　<u>day</u>. 6) And <u>God</u> said, Let there be a <u>firmament</u> in the

tavek　　*mayim*　　　*badal*　　*mayim*　　　*mayim*

<u>midst</u> of the <u>waters</u>, and let it <u>divide</u> the <u>waters</u> from the <u>waters</u>.

elohim asah　　*raqia*　　　*badal*　　*mayim*

7) And <u>God</u> <u>made</u> the <u>firmament</u>, and <u>divided</u> the <u>waters</u> which

tachath　　*raqia*　　　　*mayim*

were <u>under</u> the <u>firmament</u> from the <u>waters</u> which were above the

raqia　　　　　　　　　*elohim*　　　*raqia*　　*shamayim*

<u>firmament</u>: and it was so. 8) And <u>God</u> called the <u>firmament</u> <u>Heaven</u>.

ereb   boqer   sheni

And the <u>evening</u> and the <u>morning</u> were the <u>second</u>

yom   elohim   mayim tachath   shamayim

<u>day</u>. 9) And <u>God</u> said, Let the <u>waters</u> <u>under</u> the <u>heaven</u> be

qavah   maqom   yabbashah raah

<u>gathered together</u> unto one <u>place</u>, and let the <u>dry land</u> <u>appear</u>: and

elohim   yabbashah erets

it was so. 10) And <u>God</u> called the <u>dry land</u> <u>Earth</u>; and the

miqveh   mayim   yam   elohim

<u>gathering together</u> of the <u>waters</u> called he <u>Seas</u>: and <u>God</u> saw that

tob   elohim   erets   dasha   deshe

it was <u>good</u>. 11) And <u>God</u> said, Let the <u>earth</u> <u>bring forth</u> <u>grass</u>,

eseb   zera   ets   peri

the <u>herb</u> yielding <u>seed</u>, and the <u>fruit tree</u> yielding <u>fruit</u> after his

min   zera   erets

<u>kind</u>, whose <u>seed</u> is in itself, upon the <u>earth</u>: and it was so. 12)

erets   deshe   eseb   zera

And the <u>earth</u> brought forth <u>grass</u>, and <u>herb</u> yielding <u>seed</u> after

min   ets   peri   zera

his <u>kind</u>, and the <u>tree</u> yielding <u>fruit</u>, whose <u>seed</u> was in itself, after

min   elohim   tob   ereb

his <u>kind</u>: and <u>God</u> saw that it was <u>good</u>. 13) And the <u>evening</u> and

boqer   shelishi yom   elohim
the morning were the third day. 14) And God said, Let there

maor   raqia   shamayim   badal   yom
be lights in the firmament of the heaven to divide the day from

layelah, layil   oth   moed
the night; and let them be for signs, and for seasons, and for

yom   shanah   maor   aqia
days, and years: 15) And let them be for lights in the firmament

shamayim   or   erets
of the heaven to give light upon the earth: and it was so.

elohim asah   gadol maor   gadol maor
16) And God made two great lights; the greater light to

memsheleth   yom   qaton maor memsheleth
  rule   the day, and the lesser light to rule the   .

layelah, layil   asah   kakab   elohim
night: he made the stars also. 17) And God

nathan   raqia   shamayim   or
set them in the firmament of the heaven to give light upon

erets   mashal   yom   layelah, layil
the earth, 18) And to rule over the day and over the night, and

badal   or   choshek   elohim
to divide the light from the darkness: and God saw that it was

tob   *ereb*   *boqer*   *rebii yom*

good. 19) And the <u>evening</u> and the <u>morning</u> were the <u>fourth</u> <u>day</u>.

       elohim   *mayim*   *sharats*

20) And <u>God</u> said, Let the <u>waters</u> <u>bring forth</u> abundantly the

      sherets   *nephesh*   *oph*   *uph*

<u>moving creature</u> that hath <u>life</u>, and <u>fowl</u> that may <u>fly</u> above the

erets   *raqia*   *shamayim*   *elohim bara*

<u>earth</u> in the open <u>firmament</u> of <u>heaven</u>. 21) And <u>God</u> <u>created</u>

      tannin   *chai*   *nephesh*

great <u>whales</u>, and every <u>living</u> <u>creature that moveth</u>, which the

mayim   *sharats*   *min*

<u>waters</u> <u>brought forth abundantly</u>, after their <u>kind</u>, and every

kanaph oph   *min*   *elohim*   *tob*

<u>winged</u> <u>fowl</u> after his <u>kind</u>: and <u>God</u> saw that it was <u>good</u>.

      elohim barak   *parah*   *rabah*

22) And <u>God</u> <u>blessed</u> them, saying, Be <u>fruitful</u>, and <u>multiply</u>, and

male   *mayim*   *yam*   *oph rabah*   *erets*

<u>fill</u> the <u>waters</u> in the <u>seas</u>, and let <u>fowl</u> <u>multiply</u> in the <u>earth</u>.

      ereb   *boqer*   *chamishshi, chamishi*

23) And the <u>evening</u> and the <u>morning</u> were the <u>fifth</u>

yom   *elohim*   *erets*   *sharats*

<u>day</u>. 24) And <u>God</u> said, Let the <u>earth</u> <u>bring forth</u> the

nephesh   *min behemah remes*

living creature after his kind, cattle, and creeping thing, and

chaiyah, cheva   *min*   *elohim*

beast of the earth after his kind: and it was so. 25) And God

asah   *chaiyah, cheva*   *min*   *behemah*

made the beast of the earth after his kind, and cattle after their

min   *remes*   *erets*

kind, and every thing that creepeth upon the earth after his

min   *elohim*   *tob*   *elohim*

kind: and God saw that it was good. 26) And God

asah adam   *tselem*   *demuth*

said, Let us make man in our image, after our likeness: and let

radah   *dagah*   *yam*

them have dominion over the fish of the sea, and over the

oph   *behemah*   *erets*

fowl of the air, and over the cattle, and over all the earth, and over

remes   *remes*   *erets*   *elohim*

every creeping thing that creepeth upon the earth. 27) So God

bara adam   *tselem*   *tselem elohim bara*

created man in his own image, in the image of God created he

zakar neqebah bara   *elohim barak*

him; male and female created he them. 28) And God blessed them, *elohim*   *parah*   *rabah*   *male*

and <u>God</u> said unto them, Be <u>fruitful</u>, and <u>multiply</u>, and <u>replenish</u>

erets   *kabash*   *radah*   *dagah*

the <u>earth</u>, and <u>subdue</u> it: and have <u>dominion</u> over the <u>fish</u> of the

yam   *oph*   *chaiyah*

<u>sea</u>, and over the <u>fowl</u> of the air, and over every <u>living thing that moveth</u>

erets   *elohim*   *hinneh*

upon the <u>earth</u>. 29) And <u>God</u> said, <u>Behold</u>, I have given

eseb   *zera*   *panim*

you every <u>herb</u> bearing <u>seed</u>, which is upon the <u>face</u> of all the

erets   *ets*   *peri*   *ets*

<u>earth</u>, and every <u>tree</u>, in the which is the <u>fruit</u> of a <u>tree</u> yielding

zera   *oklah*   *chaiyah, cheva*

<u>seed</u>; to you it shall be for <u>meat</u>. 30) And to every <u>beast</u>

erets   *oph*

of the <u>earth</u>, and to every <u>fowl</u> of the air, and to every thing that

remes   *erets*   *nephesh*

<u>creepeth upon</u> the <u>earth</u>, wherein there is <u>life</u>, I have given every

yereq eseb *oklah*   *elohim*

<u>green</u> <u>herb</u> for <u>meat</u>: and it was so. 31) And <u>God</u> saw every thing

asah   *meod tob*

that he had <u>made</u>, and, behold, it was <u>very good</u>. And the *ereb*   *boqer*   *shishshi yom*

<u>evening</u> and the <u>morning</u> were the <u>sixth</u> <u>day</u>. 2:1) Thus the

shamayim   *erets*   *kalah*   *tsaba*

<u>heavens</u> and the <u>earth</u> were <u>finished</u>, and all the <u>host</u> of them.

shebii yom elohim kalah   melakah

2) And on the <u>seventh</u> <u>day</u> <u>God</u> <u>ended</u> his <u>work</u> which he had

asah   *shabath*   *shebii yom*   *melakah*

<u>made</u>; and he <u>rested</u> on the <u>seventh</u> <u>day</u> from all his <u>work</u> which

asah   *elohim barak*   *shebii yom*   *qadesh*

he had <u>made</u>. 3) And <u>God</u> <u>blessed</u> the <u>seventh</u> <u>day</u>, and <u>sanctified</u>

shabath   *melakah*

it: because that in it he had <u>rested</u> from all his <u>work</u> which

elohim bara   *asah*

<u>God</u> <u>created</u> and <u>made</u>.

WORDS AND DEFINITIONS

Hebrew Word	Hebrew Definition
asah	to do, make (applies to man or God—reworking existing material)
adam	a man, human being
badal	to separate
bara	to prepare, form, fashion, create (applies only to God. Fiat creation—a miracle)
barak	to declare blessed
behemah	cattle, beast
bohu	emptiness
boqer	morning
chai	living, alive, lively

chaiyah	living being
chaiyah, cheva	a living creature
chamishshi, chamishi	fifth
choshek	darkness
dagah	fish
dasha	to cause to yield tender grass
demuth	likeness
deshe	tender grass (lichen, algae, etc.)
echad	one, first
elohim	God, (plural—implies power of God)
ereb	evening
erets	earth, land (refers to functional planet—648 uses in O. T.)
eseb	herb (naked seed—fern—gymnosperm)
ets	a tree, wood, timber, stick
gadol	great
hinneh	see
kabash	to subdue
kakab	a star
kalah	to be completed, finished
kanaph	a wing (as covering and protecting)
layelah, layil	night
male (Eng. fill)	to fill, complete (not to refill)
male (Eng. replenish)	to fill, be full
maor	light giver (or light holder)
mashal	to rule
maqom	a place of standing (or bowl)
mayim	waters, water
melakah	work
memsheleth	rule, dominion
meod	might, very
min	kind (broad term not equal to the scientific word *species*. See 1 Corinthians 15:39)
miqveh	collection

moed	an appointed time or season
nathan	to give
nephesh (Eng. life)	living (or life) breath
nephesh (Eng. creature)	breathing creature
neqebah	a female
oklah	what is eaten, food
oph	fowl
or	light (Genesis 1:3, 4, 4, 5, 18) (See *maor*, not used here)
or	to cause or give light (Genesis 1:15, 17)
oth	a sign
panim	face
parah	to be fruitful
peri	fruit (angiosperm, see *zera*)
qadesh	to separate, set apart
qaton	little, small, young
qavah	to be gathered, bound together
raah	to be seen
rabah	to be many, abundant
rachaph	to move, shake
radah	to rule (be responsible for)
raqia	expanse (interface—zone of change)
rebii	fourth
remes	a creeping creature, close to the earth (sheep, goats, smaller mammals —Jews could eat them)
reshith	first, former (absolute beginning point)
ruach	Spirit, wind
shabath	to cease, rest, keep sabbath
shamayim	heavens, (heaved up things referring to space)
shanah	a year, repetition (identifiable cycles)
sharats	to swarm
shebii	seventh

shelishi	third
sheni	second, other, again
sherets	a teeming thing (implies a group of animals—all kinds)
shishshi	sixth
tachath	under, beneath
tannin	a great sea monster (implies any great sea creature)
tavek	middle, midst
tehom	deep place, the deep (sea)
tob	good
tohu	a ruin, vacancy (implies there was something to vacate)
tsaba	host, warfare, service
tselem	image (likeness of some kind)
uph	to fly
yabbashah	a dry place (as opposed to land that was not dry—swampy, underwater)
yam	sea, lake, pool
yereq	green herb, greenness
yom	day (or time, forever, etc. See Deuteronomy 10:10)
zakar	male
zera	seed, seed time, progeny (true seed plant—angiosperm)

ANIMALS OF GENESIS

English Name	Verses	Hebrew Name	Literal Meaning	Other Uses
moving creature	20	*sherets*	swarming creature	0
fowl	20, 21, 22, 26	*oph*	fowl	61
winged	21	*kanaph*	winged	78
whale	21	*tannin*	sea monster (See also Job 7:12; Ezekiel 32:2)	3

English Name	Verses	Hebrew Name	Literal Meaning	Other Uses
creature that moveth	21, 24	nephesh	breathing creature	8
creeping thing	24, 25, 36	behemah	cattle, beast	51
beast	24, 25, 30	chaiyah cheva	a living creature	114
fish	26, 28	dagah	fish	33
behemoth	Job 40:15	behemoth	enlarged form behemah	0
leviathan	Job 41:1	Livyathan	great water animal (Psalm 104:26)	3

Appendix

9

VISIBLE EFFECTS OF SURPLUS OXYGEN

At about 2,100 mya, we find evidence that the amount of atmospheric oxygen began to increase dramatically. This is taken to mean that oxygen-consuming reactions, such as the oxidation of soluble iron and sulphur, were probably complete. It signified that the era of the famous "red bed" land forms was over. The extensive red-orange soils we recognize today are the result of the oxidation of iron. The increased oxygen content of the atmosphere would also mean that the lakes and seas were cleansed of much of their excess dissolved iron by the formation of the distinctive banded iron deposits (Lamb and Sington 1998, 181).

Appendix

10

OXYGEN PRODUCTION STABILIZES

It should be noted that the present atmosphere is precisely balanced because the earth's systems are producing just enough oxygen to keep up with the consumption of the oxygen users. If oxygen levels get too high, the potential for fire increases significantly. This results in great forest fires earthwide. These fires quickly reduce the oxygen levels while simultaneously increasing the carbon-dioxide levels (Lamb and Sington 1998, 233).

Conversely, if there were a significant decrease in the oxygen supply, factors could be set in motion that would result in the death of all living things. Because death results in what is called respiration or decay, dead bodies quickly convert back into their elements, thereby releasing large volumes of carbon dioxide and water.

If the oxygen generating system does not keep up with demand, it is theorized that within about 100 or 200 million years the atmosphere could be completely converted back into carbon dioxide and water

(Condie and Slone 1998, 122). This is one reason why many environ-
mentalists express great concern over the loss of the rain forests and
oxygen-producing sea plants. These observations are echoed when
Lamb and Sington state:

> The system outlined [about carbon-dioxide balance] begs an
> intriguing question. Could it operate if any part was missing? For
> example, if we took away the effects of living organisms, would it
> work? The answer to this may be no. Living organisms rely on
> chemical reactions which are very sensitive to temperature. This
> sensitivity may be the ultimate thermostat on Earth. What we
> have really described here is a partnership between geological and
> biological activity. The two act together and each is dependent on
> the other. This is a truly amazing conclusion. The Earth gave birth
> to life in the first place, but life has helped to sustain the geological
> life of the planet. (1998, 233)

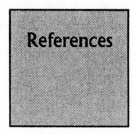

INTRODUCTION
The Need for Answers

Cothran, J. C. 1958. The Inescapable Conclusion. In J. C. Monsma, ed. *The Evidence of God in an Expanding Universe*. New York: G. P. Putnam's Sons.

CHAPTER 1
The Cosmos and the Creation

Andromeda. 1998. In *Britannica CD 99 Multimedia Edition* [CD-ROM]. Encyclopaedia Britannica, Inc.

Audouze, J., and G. Israel, eds. 1988. *The Cambridge Atlas of Astronomy*. Cambridge: Cambridge University Press.

Barrow, J. D. 1994. *The Origin of the Universe*. New York: BasicBooks (a division of HarperCollins Publishers, Inc.).

Dooling, D. 1998. Space Exploration: Unmanned Satellites. In *Britannica Book of the Year* [CD-ROM]. Encyclopaedia Britannica, Inc.

Easterbrook, G. 1998. What Came before Creation? *U.S. News & World Report* [On-line], 20 July. Available: http://www.usnews.com/usnews/issue/980720/ 20bang.htm

Hawking, S. W. 1988. *A Brief History of Time*. New York: Bantam Books.

Hubble Provides Views of How to Feed a Black Hole. 1998, May 14. *Webster's World Encyclopedia 2000* [CD-ROM], 1999. Webster Publishing.

Sagan, C. 1980. *Cosmos*. New York: Random House.

Top Scientific Advance of Year: Universe Will Keep Expanding. 1998. *CNN.com* [On-line], 18 December. Available: http://cnn.com/TECH/science/9812/18/top.science.ap/index.html

CHAPTER 2
The Design of Planet Earth

Smith. 1976. *The Human Degree*. J. B. Lippincott Co.

CHAPTER 4
Design as Evidenced in Life

Currie, C. R., J. A. Scott, R. C. Summerbell, and D. Malloch. 1999. Fungus-Growing Ants Use Antibiotic-Producing Bacteria to Control Garden Parasites. *Nature* 398.

Dawkins, R. 1986. *The Blind Watchmaker*. New York: W. W. Norton & Company.

de Duve, C. 1995. The Beginnings of Life on Earth. *American Scientist*, [On-line], September-October. Available: http://www.sigmaxi.org/amsci/ articles/95articles/CdeDuve.html

Griffiths, A. J. F., J. H. Miller, D. T. Suzuki, R. C. Lewontin, and W. M. Gelbart. 1993. *Genetic Analysis*. W. H. Freeman and Company.

Heyning, J. E., and J. G. Mead. 1997. Thermoregulation in the Mouths of Feeding Grey Whales. *Science* 278, 7 November.

Radetsky, P. 1998. Life's Crucible. *Earth*, February.

Schmidt-Nielsen, K. 1997. *Animal Physiology*. Cambridge University Press.

Schultz, T. R. 1999. Ants, Plants, and Antibiotics. *Nature* 398.

CHAPTER 5
The Nature of God

Abbot, E. 1994, reprint. *Flatland/Sphereland*. New York: Harper-Collins.

Williams, J. G. 1968. *Christian Faith and the Space Age*. New York: The World Publishing Co.

CHAPTER 6
The Language of the Earth

Bowling, S. A. 1987. The Earth's Changing Orbit. *Alaska Science Forum* [On-line], 1. Available: http://www.gi.alaska.edu/ScienceForum/ASF8/825.html

Chernicoff, S., and R. Venkatakrishnan. 1995. *Geology, an Introduction to Physical Geology*. New York: Worth Publishers.

Condie, K. C., and R. E. Slone. 1998. *Origin and Evolution of Earth, Principles of Historical Geology*. Upper Saddle River, N.J.: Prentice-Hall, Inc.

Lamb, S., and D. Sington. 1998. *Earth Story, the Shaping of Our World*. Princeton, N.J.: Princeton University Press.

Landes, K., & R. Hussey. 1956. *Geology and Man*. Prentice Hall.

MacRae, A. 1998. Radiometric Dating and the Geological Time Scale. *The Talk Origins Archive* [On-line]. Available: http://earth.ics.uci.edu/ faqs/dating.html

Schimmrich, S. 1998. Geochronology Kata John Woodmorappe. *The Talk Origins Archive* [On-line], 20. Available: http://www.talkorigins.org/ faqs/woodmorappe-geochronology.html

Smith, D. G., ed. 1981. *The Cambridge Encyclopedia of Earth Sciences*. New York: Crown Publishers.

Tarbuck, E. J., and F. K. Lutgens. 1993. *The Earth, an Introduction to Physical Geology*. New York: Macmillan.

Wolpoff, M. H. 1999. *Paleoanthropology*. Boston: McGraw-Hill.

CHAPTER 7
The Language of the Bible

Leiden, J. N. 1960. *Commentary of Nahmanides on Genesis 1-6*. New York: Brill Publishing.

Sarna, N. N. 1989. *Genesis, the JPS Torah Commentary*. New York: Jewish Publication Society.

Willmington, H. L. 1982. *Willmington's Guide to the Bible*. Wheaton, Ill.: Tyndale House Publishers, Inc.

Wiseman, P. J. 1985. *Ancient Records and the Structure of Genesis*. Nashville: Thomas Nelson Publishers.

CHAPTER 8
Let the Earth Speak

Audouze, J., and G. Israel, eds. 1988. *The Cambridge Atlas of Astronomy*. Cambridge: Cambridge University Press.

Chernicoff, S., and R. Venkatakrishnan. 1995. *Geology, an Introduction to Physical Geology*. New York: Worth Publishers.

Condie, K. C., and R. E. Slone. 1998. *Origin and Evolution of Earth, Principles of Historical Geology*. Upper Saddle River, N.J.: Prentice-Hall, Inc.

Curtis, H., and S. Barnes. 1989. *Biology Part 1 Biology of Cells*. New York: Worth Publishers.

Lamb, S., and D. Sington. 1998. *Earth Story, the Shaping of Our World*. Princeton, N.J.: Princeton University Press.

Redfern, R. 1980. *Corridors of Time*. New York: The New York Times Book Co.

Talcott, R. 1999. Water, Water Everywhere. *Astronomy Magazine* [On-line], 27 January. Avaliable: http://www.kalmbach.com/astro/News/News/swas.html

Tarbuck, E. J., and F. K. Lutgens. 1993. *The Earth, an Introduction to Physical Geology*. New York: Macmillan.

CHAPTER 9
Ask the Animals

Bowring, S. A., E. H. Erwin, Y. G. Jin, M. W. Martin, K. Davidek, and W. Wang. 1998. U/Pb Zircon Geochronology and Tempo of the End-Permian Mass Extinction. *Science* 280.

Boyle, A. 1999. Birds, Dinosaurs: No Direct Link, New Study Shows. *MSNBC News* [On-line], 23 June. Available: http://www.msnbc.com/news/123219.asp

Brownlee, S. 1997. How Do Genes Switch On? *U.S. News & World Report* [On-line], 18 August. Available: http://www.usnews.com/usnews/issue/970818/18gene.htm

Condie, K. C., and R. E. Slone. 1998. *Origin and Evolution of Earth, Principles of Historical Geology*. Upper Saddle River, N.J.: Prentice-Hall, Inc.

Dalrymple, G. B., G. A. Izett, L. W. Snee, and J. D. Obradovich. 1993. *Ar/Ar Age Spectra and Total-Fusion Ages of Tektites from Cretaceous-Tertiary Boundary Sedimentary Rocks in the Beloc Formation, Haiti* (U.S. Geological Survey Bulletin 2065). Washington, D.C.: U.S. Government Printing Office.

Dawkins, R. 1987. *The Blind Watchmaker*. New York: W. W. Norton & Company, Inc.

Gould, S. 1989. *Wonderful Life*. New York: W. W. Norton & Company, Inc.

Hartwig-Scherer, S. 1998. Apes or Ancestors? In W. A. Dembski, ed. *Mere Creation Science, Faith & Intelligent Design*. Downers Grove, Ill.: InterVarsity Press.

Hickman, C. P., Jr., L. S. Roberts, and A. Larson. 1997. *Integrated Principles of Zoology*. Chicago: Wm. C. Brown Publishers.

Kerr, R. A. 1998. Biggest Extinction Looks Catastrophic. *Science* 280.

Lamb, S. and D. Sington. 1998. *Earth Story, the Shaping of Our World*. Princeton, N.J.: Princeton University Press.

Levi-Setti, R. 1993. *Trilobites*. Chicago: University of Chicago Press.

Monastersky, R. 1993. Mysteries of the Orient. *Discover* [On-line], April. Available: http://208.226.13.177/archive/output.cfm?ID=192

Pendick, D. 1998. When Life Got Legs. *Earth* 28, August.

Poirier, F. E., and J. D. McKee. 1999. *Understanding Human Evolution*. Upper Saddle River, N.J.: Prentice-Hall, Inc.

Siegel, L. 1997. Scientists Unsure if Dinos Linked to Birds. *The Salt Lake Tribune* [On-line], 24 October. Available: http://www.sltrib.com/old/97/ oct/102497/nation_w/3772.htm

CHAPTER 10
What Is Man?

Caldwell, M. 2000. Polly Wanna Ph.D.? *Discover* 21 (1): January.

Clark, J. D. 1993. African and Asian Perspectives on Modern Human Origins. In M. J. Aitken, C. B. Stringer, and P. A. Mellars, eds. *The Origin of Modern Humans and the Impact of Chronometric Dating*. Princeton, N.J.: Princeton University Press.

Goldschmidt, R. B. 1940. *The Material Basis of Evolution*. New Haven, Conn.: Yale University Press.

Hauser, M. D. 2000. Morals, Apes, and Us. *Discover* 21 (2): February.

Hublin, J. J. 2000. An Evolutionary Odyssey [Review of the book *The Human Career: Human Biological and Cultural Origins* (second edition)]. *Nature* 403, 27 January.

Jones, S., R. Martin, and D. Pilbeam, eds. 1992. *The Cambridge Encyclopedia of Human Evolution*. Cambridge: Cambridge University Press.

Klein, R. G. 1999. *The Human Career: Human Biological and Cultural Origins*. Chicago: The University of Chicago Press.

Lewin, R. 1987. *Bones of Contention*. Chicago: The University of Chicago Press.

Renfrew, C. 1998. The Origins of World Linguistic Diversity: An Archaeological Perspective. In N. G. Jablonski and L. C. Aiello, eds. *The Origin and Diversification of Language*. San Francisco: California Academy of Sciences.

Tattersall, I. 1995. *The Fossil Trail*. New York: Oxford University Press.

Tattersall, I. 1998. *Becoming Human*. San Diego: Harcourt Brace & Company.

Thorndike. 1978. *Science News* 117, 19 August.

CHAPTER 11
Let Humans Speak

Cavalli-Sforza, L., and F. Cavalli-Sforza. 1995. *The Great Human Diasporas*. Reading, Mass.: Perseus Books.

Dalton, R. 2000. Biologists Flock to 'Evo-Devo' in a Quest to Read the Recipes of Life. *Nature* 403, 13 January.

Dickson, D., and C. Macilwain. 1999. "It's a G": the One-Billionth Nucleotide. *Nature* 402, 25 November.

Jones, S. 1993. *The Language of Genes*. New York: Doubleday.

Jones, S., R. Martin, and D. Pilbeam, eds. 1992. *The Cambridge Encyclopedia of Human Evolution*. Cambridge: Cambridge University Press.

Poirier, F. E., and J. D. McKee. 1999. *Understanding Human Evolution*. Upper Saddle River, N.J.: Prentice-Hall, Inc.

Ryan, W., and W. Pitman. 1998. *Noah's Flood*. New York: Simon and Schuster.

Tattersall, I. 1995. *The Fossil Trail*. New York: Oxford University Press.

Tattersall, I. 1998. *Becoming Human*. San Diego: Harcourt Brace and Company.

Whitcomb, J., and H. Morris. 1961; 42nd reprint 1998. *The Genesis Flood*. Phillipsburg, N.J.: P and R Publishing.

CHAPTER 12
God's Permission of Evil

Sayers, D. L. 1969. *Christian Letters to a Post-Christian World*. Grand Rapids, Mich.: William B. Eerdmans Publishing Company.

CHAPTER 13
Why Choose the Bible as the Word of God?

Branley and Wimmer. 1970. Concepts of the Universe. *Natural History Magazine*, December.

DeHoff, G. 1959. *Why We Believe the Bible*. DeHoff Publications.

Prophecies Concerning the Messiah. 2000. [On-line], 17 March. Available: http://www.ccobb.org/prophecies_introduction.asp

CHAPTER 14
Conclusion

Sheler, J. L., and J. M. Schrof. 1991. Religions's Search for a Common Ground with Science. Creation. *U.S. News & World Report* [On-line]. Available: http://www.usnews.com/usnews/news/create.htm

APPENDIX 3
String Theory

Green, B. 1999. *The Elegant Universe*. New York: W. W. Norton and Company, Inc.

Hawking, S. W. 1988. *A Brief History of Time*. New York: Bantam Books.

APPENDIX 7
Discussion of Flood Geology

Brown, G. (Director and Editor), H. Morris, D. Gish, S. Austin, and A. Snelling (Moderators). 1996. *The Grand Canyon Catastrophe* [Videocassette]. (Available from Keziah and American Portrait Films, P. O. Box 19266, Cleveland, OH 44119).

Kuban, G. 1986. Review of ICR Impact Article 151 [On-line]. Available: http://member.aol.com/paluxy2/sor-ipub.htm

Morris, H. 1986. *Time*, 30 June.

Nelson, P., and J. Reynolds. 1999. Young Earth Creationism: Conclusion. In J. Moreland and J. Reynolds, eds. *Three Views on Creation and Evolution*. Grand Rapids, Mich.: Zondervan Publishing House.

Poythress, V. 1999. Response to Paul Nelson and John Mark Reynolds. In J. Moreland and J. Reynolds, eds. *Three Views on Creation and Evolution*. Grand Rapids, Mich.: Zondervan Publishing House.

Robinson, B. 1996. Proving Evolution or Creation Science [On-line]. Available: http://www.religioustolerance.org/ev_proof.htm

Whitcomb, J., and H. Morris. 1961; 42nd reprint 1998. *The Genesis Flood*. Phillipsburg, N.J.: P & R Publishing.

APPENDIX 9
Visible Effects of Surplus Oxygen

Lamb, S., and D. Sington. 1998. *Earth Story, the Shaping of Our World*. Princeton, N.J.: Princeton University Press.

APPENDIX 10
Oxygen Production Stabilizes

Condie, K., and R. Slone. 1998. *Origin and Evolution of Earth, Principles of Historical Geology*. Upper Saddle River, N.J.: Prentice-Hall, Inc.

Lamb, S., and D. Sington. 1998. *Earth Story, the Shaping of Our World*. Princeton, N.J.: Princeton University Press.

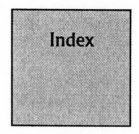

Index

Printed in the United States
23090LVS00003B/211